The Arms Race:
Economic and Social
Consequences

The Arms Race: Economic and Social Consequences

Hugh G. Mosley
University of Maryland

LexingtonBooks
D.C. Heath and Company
Lexington, Massachusetts
Toronto

Library of Congress Cataloging in Publication Data

Mosley, Hugh G.
  The arms race: Economic and social consequences

  Includes index.
  1. Arms race—Economic aspects—United States. 2. Armaments—
Economic aspects—United States. 3. Disarmament—Economic apsects—
United States. I. Title.
HC110.D4M67   1984   338.4'76234'0973   81–48005
ISBN 0–669–05237–X

Copyright © 1985 by D.C. Heath and Company

Published simultaneously in Canada

Printed in the United States of America on acid-free paper

International Standard Book Number: 0–669–05237–X

Library of Congress Catalog Card Number: 81–48005

For Isabella

Contents

Figures and Tables   ix

Preface and Acknowledgments   xiii

Introduction   1

Chapter 1   The Cold War Origins of Military Keynesianism   5

             The Old Orthodoxy on Military Spending   5
             NSC-68 and Military Keynesianism   7
             Military Keynesianism and the Korean
                 Rearmament   12

Chapter 2   Military Expenditure: Some Basic Concepts   17

             Military Expenditure and Economic Utility   18
             Military Expenditure and GNP Accounting   20
             Defining Military Expenditure   23
             Opportunity Costs and Military Spending   32
             Military Keynesianism and Opportunity Costs   34

Chapter 3   The Military Use of Resources   41

             Other Military-Related Expenditures   41
             The Military Burden   45
             Real Resources Utilized for Military Purposes   47
             Guns vs. Butter: Tradeoffs in the U.S. Budget   55
             The Making of the Pentagon Budget   56

Chapter 4   Military Expenditure and Economic Growth   63

             Global Comparisons of the Military Burden   63
             Military Expenditure and the Components of
                 Economic Growth   65
             Military Expenditure and Investment   66
             Military Expenditure and Productivity   73
             Civilian Spinoffs of Military R&D   80

Chapter 5   **Military Expenditure and Employment**   89

Employment Opportunity Costs of Military
    Spending   89
Employment Opportunity Costs of Specific
    Weapon Systems   95
Industrial, Regional, and Occupational Effects   100

Chapter 6   **Military Expenditure and Inflation**   113

Military-Related Inflation   113
The Political Context: Vietnam Inflation and
    Policy Stress   119
Cost-Push Inflation in the Military Sector   122

Chapter 7   **Impact on Balance of Payments and**
                  International Competitiveness   135

Structural Impact on International
    Competitiveness   137
Foreign Military Sales   139
The Price of Hegemony   141

Chapter 8   **The Reagan Military Buildup and Reaganomics**   145

The Reagan Economic Program   145
Military Buildup vs. Economic Goals   148
Reagan Buildup vs. the Korean and Vietnam
    Buildups   151
Economic and Social Consequences of the
    Reagan Military Buildup   155

Chapter 9   **The Economic and Social Consequences of**
                  Disarmament   161

The Conversion Problem   162
U.S. Experience with Postwar Conversion   167
Conversion Planning   177

Appendix A   **Components of the U.S. Military Burden**   183

                  Selected References   187

                  Index   195

                  About the Author   205

Figures and Tables

Figures

2–1   The Relationship of Budget Authority to Outlays   24

Tables

2–1   U.S. Military Expenditure: Four Official Definitions   25

2–2   DOD Constant Price Outlays Based on Defense Deflator and GNP Deflator   29

3–1   Military Expenditure Conventionally and Broadly Defined   44

3–2   Components of the Military Burden   46

3–3   U.S. Military-Related Employment, 1983   49

3–4   U.S. Military Production and Employment by Industrial Sector, 1980   51

3–5   Concentration of Defense Employment in Industry by Metropolitan Areas, 1980   52

3–6   Military Consumption of 32 Nonfuel Minerals, 1969–1972   54

4–1   The Military Burden and Economic Performance of Selected OECD Countries   64

4–2   Estimates of the Opportunity Costs of Military Spending, 1939–1968   67

4–3   Opportunity Costs of Military Spending, 1939–1968: Alternative Estimates for Selected Subperiods   69

4–4   Composition of the Gross Capacity Product, 1929 and 1969   69

4–5   Lead Times for Selected Aircraft Components   72

4–6   Output per Employed Person in Selected OECD Countries   74

4–7   Defense and Civilian R&D Expenditures in Selected OECD Countries   77

4–8	Sectoral Distribution of R&D Expenditure in Manufacturing in Selected OECD Countries	79
4–9	U.S. Defense Department R&D, 1982	81
4–10	Fighter Aircraft Readiness Indicators	82
5–1	Employment Effects of Military Expenditures	91
5–2	Summary Effects of a Compensated 20 Percent Defense Contraction	96
5–3	Employment Impact of Alternative Uses of $1 Billion of New Final Demand	97
5–4	Labor Requirements Generated by B–1 Bomber and by Alternative Federal Expenditures	99
5–5	Effect of Compensated Increases and Decreases in Military Spending on Forecast 1980 Industry Output and Employment	101
5–6	Regional Distribution of Domestic Military Employment, 1980	103
5–7	Estimated 1980 Regional Employment Before and After Compensated Increases and Decreases in Defense Expenditures	104
5–8	Effects of Changes in Defense Expenditures on 1980 Requirements for Selected Occupations	106
6–1	National Defense Expenditures as a Percentage of U.S. Budget and Source of Budget Deficits, 1950–1980	116
6–2	Monetization of the Federal Debt	117
6–3	Market Imperfections in Defense Industry	124
6–4	Price-Increases and Official Explanations for Selected Items	125
6–5	Composite Inflation Rates by DOD Appropriation Category	127
6–6	Implicit Price Deflators for National Defense Purchases	128
7–1	Impact of Military-Related Transactions on U.S. Balance of Payments	135
7–2	U.S. Arms Sales, 1970–1980	140

8–1   Reagan Defense Budget 1981–1986   149

8–2   Three U.S. Military Buildups: Korea, Vietnam, and
            Reagan   154

9–1   Three U.S. Postwar Conversion Experiences: World
            War Two, Korea, Vietnam   174

Preface and Acknowledgments

The maintenance of a large and permanent military establishment has been the principal activity of the U.S. government for more than thirty years. Nevertheless, the economic and social consequences of the arms race have received surprisingly little attention from U.S. political scientists and economists concerned with public policy issues. There are a number of reasons for this state of affairs, but probably the most important has been a rather complacent attitude toward the domestic economic effects of military spending, which have been widely perceived as being largely beneficial.

However, a small but growing body of literature is concerned with identifying and analyzing the economic and social consequences of the arms race. These writers are increasingly critical of the sanguine assumptions on which the conventional wisdom is based. In the past, the U.S. Arms Control and Disarmament Agency has been an important impetus for such research. Nongovernmental institutions, such as the Defense Information Center and the Council on Economic Priorities, have provided significant independent research, as have many individuals whose work is cited in this book. Peace research institutes abroad like the Stockholm International Peace Research Institute (SIPRI) have also devoted considerable attention to such issues. Finally, the United Nations has carried out a continuing series of studies and reports on this subject.

This book was conceived as a contribution to this developing critical discussion of the economic and social consequences of the arms race. Drawing on both U.S. and international sources, it examines the domestic consequences of the arms race in the United States. Its purpose is twofold: to present the analytic framework that has been developed for the study of the economic and social consequences of the arms race; and to apply this framework in a systematic way to study these consequences in the United States.

The United States was selected for several reasons: it is the largest Western military power, it is the most studied, and more official information is available than for any other country. Although the United States is the particular focus, the analysis is also applicable to other market economies. The U.S. focus also represents a certain methodological choice. An in-depth, qualitative study of the domestic effects of military spending in one major country seemed more fruitful than a cross-national, macrostatistical approach.

The economic and social consequences of the arms race straddle the boundary between political and economic analysis. Perhaps the best designation for it would be public policy analysis. For the past thirty years, the U.S. policy of military priorities in public spending and investment has been the implicit U.S. industrial policy. This book is a critical account of the domestic effects of this policy and a critique of its domestic rationale, military Keynesianism.

I have attempted to present the sometimes rather technical subject matter in a way that is also understandable and interesting for students, journalists, and other interested readers as well as for a more specialized academic audience. I would be happy to receive comments, suggestions, and criticism from readers. This book originates with work I did as a consultant for the UN *Study on the Relationship between Disarmament and Development* during 1980 and 1981. I am greatly indebted to my association with the collective effort of this international project. I would like to thank my colleagues at the UN Centre for Disarmament for their support—particularly Abdelkader Bensmail, Ron Huisken, and Swadesh Rana. I would like to acknowledge my special indebtedness to Ron Huisken for our discussions and for many ideas drawn from his contributions to the *Disarmament and Development* study. The ideas and comments of many of the distinguished international group of governmental experts who participated in the UN study have also found their way directly or indirectly into this book. The contributions of Daniel Gallik, Klaus Engelhardt, Hendrick de Haan, and Robert Haselden merit particular acknowledgment. Finally, I would like to thank Inga Thorsson, who chaired the *Disarmament and Development* study, for her example of courage, integrity, and commitment to disarmament.

I would also like to thank all those who have been kind enough to read parts of the manuscript and give me the benefit of their comments and suggestions. The final responsibility for the contents is of course a personal one.

Mrs. Rita Ehret and Elizabeth Miller typed the manuscript expertly, under sometimes hectic circumstances, with a great deal of interest and patience. I would like to thank them here.

Introduction

For more than thirty years, the United States has been involved in an arms race without precedent. Never before has the nation devoted such a large share of its resources for a sustained period to maintain a war-ready military establishment and a permanent military-industrial base. In World War Two and more briefly in World War One, a higher percentage of national output was allocated to military uses, but for a limited period and in the context of full wartime mobilization. In contrast to these temporary military mobilizations of an essentially civilian economy, today's large, permanent military sector has consumed, if at a slower pace, many times the resources of the U.S. military effort in World War Two.

The Arms Economy in Conventional Wisdom

The American self-image has changed as a result of the domestic turmoil of the 1960s and the economic crises and foreign policy setbacks of the 1970s. Yet one important piece of ideological baggage remains: a remarkable belief in the possibility of producing both swords and plowshares, both guns and butter. Although there has been widespread awareness that military expenditures are at the expense of other domestic programs and sometimes, especially in the 1970s, even successful opposition to expensive new weapon systems, it was largely based on moral disapproval of military priorities and concern about the dangers of the arms race.

Until recently, there has been very little public concern about the possibly damaging economic effects of a permanent arms economy. On the contrary, the conventional wisdom on the economic implications of military spending is typically highly positive. For example, a recent report by the Carnegie Foundation Endowment for International Peace concluded that the United States would have "little problem in being able to allocate more economic resources to defense spending" as envisioned by the Reagan program and dismissed the issue as being "more a question of political priorities than of economic resources."[1]

The beneficial effects ascribed to military spending are as many and varied as their spokesmen. Military expenditure, it is frequently argued, spurs economic growth rather than retarding it and acts as an economic stabilizer. This perception of the growth benefits of military spending has been rationalized in terms of vaguely Keynesian assumptions about military spending as the answer to chronic problems of insufficient aggregate demand in the U.S. economy.[2] This rather positive conception of the impact of military spending has been, ironically, also largely accepted by the American Left, which was influenced by Baran and Sweezy's analysis of the U.S. economy in terms of "underconsumption" and the problems of "surplus absorption." In their view military spending has been a necessary, if wasteful, crutch for the stabilization and expansion of U.S. capitalism.[3]

It is also widely assumed that military expenditures create jobs, both directly in industries producing goods and services for the military and indirectly through the multiplier effect. This belief is assiduously fostered by the proponents of new weapon systems. For example, Rockwell International, the prime contractor for the B-1 bomber, routinely circulated a state-by-state breakdown of the value of contracts and subcontracts to gain support for the multibillion dollar project, which was initially canceled in 1978 and resurrected by the Reagan administration.[4] Finally, research and development (R&D) expenditures for military purposes, which may account for 30 to 50 percent of the total costs of major weapon systems, are said to create a dynamic technological environment and spinoffs that improve the productivity and competitiveness of U.S. industry.[5]

The significance of Keynesian economic theories in providing intellectual support for the acceptance of military expenditures as benign or even beneficial is of particular importance. In the Keynesian macroeconomic universe, which focuses on the total circulation process and problems of aggregate demand, military expenditures are beneficial insofar as they lead to fuller employment of available resources. World War Two seemed to provide a model for military Keynesianism. Civilian employment increased from 46 million in 1939 to 53 million in 1945, at the same time that the armed forces expanded from 370,000 to over 11 million persons. Not only did GNP expand rapidly as wartime prosperity finally put an end to the depression, but personal consumption actually rose during the war by about 25 percent.[6]

After World War Two, the U.S. economy entered a period of unprecedented prosperity. The Korean and Vietnam military buildups and the new peaks in peacetime military expenditures during the postwar period seemed, both to professional economists and to the general public, an integral part of a new and beneficent economic order.

The Reagan administration, though it prides itself on breaking with the habits of government and economic policies of the last three decades of triumphant liberalism, remains a captive of this one essential premise. It believes, like its predecessors, that the allocation of a large share of national resources to the military effort is, if not neutral, actually beneficial for overall economic growth and development. Reagan's foremost domestic goal on taking office was to restore the U.S. economy, at the same time embarking on the largest armaments program ever undertaken in peacetime. The increase in the military budget proposed by the Reagan administration is even greater than the Vietnam war buildup. But its central premise—that military expenditures are benign or even beneficial—is false, which may well be the principal contradiction of Reaganomics.

Notes

1. Carnegie Endowment for International Peace, *Challenges for U.S. National Security* (New York: Carnegie Endowment, 1981), pp. 37, 39. For the World War Two period see Jack Stokes Ballard, "The Shock of Peace: Military and Economic Demobilization after World War II" (Ph.D. Dissertation, UCLA, 1974), Chapter 2, "Fears about the Postwar Era." For the immediate postwar period see the account of NSC-68 and military Keynesianism in Chapter 1 in this book as well as the references in note 1 therein. This complacent attitude toward the economic effects of military spending has been criticized in studies conducted by the United Nations. In the U.S. the Center for Defense Information in Washington, Employment Research Associates in East Lansing, Michigan, and the Council on Economic Priorities in New York have been conspicuous critics of the economic effects of military spending; many of their publications are cited in following chapters. Seymour Melman is perhaps the single most prominent U.S. critic of the economic effects of military spending in numerous books and articles. See *The Permanent War Economy* (New York: Simon and Schuster, 1974) for a statement of his views.

2. "Vaguely" at least among the American public and policy elites, but sometimes also more explicitly. See chapter 1, note 1.

3. See Paul Baran and Paul Sweezy, *Monopoly Capital* (New York: Monthly Review, 1966); James O'Connor, *The Fiscal Crisis of the State* (New York: St. Martin's, 1973); and more recently, for example, James Cypher, "The Basic Economics of Rearming America," *Monthly Review* (November 1981), pp. 11–27.

4. This practice is routine. For example, on Rockwell International, see Gordon Adams, *The B-1 Bomber: An Analysis of Its Strategic Utility, Coast, Constituency, and Economic Impact* (New York: Council on Economic Priorities, 1976), table 7 and appendix. Rockwell has made similar data available for the B-1B.

5. See, for example, Charles Hitch and Roland McKean, *The Economics of Defense in the Nuclear Age* (Cambridge: Harvard University Press, 1960), pp. 82–83.

6. Data as reported in *Economic Report of the President, 1982* (Washington, D.C.: GPO, 1982, tables B-1, B-2, and B-29.)

1 The Cold War Origins of Military Keynesianism

The origins of military Keynesianism are intertwined with the origins of the cold war. "Military Keynesianism" is a diffuse set of ideas and assumptions about the compatibility, and even beneficial effects, of a high level of military spending and economic prosperity. Since the 1950s, it has become part of the conventional wisdom held by U.S. policymakers.[1]

Military Keynesianism as a more or less explicit conception of economic policy entails the use of military expenditures to promote economic stabilization and growth within a broadly Keynesianism framework. Its five basic elements are:

1. A demand management perspective on the economy and a concern with the problems of insufficient aggregate demand.
2. The willingness to use government fiscal and monetary policy to stimulate aggregate demand to maintain employment and spur growth.
3. The willingness to engage in planned deficits to support continued or expanded countercyclical government demand, in contrast to the older fiscal orthodoxy of the necessity for balanced budgets.
4. Reliance on government military expenditures to create such demand.
5. The assumption that the government-subsidized high-technology component of military-industrial production contributes significantly to innovation and growth in the economy as a whole.

The Old Orthodoxy on Military Spending

Before the Korean war and the policy shifts it precipitated, the conventional wisdom on military expenditures was very different. Policymakers then stressed the limits on the military burden that the economy could support without such serious consequences as declining civilian consumption, lost economic growth, runaway inflation, and the necessity of onerous controls. For example, the Truman administration budget requests before the Korean war, allocated a fixed one-third of the federal budget to the military. In spite of a growing cold war climate, the administration's budget request for fiscal year 1951 reduced planned military spending by 8 percent because revenues had declined as a result of the economic recession and Truman was determined to balance the budget.[2]

5

The military share of the Truman budget was arrived at by a "remainder method"—that is, after essential domestic programs were subtracted from anticipated revenues, the military got what was left over.[3] The director of the Bureau of the Budget, Frank Pace, was the chief proponent of this policy, which, with Truman's backing, prevailed until the outbreak of the Korean war in June, 1950.[4]

Edwin G. Nourse, Truman's chairman of the Council of Economic Advisers, acknowledged "the difficulties of peace"—that is, the problems of postwar economic stabilization after the expiration of pent-up wartime demand and savings—but warned that further increases in military spending would raise the problem of reconciling economic supply with significantly increased military demand.[5] Contemplating the prospect of an increase in defense expenditures to as much as $15 billion (considered by many at the time, including Nourse, Pace, and Secretary of Defense Louis Johnson, to be the upper limit that the economy could stand[6]) Nourse listed four possible impacts: inflation, labor diversion, materials shortage, and controls. Nourse considered military expenditures as the source of strong inflationary forces operating through monetary mechanisms, market processes, and psychological reactions that may be disproportionate to the actual financial sums involved. Without strong antiinflationary government policies, he foresaw grave danger of engendering a cumulative or spiraling inflationary trend. Even if military spending were financed by higher taxes and increased savings, Nourse thought that there would be significant bottlenecks and other types of controls would be necessary to meet shortages of labor and materials. Controls to facilitate military production would "force us out of the free market procedures of a peacetime economy." Peacetime economic objectives would not only have to be deferred; they would be made "more difficult of attainment over an indefinitely long future period."

This sensitivity to the economic context and limits of military spending and military potential was, in a slightly different form, shared by the military itself. Historically, the U.S. military had relied on a strategy of mobilization—the maintenance of a small peacetime military establishment and the mobilization of citizen-soldiers and civilian industries in case of war.[7] This traditional strategy, which has been proved in World War Two, still prevailed after the war, although military leaders recognized that the postwar world required a higher degree of U.S. readiness than in the past. As Huntington observes, "In the immediate postwar years the concept of deterrence by forces-in-being had little place in military planning."[8]

The Army was particularly sensitive to economic issues. Both George Marshall and Eisenhower had been personally involved in interwar mobilization planning.[9] These leaders felt that military planning must be geared to what is feasible for the economy and that economic strength was the ultimate source of military power. It was an army general, Omar Bradley, who, as chairman of the Joint Chiefs of Staff, dissented from the State Department's advocacy of a massive rearmament program before Korean hostilities began. In Bradley's view, such lavish spending threatened the nation's economic system as much as the Soviet Union.[10]

Eisenhower's later warning about the danger of a military-industrial complex and his many remarks about the economic and social costs of military spending were also rooted in this earlier orthodoxy on military spending.[11] Eisenhower, who considerably reduced military spending during his presidency, sharply criticized the Kennedy administration's escalation in military-space expenditures, which were made in the context of Keynesian planned deficits to stimulate economic growth. Eisenhower said:

> there is no way in which a country can satisfy the craving for absolute security—but it can easily bankrupt itself, morally and economically, in attempting to reach that illusory goal through arms alone. The military establishment, not productive in itself, necessarily must feed on the energy, productivity, and brainpower of the country, and if it takes too much, our total strength declines.[12]

NSC-68 and Military Keynesianism

The origins of Military Keynesianism coincide with the origins of the cold war. Truman's call for increased military expenditures in March 1948 signified a politically significant turn in policy, but only an additional $3 billion was requested. The administration had still not fully accepted the need for political and military mobilization of U.S. resources as a consequence of the deterioration in U.S.–Soviet relations. Moreover, the administration was severely constrained by congressional and public opposition to increased government spending.

In January 1950, in response to the explosion of a nuclear device by the Soviet Union, the secretaries of State and Defense were directed by the president "to undertake a reexamination of our objectives in peace and war and of the effect of these objectives on our strategic plans."[13] This exercise, which subsequently became known under its National Security Council designation NSC-68, was the policy instrument of those in the administration who were advocating a far-reaching U.S. military build-up.[14]

The State Department representatives, led by Paul Nitze, Director of the Policy Planning Staff, were the principal advocates of such views, while the Department of Defense was by all accounts a somewhat reluctant participant. The April 1950 report, submitted before the Korean war, espoused a Manichaean view of historic confrontation between an aggressive and expansive Soviet Union and the "free world" led by the United States. More significantly, it called for a comprehensive build-up of U.S. military forces, as well as other measures, to counter the supposed Soviet threat.

Although all participants generally agreed on the political and ideological tenor of the report and the need for increased military spending, the State Department representatives envisioned a doubling or tripling of levels of military spending. The Department of Defense representatives favored much more modest, marginal increases. As a result, no dollar estimates were included in the original report.

The initial NSC-68 report and the ensuing policy discussion within the administration also mark the beginnings of a new perception of the economic implications of military spending. The advocates of massive rearmament had to dispel the then established view that military spending itself threatened the economy. They cited the performance of the economy during World War Two and the expansionary, vaguely Keynesian economic views espoused in particular by Leon Keyserling, who succeeded Nourse as chairman of the Council of Economic Advisers.

The drafters of NSC-68 contrasted the high levels of employment and production achieved during World War Two to the shrunken economy and recessionary tendencies prevailing in 1950:

> Furthermore, the United States could achieve a substantial absolute increase in output and could thereby increase the allocation of resources to a build-up of the economic and military strength of itself and its allies without suffering a decline in its real standard of living. Industrial production declined by 10 percent between the first quarter of 1948 and the last quarter of 1949, and by approximately one-fourth between 1944 and 1949. In March 1950 there were approximately 4,750,000 unemployed, as compared to 1,070,000 in 1943 and 670,000 in 1944. The gross national product declined slowly in 1949 from the peak reached in 1948 ($262 billion in 1948 to an annual rate of $256 billion in the last six months of 1949), and in terms of constant prices declined by about 20 percent between 1944 and 1948.[15]

In their view, the economic lesson of World War Two is clear:

> From the point of view of the economy as a whole, the program might not result in a real decrease in the standard of living, for the economic effects of the program might be to increase the gross national product by more than the amount being absorbed for additional military and foreign assistance purposes. One of the most significant lessons of our World War II experience was that the American economy, when it operates at a level approaching full efficiency, can provide enormous resources for purposes other than civilian consumption while simultaneously providing a high standard of living. After allowing for price changes, personal consumption expenditures rose by about one-fifth between 1949 and 1954, even though the economy had in the meantime increased the amount of resources going into government use by $60–$65 billion (in 1939 prices).[16]

The proponents of increased spending drew a number of conclusions about the economic implications of the military buildup: (1) there was significant unused capacity in the U.S. economy; (2) a further dynamic expansion of the economy might be achieved analogous to that in World War Two; (3) increased military expenditures are not a drag on the economy but may stimulate such an expansion; and (4) higher levels of military spending need not be at the expense of current living standards but are more than offset by the increment in GNP that they generate:

> With a high level of economic activity, the United States could soon attain a gross national product of $300 billion per year, as was pointed out in the President's Economic Report (January 1950). Progress in this direction would permit, and might itself be aided by, a build-up of the economic and military strength of the United States and the free world; furthermore, if a dynamic expansion of the economy were achieved, the necessary build-up could be accomplished without a decrease in the national standard of living because the required resources could be obtained by siphoning off a part of the annual increment in the gross national product. These are facts of fundamental importance in considering the courses of action open to the United States.[17]

The NSC-68 authors also suggest that without such government spending for military rearmament, the United States and the international economy might relapse into the kind of economic stagnation that characterized the interwar period:

> there are grounds for predicting that the United States and other free nations will within a period of a few years at most experience a decline in economic activity of serious proportions unless more positive governmental programs are developed than are now available.[18]

NSC-68 was not only the source of a militarization of foreign policy and of the corresponding new military strategy of defense through the maintenance of large peacetime forces, but also the beginning of the militarization of economic policy. Military Keynesianism was forged in an ad hoc and eclectic manner under the exigencies of the policy formulation process, but it was neither accidental nor ephemeral. It appealed powerfully to fears of recurring economic stagnation in the interwar years and to hopes for the full employment and prosperity of the war years. Nevertheless, military Keynesianism was not the principal justification for the advocacy of rearmament by the NSC-68 drafters.[19] Rather, the political and military considerations of national security policy are clearly predominant; to implement a massive rearmament in a peacetime economy, proponents had to counter the prevailing orthodoxy within the administration about military expenditures.

The drafters of NSC-68 drew heavily on the expansionist left Keynesianism advocated by Keyserling.[20] Although Keyserling and the Council of Economic Advisers did not directly participate in the original report, its views on the economic potential for the employment of unused capacity and economic expansion bear their imprint.[21]

After receiving the original report, Truman requested a full National Security Council review, including estimates of its probable costs. An ad hoc interagency committee was then set up within the NSC framework, in which Keyserling and the Council of Economic Advisers were direct participants. Their initial response, apart from some precise and technical observations, was distinctly favorable. They endorsed the proposition "that 'a very rapid absolute expansion could be realized' in *total* United States production of all goods and services,"[22] and rejected the orthodox view "that increased defense must mean equivalently lowered living standards, higher taxes and a proliferation of controls."[23] In endorsing its economic arguments, the Council of Economic Advisers allied itself politically with the Department of State, the National Security Resources Board, and the Economic Cooperation Administration against the Department of Defense, the Joint Chief of Staff, and the Bureau of the Budget.

Internal Critics

However, NSC-68 and its facile economic assumptions about military spending were vigorously criticized in the National Security Council review process. The Bureau of the Budget, for example, questioned the Manichaean "free world" versus "slave world" formulation of the Soviet-U.S. rivalry: "it is not true that the U.S. and its friends constitute a free world. Are the Indo-Chinese free? Can the peoples of the Philippines said to be free under the corrupt Quirion government?[24]

Moreover, the Bureau of the Budget severely criticized the economic analysis that the Council of Economic Advisers so blithely accepted. The World War Two economic analogy was rejected as inappropriate for evaluating the capability of the U.S. economy for a sustained peacetime military capability:

> The comparison of the present situation with that of the peak of World War II is misleading. Apart from statistical difficulties in computing GNP in wartime on a basis comparable to peacetime, the effort achieved in 1944 was possible only under wartime conditions, with widespread controls, heavy deterioration in many types of capital assets, and bulging inflationary pressure subject to only short-range restraints. Under a total war effort the United States might, in time and barring internal destruction, exceed its World War II performance, but this effort would not be sustained for a long period and is hardly relevant to the task of a long drawn-out cold war."[25]

The Bureau of the Budget was similarly skeptical about the argument that current unused capacity might be drawn upon for increased military effort. It faulted NSC-68 for failing to see the economy in terms of specific sectors as well as aggregates:

> It would be difficult to conclude categorically that under current conditions substantial further armament demand could be placed upon durable goods' industries without requiring a diversion from present civil purposes either through inflation or through taxes or direct controls.[26]

These critics rejected the view that increased military expenditures would themselves stimulate economic growth and hence be painlessly paid for out of the augmented national product. Instead, they argued that the rearmament program would divert resources from civilian purposes with more subtle long-term effects on the economic system:

1. The necessary higher taxes would dampen incentives without offsetting productive impact from the expenditures.
2. The rate of investment might be slowed.
3. Public expenditures for social and economic development purposes vital to the long-term strength of the economy would be sacrificed.

The Bureau of the Budget thus reached conclusions diametrically opposed to those of the drafters of NSC-68:

> The implications of higher military expenditures are of course mainly a matter of degree. It cannot be said that at any point such expenditures are "too high." They must be sufficient to meet minimum requirements for the security of the nation. But security rests in economic as well as military strength, and due consideration should be given to the tendency for military expenditures to reduce the potential rate of economic growth, and at an advanced stage to require measures which may seriously impair the functioning of our system.[27]

This controversy about the necessity and economic feasibility of a large-scale buildup of U.S. military forces was resolved by the outbreak of the Korean war in June 1950 and the subsequent Chinese intervention. Rearmament became both a practical necessity and politically feasible. The size and scope of the rearmament program went far beyond the immediate requirements of the Korean war and reflected the larger NSC-68 design for forces sufficient to confront and deter the Soviet threat as perceived by U.S. policymakers on a worldwide scale. The conclusions of NSC-68 were officially accepted by the president and National Security Council as a statement of national policy on September 30, 1950.

Even though the size of the Korean buildup was far beyond the outside NSC-68 estimates, Keyserling remained optimistic about the long-term capacity of the U.S. economy to absorb such high levels of military spending. He emphasized the need for government planning and programs for the expansion of productive capacity as the basic economic approach to the military rearmament program, and he initially opposed direct wage and price controls. Subsequent government policy reflected this approach by providing for accelerated tax amortization and direct loans for expanded productive capacity under the Defense Production Act.[28] These arguments were repeated for the public record in the *Annual Economic Review* of the Council of Economic Advisers of January 1951. Although then conceding that the current military force projections would require drastic cutbacks in durable consumer goods production, Keyserling saw this as only a short-run consequence of the intensity of the buildup, and he continued to combat the old orthodoxy "sometimes expressed that if the military buildup should advance above some stated size it would within a few years 'bleed our economy white' and thus accomplish through our own actions the purposes of the Russians."[29]

Military Keynesianism and the Korean Rearmament

The expansionary impact of military spending on the U.S. economy envisioned by NSC-68 advocates may be described as vaguely Keynesian. There is a clear perception of unused capacity and growth potential in the economy which military expenditures may stimulate, as in the Second World War, and thus military expenditures are not seen as simply competing with civilian economic production but as potentially positively augmenting it. However, NSC-68 lacked conceptual clarity and the specific language of "demand management" for articulating economic policy. For example, NSC-68 also proposed tax increases as necessary for military rearmament; new taxes, as the Bureau of the Budget commented, were inconsistent with the NSC-68 depiction of military rearmament in the context of an expansionary economic policy.

Such inconsistency and lack of conceptual precision is in part a consequence of the compromises and accommodations inherent in the policy-making process and in part a result of the relatively early phase of the development of Keynesian orthodoxy. Moreover, military Keynesianism is seldom an explicit program, but rather a more diffuse ideological set of ideas and assumptions that shape and rationalize governmental policy. Finally, both the NSC-68 drafters and their critics were clearly more concerned with the long-term implications of high levels of military spending, rather than with the response of government policy to fluctuations in the business cycle.

While the first postwar economic recession certainly caused widespread concern about the future course of the U.S. economy in 1949 and 1950, it would be farfetched to interpret the administration's decision to intervene in Korea as a consequence of domestic economic problems. NSC-68 did argue that increased military spending could play a positive economic role, both domestically and internationally, but this assessment was a minority view within the administration. The military rearmament recommended by NSC-68 was adopted only after the outbreak of the Korean war and the U.S. decision to intervene. It seems clear that, for the immediate decision-makers, political considerations in the developing cold war confrontation were more important than the economic issues, and that the magnitude and pace of the rearmament program was a response to the politico-military situation. The threats posed by Korea, the Soviet Union, and "world communism" were also certainly related to a broader political and economic conception of U.S. interests in the postwar world, but these issues are quite different from a simplistic economic interpretation of military spending as a response to domestic economic difficulties.

Moreover, the fact that the 1948–1949 recession had already given way to recovery by Spring 1950 weighs heavily against any such interpretation. As the *Economic Report of the President* for January 1951 reflected, the administration regarded increased military demand as impacting on an economy already at a high level of capacity utilization. Controls were instituted to rechannel production in the short run from civilian uses to the requirements of military production; tax and loan programs were instituted to expand capacity to meet military needs.[30] These responses are inconsistent with an interpretation of the rearmament program as a Keynesian or military Keynesian response to problems of deficient aggregate demand. On the other hand, military Keynesianism was advocated at the highest levels and did help rationalize massive rearmament to policymakers and the public.

Even after the adoption of NSC-68 and the Korean rearmament program, the Truman administration continued to espouse the fiscal orthodoxy of balanced budgets and proposed tax increases to cover the increased expenditures. In FY 1947 to 1949, the budget was balanced, but in FY 1950 there was a $3 billion deficit, largely related to the economic recession. By FY 1951, the first year of the war, tax increases contributed to a $6 billion budget surplus. In FY 1952, the deficit was $1.5 billion as the tax revenues failed to keep pace with the increase in military expenditures. Although the administration's fiscal practice was not as orthodox as its principles, it was in part hampered by congressional reluctance to increase taxes. The NIPA federal surplus reached $15.7 billion for the first two years of the Korean buildup; in the following three years, the deficit only reached $16.8 billion.[31]

The Eisenhower administration was even less ready than its predecessor to embrace an explicitly Keynesian conception of the role of government fiscal policy. Furthermore, Eisenhower was personally convinced of the negative economic implications of high levels of military expenditure and the "New Look" national defense strategy of the early 1950s was significantly shaped by these views. To control military spending, Eisenhower's strategic doctrine relied heavily on nuclear weapons ("more bang for the buck"), a strategy that has persisted until now.[32]

The Kennedy administration was the first to endorse the new economics of Keynesian demand management. It was also the first to practice military Keynesianism in an explicit and intentional form. The sharp expansion of government spending from 1962 to 1964, accompanied by the Kennedy-Johnson tax cuts, was largely an expansion of military and related space programs. The Kennedy era is the paradigm of military Keynesianism in recent U.S. economic policy.

After the Korean rearmament, the level of military expenditure never returned to its prewar lows as the cold war arms economy became permanently established. The old orthodoxy on military expenditures still lingered on, especially in the pronouncements of the Eisenhower administration. On the other hand, the new arms economy had brought about a structural change in the face of the economy and alterations in the relationship of government to the economy as well as within the federal budget. Interventionist government—that is, a fiscal policy with significant leverage on the economy—is largely the result of the rise of the arms economy. Even such liberal analysts as Galbraith recognized these new structural features in the U.S. political economy:

> If a large public sector of the economy . . . is the fulcrum for the regulation of demand, plainly military expenditures are the pivot on which the fulcrum rests. . . . Military expenditures are what now makes the public sector large. Without them the federal government would be rather less than half of its present size. It is most unlikely that this would exercise the requisite leverage on the economy.
>
> Nor is it sufficient that other public outlays make up the quantitative total. For in addition to the problem of obtaining them in the necessary volume, there is also that of underwriting technology and therewith the planning of the industrial system. Spending for schools, parks and the poor would not do this.[3]

Military Keynesianism thus became, even when Keynesian theory was not yet fully accepted, a de facto policy for shoring up demand in the U.S. economy. It also created the essential institutional preconditions for government intervention in the form of countercyclical demand management through marginal shifts in military expenditure, even when it was not fully acknowledged or ineptly practiced—as during the Eisenhower administration.

Notes

1. Writing in the *New Republic* in the Summer of 1940, Keynes himself clearly perceived the implications of his economic theories for a new and positive assessment of military spending. He expressed the view that a capitalist democracy such as the United States could only in wartime undertake the scale of expenditures necessary to prove his case and predicted that: "war preparations, so far from requiring a sacrifice, will be a stimulus . . . to greater individual consumption and a higher standard of life." *New Republic,* 103:5 (July 29, 1940), p. 158. On military Keynesianism, see David Gold, "The Rise and Decline of the Keynesian Coalition," *Kapitalistate,* no. 6 (Fall 1977), pp. 129–161; and Clarence Y.H. Lo, "The Conflicting Functions of U.S. Military Spending after World War II," *Kapitalistate,* no. 3 (Spring 1975), pp. 26–44. The reasons why military expenditure may be particularly appropriate for the purposes of Keynesian demand management are summarized in chapter 2.

2. Lawrence J. Korb, "The Budget Process in the Department of Defense, 1947–77: The Strengths and Weaknesses of Three Systems," *Public Administration Review* (July/August 1977), pp. 334–335.

3. This term is from Samuel Huntington, *The Common Defense* (New York: Columbia University Press, 1961) p. 4.

4. Paul Y. Hammond, "NSC-68: Prologue to Rearmament," in Warren R. Schilling and others, *Strategy, Politics and Defense Budgets* (New York: Columbia University Press, 1962), p. 328.

5. Published in Edwin G. Nourse, *Economics in the Public Service* (New York: Harcourt, Brace, 1953), appendix E.

6. Edward S. Flash, *Economic Advice and Presidential Leadership* (New York: Columbia University Press, 1965), p. 37.

7. Huntington, *The Common Defense,* p. 26.

8. Ibid.

9. Paul A. Koistinen, *The Military-Industrial Complex, A Historical Perspective* (New York: Praeger, 1980), p. 13.

10. Koistinen, p. 13.

11. See Huntington, *The Common Defense,* and Schilling, *Strategy, Politics, and Defense Budgets,* for discussions of Eisenhower's conception of the relationship between military spending and the economy.

12. Eisenhower, "Spending into Trouble," *Saturday Evening Post,* May 18, 1963, p. 17.

13. *Foreign Relations of the United States 1950* (Washington, D.C.: GPO, 1977), vol. 1, p. 236.

14. For the context and development of NSC-68 see Fred Block, "Economic Instability and Military Strength: The Paradoxes of the 1950 Rearmament Decision," *Politics and Society,* 10:1 (1980), pp. 35–58; Hammond, "NSC-68"; and Samuel Wells, Jr., "Sounding the Tocsin: NSC-68 and the Soviet Threat," *International Security,* 4:2 (Fall 1979).

15. *Foreign Relations of the United States 1950,* vol. 1, p. 258.

16. Ibid., p. 286.

17. Ibid., p. 258.

18. Ibid., p. 261.

19. Block, "Economic Instability and Military Strength," for example, tends toward this view.

20. For an overview of Keyserling's stewardship see Flash, *Economic Advice.*

21. See, for example, the Council's *Annual Economic Review* in *Economic Report of the President* (Washington, D.C.: GPO, 1950), January 1950 in which Keyserling's arguments for increasing GNP through fuller utilization of the nation's productive resources are set forth in "Pathways to Economic Growth."

22. *Foreign Relations of the United States 1950,* vol. 1, pp. 308ff.

23. Ibid., p. 311.

24. Ibid., p. 300.

25. Ibid., p. 304.

26. Ibid., p. 304.

27. Ibid., p. 305.

28. These views are contained in the Council of Economic Advisers' comments on the rearmament program: "Economic Implications of the Proposed Programs: Required Fiscal Policy, Budgetary and Other Economic Policies," in *Foreign Relations of the United States 1950,* vol. 1, p. 430.

29. "Annual Economic Review," in *Economic Report of the President* (Washington, D.C.: GPO, January 1951), pp. 81–82.

30. Ibid.

31. *Economic Report of the President, February 1982* (Washington, D.C.: GPO, 1982), tables B-73, B-74.

32. See Huntington, *The Common Defense,* pp. 64ff. and Schilling, *Strategy, Politics, and Defense Budgets.*

33. John Kenneth Galbraith, *The New Industrial State* (New York: New American Library, 1968), pp. 238–239, 240.

2

Military Expenditure: Some Basic Concepts

Increasing attention has been given in recent years to the economic and social consequences of the arms race, both within the United Nations and by scholars and institutes associated with the growing field of peace research.[1,2] Military expenditure and measures of the military burden have been basic terms. Yet this research is plagued by two problems: the unreliability of the available comparative data and the lack of an agreed-upon definition of military expenditure. Even for the United States, about which rather too much than too little financial data are available, there is no agreement on the definition of military expenditure.

The definitional problem has several sources: the difficulties inherent in measuring a phenomenon as complex as military expenditure, divergent perspectives of the researchers, and in many cases, their institutional and political interests. The national security establishment's policy discussions of military expenditure, which focus primarily on military preparedness and the military balance, are very different from research conducted by those more concerned with the economic and social consequences of the arms race (such as the U.S. Arms Control and Disarmament Agency and the Stockholm International Peace Research Institute). Both the Carter and Reagan administrations have cited CIA estimates of increases in Soviet military spending to justify their own proposed increases. That is, they have used military expenditure data as an index of relative military effort; their institutional-political bias has been to exaggerate Soviet expenditures and to minimize the U.S. military effort.

Moreover, institutional interest and definitional bias may vary in an ad hoc way. Within NATO, for example, there has been an intense discussion about military expenditures in terms of burden sharing—that is, the relative contributions of the member states to the alliance's collective military effort. Both the Carter and Reagan administrations have increased U.S. military spending and pressured NATO allies and Japan to make corresponding increases. In this case, the issue is relative burden sharing, and the institutional interest of the parties in defining military expenditure is to emphasize the national contribution. According to one account, the Carter administration applied three different yardsticks to show that it was increasing defense expenditures by 3 percent a year in real terms.[3]

This chapter examines some major issues concerning the definition and measurement of military spending in terms of its economic and social consequences. Although the focus is on U.S. military spending, the conclusions are also applicable to other developed market economies.

Military Expenditure and Economic Utility

Military expenditure is an economic burden for a nation's economy. Such expenditures represent a government allocation of national resources for a military product that flows neither into consumption, which increases the general standard of living, nor into investment, which benefits society's future productive capacity. Military expenditures are both economically unproductive and socially wasteful. Indeed, military goods and services are unique in that this output leaves the economic cycle almost entirely. If all U.S. military equipment purchased and produced in a given year were thrown into the sea it would have no significance for either the standard of living of the American people or for the productive capacity of American industry.[4]

Military expenditure is thus distinctive among other types of public consumption expenditures. Most U.S. federal budget expenditures for goods and services benefit the standard of living, either individually or collectively (such as social outlays for health care, education, and social services), or are social investments (such as outlays for transportation, community and regional development, science, and technology).[5] Such nonmilitary programs, of course, are not free from waste or inefficiency, but they are not inherently economically unproductive and socially wasteful like military outlays are.

Some other governmental overhead expenditures may not directly benefit either consumption or investment, such as costs for the administration of justice, the conduct of foreign affairs, and operation of the legislative branch. However, such expenditures are both relatively small (approximately 10 percent of recent military outlays) and contribute positively to the operation and maintenance of a large and complex society. At best, military expenditures can be said to be imposed by external political requirements and represent a burden for the domestic economy and society—a distinction consistently emphasized by liberal critics of the social and economic effects of military spending,[6] as well as some neo-Marxists.[7]

However, the predominant tendency in defense economics regards military spending as the purchase of the public good "defense" or "national security" and, therefore, similar to other public choices.[8] Once the military expenditure has been transmuted in this fashion, there is by implication a practically inelastic demand function for national security that takes precedence over all others. But, as one critic has argued:

we don't know what quantity of defense results from a given defense budget; we don't know whether a larger defense budget will deter an attack or provoke an arms race, whether antiballistic missiles will be effective or not, whether it is better to use tanks or Maginot lines, to carry a big stick or to sign a non-aggression pact. We do not, in short, know the production function for the collective good of national security, so that belief about that production function rests as much upon ideology and fashion as upon empirical estimation.[9]

The actual relationship of military expenditure to defense or national security is at best controversial and speculative. In practice, political decision-makers have usually been aware of this. Although they have accorded a high priority to military needs, by no means do they allow an unlimited claim. The theory of public goods as applied to military expenditure obfuscates this basic fact. Moreover, whether military expenditures are wisely or even necessarily spent is another issue; for our purposes, it is important merely to stress that in economic terms ships, tanks, guns, troops, and so forth are being purchased that contribute neither to production nor to social consumption.

The armed confrontation between the East and West since World War Two has produced novel ways of thinking about military force and military expenditure. The conventional wisdom now holds that the arms race is a strategy for peace (marked by familiar slogans such as "arming for peace" and "peace through strength") and that military expenditure begets economic prosperity as well as national security. In this context, the characterization of military expenditure as unproductive and wasteful may seem strident and vaguely radical. In fact, however, this view has been predominant throughout the history of economic thought. For example, Adam Smith, while regarding the protection of society from violence and invasion by other societies as "the first duty of the sovereign," considered the growing expense entailed by standing armies and increasingly more specialized and expensive armaments to be a burden on the labor of the rest of society who must maintain them.[10] The economic burden of the arms race is, of course, only a limited aspect of the economic implications of military spending. As Say, the French economist and contemporary of Smith, observed, the soldier is not merely an unproductive worker but a "destructive worker":

not only does he *not* enrich society with any product, not only does he consume the products necessary for his maintenance, but only too often he is called upon to destroy . . . the fruits of others' hard labor.[11]

The mainstream of classical economic theory until the end of World War Two held that military spending absorbed resources or distorted their allocation without any utility for the civilian economy.[12]

Obviously, the characterization of military expenditures as unproductive and socially wasteful is subject to some qualifications. First, it applies most strongly to expenditures for military equipment. Expenditures for weapon systems, labeled "procurement" in the Defense budget, are only a fraction of the total budget. Weapons and equipment spending amounted to 25.7 percent of total Department of Defense (DOD) outlays in 1980. Personnel costs were 46.9 percent; operations and maintenance, 18.9 percent; and research and development, 9.8 percent.[13] Operations and maintenance includes, in addition to specialized military products, such items as fuel, automobiles, office machines, food, and clothing that are similar to or identical to corresponding civilian products. Although such items have some potential for conversion to civilian use, it is their actual military end use that contributes to the military burden on government budgets and the gross national product.

Second, military expenditures do have spillover benefits for the civilian economy. For example, health and welfare programs for military personnel benefit individuals, and military training may impart skills relevant to the needs of the civilian economy. As discussed later, it has been argued in particular that military research and development has such secondary benefits for the civilian economy. In addition, military institutions sometimes perform purely civilian functions. For example, the U.S. Army Corps of Engineers carries out extensive river and harbor construction projects.

Military Expenditure and GNP Accounting

The economic significance of military expenditure becomes a practical problem for economists and for government in defining gross national product (GNP) in U.S. national income accounting. The definition of GNP is predicated on strongly conventional and even ideological assumptions: it reflects the world view and the particular policy concerns of a society.[14]

GNP is used to measure national income and product. It can be defined as the current value of all final goods and services produced by the economy in a year. The major components of U.S. national income accounts are personal consumption (C), gross private domestic investment (I), government purchases of goods and services (G), and net exports (E). Government purchases of goods and services, it should be noted, are distinguished from government transfer payments, such as social security, in which government makes payments without receiving goods or services in return.

GNP has come to be identified with prosperity and economic well-being. Beginning in the 1970s, however, many critics have argued that traditional GNP accounting fails to capture important dimensions of the quality of life. The problem is that GNP, as used as an economic indicator in the

United States and other countries in the last forty years, principally measures economic product in terms of exchange or market value in the money
economy. This definition of the economic product both excludes certain
external costs and fails to include the value of other work performed outside
the cash nexus. Such social costs as the effects of environmental pollution
and traffic congestion are not fully taken into account; neither are many
utilities or use values that occur outside of the money economy (such as
unpaid housework or the product of backyard vegetable gardens). Some
corrections are made for such factors—U.S. GNP imputes the value of
owner-occupied housing, for example.

With respect to military expenditure, what GNP concepts include is
more important than what is excluded. GNP incorporates all goods and services purchased without regard to their actual ordinary economic use
value—that is whether they benefit our standard of living as do consumer
goods and services or whether they contribute to further production, such
as machinery and facilities for making other useful articles. For that matter,
no consideration is given to their actual military utility. Thus, whether a billion dollars is spent to purchase school equipment, install modern steel-
making facilities, or train and equip a new Army division, it is treated as an
addition to the national product.

National income accounting incorporates the conventional view in neo-
classical economics that market price measures the worth of a thing: caveat
emptor! Any distinction between use value and exchange value, such as
posited by Smith, Ricardo, and Marx, is precluded.

This approach is sometimes questionable as applied to market transactions themselves—so-called market imperfections being always present. As
applied to the valuation of government purchases it represents merely an
accounting convention. That is, because there is no market determination
of the value of government goods and services, they are valued in GNP
accounting at the price that government pays for them. This accounting
practice is fraught with potential anomalies. By definition, the government
employee is worth what he or she is paid; government purchases are worth
in GNP terms their cost to the government. The more they cost the greater is
the government sector's contribution to GNP, and GNP accounting is indif-
ferent to whether these expenditures are for military or civilian purposes.
Clearly, this practice violates our intuitive understanding of military spending in relation to other alternative government expenditures, i.e. that it is in
fact an economic burden.

The U.S. economics establishment has voiced similar misgivings about
GNP accounting. For example:

> as social accountants we have to recognize that a society which spends 10
> percent of its total output to provide for defense against potential external

enemies, and another several percent to protect itself against domestic violence, is less well off than a comparable society which can achieve the same level of national and personal security without the need to incur such costs.[15]

Nordhaus and Tobin have also argued that GNP in the case of military expenditure measures production but not welfare, and that military and other similar expenditures, such as police and sanitation services, are "instrumental expenditures" that are "not directly sources of utility themselves but are regrettably necessary inputs to activities that may yield utility"[16] On the basis of this and other similar criticisms, they proposed to amend the national income accounts to construct a measure of economic welfare (MEW) that incorporates the "amenities and disamenities of economic growth" as well as treating defense expenditure and other "regrettable and instrumental" expenditures as overhead costs to be deducted from MEW.

The strongest technical argument made against the inclusion of military expenditures in GNP is that GNP is a measure of final output and excludes intermediate output. For example, the cost of guards, watchmen, weapons, and equipment spent by a private business to protect itself does enter final output as presently defined; on the other hand, the cost of these activities does enter into final output in national income accounting if governments hire policemen or consumers purchase locks and guns:

> If all of the business firms in the community got together and decided to form a private army to defend their property against external aggression, the national accounts would faithfully register the fact that national defense outlays were intermediate product and not final product. But if the citizens of the community band together through their government and decide to hire a public army, it's final output.[17]

Military product is treated as interchangeable with all other possible types of government consumption expenditure and counted for GNP purposes as an additional component of output rather than as a social expense. As we have seen, these two characteristics—interchangeability and additionality—of military product in GNP accounting are questionable. The definite bias in the way in which military expenditures are treated in U.S. national economic accounting has implications for the economic and social consequences of the arms race. It represents both an indifference to this pattern of resource allocation and even a subtle legitimation of such expenditures. Moreover, it obscures analysis of their actual significance even in an economic sense. However necessary such military expenditures may be, they constitute an economic burden rather than an addition to the social product. A system of national income accounting in a democratic society should express that clearly and provide the basis for an analysis of the military burden.

Defining Military Expenditure

To assess the burden of military spending on the U.S. economy and society, there has to be some agreed upon definition of military expenditure. However, even the measurement of U.S. military expenditure is controversial, not to mention the difficulties of comparing miliatary expenditures of different countries and different social systems (such as the USSR). The U.S. federal budget and other goverment reports employ four different definitions of the scope of military expenditure:

1. Department of Defense military spending.
2. National defense function expenditures.
3. Defense purchases of goods and services as defined in the National Income and Product Accounts (NIPA) of the Department of Commerce.
4. The NATO definition of U.S. military expenditure developed to measure burden-sharing within the alliance.

The latter two definitions refer to military expenditure as current outlays within a given year. However, DOD and defense spending may refer either to budget authority, obligations incurred, or actual outlays. In general, Congress grants budget authority in the form of appropriations, which permit DOD or other government agencies to incur obligations. Military or defense appropriations in the budget represent the amount of new budget authority. Outlays are the payments made during the fiscal year for obligations incurred. Not all budget authority in appropriations for a given year will be obligated or spent in that year.

In the case of major military procurements and construction, the initial budget authority in the Congressional appropriation covers the estimated cost of the project even though obligations incurred and actual outlays may take place over a period of many years.[18] Figure 2–1 illustrates the relationship between budget authority and outlays. In periods of increasing military expenditure, budget authority in a given year may be considerably in excess of actual outlays. These distinctions become significant in the subsequent analysis of military expenditure and its economic and social consequences.

In turn, each category of military expenditure has several major components (see table 2–1):[19]

1. DOD military spending includes personnel costs (including military retirement pay), operations and maintenance, procurement, research and development, and military construction (including family housing). Not included are DOD civil expenditures, primarily funds for the Army Corps of Engineers.

2. The national defense budget category is a second, broader functional definition of military spending. In addition to DOD military spend-

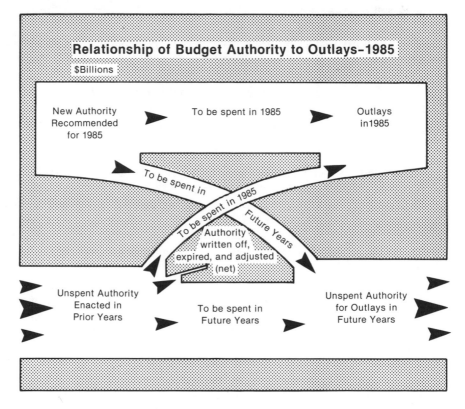

Source: *Budget of the United States Government, Fiscal Year 1985* (Washington, D.C.: Government Printing Office, 1984).

Figure 2-1. The Relationship of Budget Authority to Outlays

ing, it also includes some related expenditures by other departments and agencies: Department of Energy (DOE) expenditures for nuclear weapons and nuclear reactors for Navy vessels, plus the cost of maintaining strategic stockpiles, the costs of the Selective Service System, and emergency planning. This definition of national defense expenditures is clearly rather narrow, suggesting much more than it actually includes. It is the most widely quoted official figure on U.S. government military spending and has been frequently criticized for being too restrictive and hence misleading about the magnitude and impact of U.S. military expenditures, as discussed later.

3. National income accounts data on military spending measures government military purchases of goods and services according to the conventions of U.S. GNP accounting. NIPA both includes some items in the national defense budget category and excludes others. The major exclusion is

Table 2-1.
U.S. Military Expenditure: Four Official Definitions
($ billions current)

	DOD-Military		National Defense				NATO
	Budget Authority	*Outlays*	*Budget Authority*	*Outlays*	*NIA Defense Purchases*	
1950	14.1	11.7	16.5	12.4	12.9	14.6
1955	30.4	35.2	32.9	39.8	38.7	40.4
1960	40.9	41.5	44.3	45.2	44.6	45.4
1965	49.1	45.9	50.6	47.5	48.1	51.8
1970	74.1	77.1	75.3	78.6	75.8	77.9
1975	85.7	84.9	86.2	85.6	80.2	90.9
1980	142.6	132.8	145.8	135.9	126.1	144.0

Sources: DOD-Military, National Defense Budget Function and National Income Account Defense Purchases taken from Office of the Assistant Secretary of Defense (Comptroller), *National Defense Budget Estimates for FY 1983*, pp. 77, 81; budget authority data is from *National Defense Budget Estimates for FY 1982*, p. 5, NATO definition of U.S. military expenditures from *World Armaments and Disarmament: SIPRI Yearbook 1983* (calendar year basis).

retirement pay for military personnel, which is considered a transfer payment and not payment for current services. Foreign military assistance, which is included in the international affairs rather than the national defense function in the U.S. budget, is considered to be a defense purchase for GNP accounting purposes. There is also an important difference in the time at which military purchases are recorded. Defense purchases are entered in the national income accounts only when the finished product is delivered; whereas data on appropriations, obligations incurred, and even outlays, which usually take the form of progress payments and then final payment on delivery, will record military procurement expenditures earlier.

4. The NATO definition includes, in addition to direct military costs, military research and development, and retirement pensions for military personnel. It is thus roughly equivalent to the defense function category in the U.S. government budget. However, it also includes foreign military assistance and paramilitary or police forces trained and equipped for military operations. Such items as war pensions, civil defense expenditures, and payments on war debts are not included within the scope of the NATO definition.

Selectivity in Defining Military Expenditure

Definitions of military expenditure are typically selective and often politically biased. Although the military usually minimizes its expenditures in relation to other government outlays (and maximizes the expenditures of potential foes), critics are more inclined to count all credible military-related costs. The national defense budget category, for example, represents only a fraction of military-related expenditures; it does not include veterans benefits, retirement pay for DOD civilian personnel, foreign military assistance, and interest payments on a national debt largely due to past military expenditures. The argument for including such additional items is considered in chapter 3.

A current effort to change the way in which military retirement costs are calculated within the Pentagon budget illustrates the politics of defining military expenditure.[20] In 1980, military pensions reached $11.9 billion (in comparison to $30.8 billion in personnel costs for active-duty personnel), roughly 9 percent of 1980 DOD outlays. Because military retirement costs will rise much faster in the early 1980s than total compensation for active-duty personnel, the Carter and Reagan administrations proposed that DOD retirement costs be calculated in a different way.[21] In the past, the DOD budget reflected the costs of current retiree payments. The change that went into effect with the FY 1985 budget shifted this to an accrual accounting basis; the budget now reflects liabilities currently being accrued for future retirement pay obligations (rather than current payments for past service). The effect will be to significantly reduce the Pentagon budget. For example, DOD retirement costs would have been an estimated $15.9 billion lower for the 1980–1984 budget period.

Retirement pay for civil service employees is not included in the DOD budget, nor in the budget of any agency, nor in the national defense function within the federal budget. During FY 1980, the federal government paid an estimated $14 billion to 1.7 million retired federal employees; the unfunded liability of the Federal civil service system had reached an estimated $124 billion by 1982. Because the DOD and other defense-related agencies account for approximately one-half of civil service employment in the postwar period, such retirement pay represents a very significant cost factor that does not appear in official calculations of defense costs. There are no indications that DOD intends to push for an extension of accrual accounting principles to civil service retirement or to include veterans benefits, now excluded entirely from its budget. Therefore, the proposal to apply accrual accounting only selectively to military retirement payments appears opportunistic.

Selective Data Presentations

Not only has the scope of defense expenditure been narrowly defined, DOD publications and other official documents also understate military spending in other ways.[22] First, relative rather than absolute numbers are used. Thus defense spending may be declining as a percentage of GNP or of total federal expenditures while expenditures are in fact rising. Second, real or constant dollar data are employed for military expenditures, and usually a recent year price level is selected, which has the statistical effect of reducing rates of increase in recent years in comparison with the past. Third, the choice of the base year in terms of which the current level of military spending is located is often misleading. As a result, current reports of the real or constant dollar decline in U.S. military expenditures in the 1970s fail to point out that the 1969–1970 fiscal year was the spending peak of the Vietnam war.

Finally, all federal spending is totaled and military spending is given as a percentage of the unified budget, which is somewhat misleading. A large proportion of the unified budget, developed with Keynesian management of the economy in mind, consists of trust funds earmarked for specific purposes (such as social security). The military competes directly for funding only within the federal funds segment of the budget. Even here some expenditures are relatively uncontrollable, such as interest payments on the debt. The share of military expenditures in the unified budget does not adequately reflect the political opportunity costs of military spending in the appropriations process.[23]

More Is Less: Current and Constant Dollars

The expression of military expenditures in real terms—that is, in constant dollars as opposed to current dollars—is especially important when dealing with timeseries data and considering trends in military spending. The Department of Defense and those concerned with the purchasing power in real terms of military expenditure strive to eliminate the distorting effects of inflation in comparing military expenditures over time by developing a special deflator or price index for each major category of military spending (personnel, procurement, operations and maintenance, research and development, construction) and a composite deflator for military spending as a whole. Military expenditures in different years are compared by expressing them in terms of their purchasing power in a base year.

Because the inflation rate for military purchases is significantly above that in the economy as a whole, the military establishment attempts to have this inflation factor fully reflected in assessing increasing military expenditures. The military deflator shows that more is less in real terms. Although current dollar expenditures show military outlays increasing from $75.8 billion to $159.9 billion between 1971 and 1981, in constant 1972 dollars defense outlays are reported to have declined from $81.5 to $76.6 billion.[24] Similarly, the Department of Defense is inclined to attribute the spiraling costs of weapon programs to inflation for which it can not be held responsible.

Several technical problems are associated with the construction of a defense deflator. A price index measures the change in the price of a cross-section of identical goods at different times. However, military purchases, particularly those for military equipment, are subject to high rates of technical change. That is, the nature of the goods purchased change significantly from year to year. It is difficult to distinguish between price increases resulting from qualitative improvements and those caused by inflation.[25]

More fundamentally, however, the use of a specific defense deflator is designed to compare the purchasing power of monies allocated to the military over time. The higher the rate of inflation in defense purchases, the more funds must be allocated to maintain the same real level of military effort. A special defense deflator is perhaps appropriate for measuring military effort in terms of material and personnel inputs but not for measuring the real social costs of military expenditure. In this case, the GNP deflator, which is a composite of rising price levels in the entire economy, is more appropriate for comparing trends in military spending.

Table 2-2 compares the results of using a defense deflator and a GNP deflator on defense spending for the 1970–1980 period. By FY 1981 real or constant 1972 dollar expenditures are actually 10 percent higher than the defense-deflator figures. Pre-1972 data indicate that DOD outlays were lower in the past and higher in the present in terms of real GNP constant dollars than the official figures indicate. No matter which deflator is used, the "decline" of DOD outlays in the 1970s is only relative to the Vietnam war highs.

Analytic Criteria

The relevance of a given category of military-related expenditure (or the type of financial transactions measured) depends on the hypothesis or relationship being investigated within some analytic framework. Three principal types of inquiry occur in discussions of military expenditure and should be distinguished:

1. To investigate the significance of military expenditures for Keynesian demand management of the economy by the Federal government.

Table 2-2
DOD Constant Price Outlays Based on Defense Deflator and GNP Deflator

	Deflators (1972 = 100)			Constant Prices (billions)	
Fiscal Year	DOD Composite	GNP	Current $ (millions)	DOD Deflator	GNP Deflator
1950	40.1	53.5	11,674	29.1	21.8
1955	50.0	61.4	35,169	70.3	57.3
1960	60.3	69.5	41,494	68.6	59.7
1965	66.1	74.9	45,880	66.2	61.3
1970	87.1	90.9	77,070	88.5	84.8
1972	100	100	75,076	75.1	75.1
1973	107.4	104.4	73,223	68.2	70.1
1974	116.2	112.0	77,550	66.7	69.2
1975	127.4	123.1	84,900	66.6	70.0
1976	136.8	131.7	87,891	64.2	66.7
1977	146.0	140.6	95,557	65.4	68.0
1978	156.7	150.0	103,043	66.8	68.7
1979	168.3	162.9	115,013	68.3	70.6
1980	187.4	176.8	132,840	70.9	75.1
1981	211.5	193.5	156,096	73.8	80.7

Source: DOD 1972 outlays from *National Defense Budget Estimates for FY 1983*. Constant prices for GNP deflator are based on author's calculations.

2. To use military expenditure data as a basis for assessing national military effort and, indirectly, the military potential of states. This inquiry is the primary focus, for example, of the International Institute of Strategic Studies, annual report, *The Military Balance,* and UN disarmament strategies that focus on reduction of military budgets are also primarily concerned with military potential.[26]
3. To examine the social and economic effects of military spending.

Depending on the focus of the inquiry, different definitions of military expenditure with somewhat different scopes will be appropriate.

The Military Keynesianism Focus. Military expenditure is particularly suited for Keynesian management of the U.S. economy for a number of reasons. First, while there is resistance to the general expansion of the government sector and government spending, it is easier to gain congressional and public support for defense spending, which does not compete with the private sector or undermine business confidence.

Second, defense spending is highly flexible because there is no readily conceivable general state of oversupply of military goods with a rapid rate of technological obsolescence in a competitive arms race. That is, the United States can have too many schools, hospital beds or, even highways, but military spending for national security is subject to no such manifest limits. Furthermore, military procurement programs can be accelerated or stretched out to conform to the short-run requirements of economic policy and new weapon systems can be initiated or dropped with great flexibility, because they play no functionally constrained role in the economy.

Third, military expenditure represents government purchases of goods and services that stimulate the economy in a direct and immediate way; the economic effect begins as soon as contracts are let or "obligations incurred," in contrast to the more indirect stimulation of a tax cut, reduced interest rates, or increased transfer payments, all of which take much longer to affect employment. Because defense purchases of goods and services account for more than two-thirds of all federal purchases, this instrument is ready at hand for U.S. policymakers.

Fourth, in contrast to increased consumer spending and to many government social programs, military demand is particularly focused on the stagnation-prone capital goods sector because of the high ratio of hardware and construction in military spending and the specialized and shifting channels of military final demand.[27]

The military Keynesianism thesis stresses the controllability of military spending and its direct impact, particularly on capital goods industries. It thus implies a strong distinction between government purchases of goods and services and transfer payments. Government purchases are a more controllable expenditure in contrast to transfer payments, which are based on entitlements. They entail a higher component of demand for investment goods and stimulate production more directly than increases in individual disposable income that must work their way through the economy.

However, studies with this focus typically employ broad definitions of military expenditure. Cypher, for example, includes the national defense budget, 50 percent of the international affairs budget (to embrace military assistance and part of foreign economic assistance), veterans benefits, 75 percent of interest payments on the federal debt, and all NASA expenditures.[28]

This type of expansive definition in fact confuses military-related expenditures with quite different characteristics. Veterans benefits, for example, are primarily transfer payments, not government purchases.[29] The level of expenditures is largely based on entitlements acquired through past military service in wartime and is not easily manipulable for purposes of short-term Keynesian demand management.

Interest on the U.S. debt, whatever the origins of that debt, is also a transfer payment and also relatively uncontrollable. Similarly, military retirement pay (which Cypher includes) and civilian retirement pay (which he does not) are transfer payments in national income account terms; these entitlements are fixed by law and cannot be easily varied in the short-run for purposes of economic policy. The inclusion of such extraneous elements would seem likely to distort any effort to examine this thesis empirically. On the other hand, Cypher does employ "obligations incurred" as the government transactions category, which is more appropriate than outlays to measure how military spending stimulates the economy. The inclusion of foreign economic assistance, military assistance, and NASA expenditures also seems to be appropriate, as would the addition of foreign military sales. Although such sales are not a cost for the U.S. federal budget, they represent a constrollable stimulus that can help to stabilize production in both the U.S. military-industrial sector and related capital goods industries.

The Social and Economic Effects Focus. To determine the economic resources utilized for military purposes it is generally important, first, to distinguish between the societal use of real resources for military purposes and the use of government financial resources as expressed in budget allocations, and second, to distinguish between the current burden of past military efforts on both real resources and financial resources and the current cost of present and continuing military efforts. For example, military procurement purchases represent not only a financial burden on the government budget but also the societal use of real resources for current military effort. Military retirement pay, on the other hand, represent a significant financial drain on government resources but is merely a transfer payment rather than an allocation of material resources; moreover, it represents a current financial burden resulting from past military efforts and would not be affected by even total disarmament. These considerations are of central importance for an evaluation of the social and economic implications of military spending and are considered in detail in chapter 3.

The Military Potential Focus. If the focus of an inquiry is the military potential of states, the relevance of various military-related expenditures changes accordingly. All costs that result from past military efforts (such as veterans benefits, military retirement pay, interest payments on war debt) are no longer relevant. Similarly, the inquiry must distinguish between military purchases of goods (such as hardware) and personnel costs. U.S. military personnel costs have increased sharply as a consequence of the shift to an all-volunteer force (which, some critics argue, may have reduced the quality of U.S. preparedness even as costs increase). A detailed consideration of the use of data on military expenditure to assess the military potential of states is beyond the scope of this book.

Opportunity Costs and Military Spending

The concept of opportunity costs is particularly important for the analysis of the economic and social consequences of military expenditure. Benoit credits Frederich von Wiesner as being the first economist to employ the modern conception of opportunity costs as foregone opportunities to produce something else.[30] In preindustrial Western societies the costs of maintaining a military establishment were often economically prohibitive. According to Adam Smith it was commonly thought that not more than one hundredth part of the inhabitants of any country can be employed as soldiers, without ruin to the country which pays the expense of their service."[31]

The economic constraints on government allocation of scarce resources to the military are no longer so restrictive in developed industrial societies. The United States allocates a significant part of its labor force and other economic resources for military purposes—averaging over 8 percent of the work force and 8 percent of total GNP in the 1950–1980 period—without catastrophic effects on the civilian economy. Although the U.S. standard of living has not declined in absolute terms as a result of high military expenditures, it has foregone rather significant increases in the standard of living and quality of life.

The concept of opportunity costs reflects above all the economic fact that resources are limited and their allocation for one purpose, the national military effort, precludes other alternative uses. In evaluating the economic and social effects of military expenditures, it enables researchers to understand the alternative, necessarily hypothetical, patterns of civilian expenditure and resource use that are foregone.[32]

The literature focuses on three major uses of the concept in relation to military spending: budgetary opportunity costs in terms of the political allocation of government financial resources; resource opportunity costs in terms of the allocation of real economic resources; and finally, performance opportunity costs in terms of foregone economic performance.

The concept of budgetary opportunity costs is captured in a quotation from a speech by President Eisenhower:

> The cost of one modern heavy bomber is this: A modern brick school in more than thirty cities. It is two electric power plants, each serving a town of 60,000 population. It is two finely equipped hospitals. It is some fifty miles of concrete highway.[33]

Such examples are based on calculating the budgetary costs of a weapon system or other military equipment in comparison with a useful civilian expenditure of comparable cost. This manner of expressing opportunity costs of military expenditures is widespread and effective. Sivard's annual *World Military and Social Expenditures* includes many similar examples.[34]

Resource opportunity costs issues focus on the specific character of real resources in an economic sense. Smith has sensibly cautioned that such simple statements of opportunity costs based on alternative expenditures are misleading.[35] He emphasizes that the economic resources used to produce specialized military equipment (such as specific materials, skilled labor, R&D facilities, specialized machine tools) could not be used to build and staff schools, power plants, or hospitals. It is not merely a question of alternative expenditures: "in calculating opportunities foregone it is necessary to compare only real substitutes, where the economic resources can be transferred from one use to another."

Smith called this approach a "resource cost" analysis that takes into account "the existing structure of production and the specific nature of many inputs and outputs." There is a strong tendency to dwell on military expenditures rather than on the real resources in raw materials, capital, and labor and their potential alternative uses. In this respect Smith's critique of such simple juxtapositions of military hardware and civilian goods is well taken. As he points out, this money illusion is also fostered by the Keynesian income expenditures framework of government economic management, which he criticizes as a one-commodity model that "encourages the perception of aggregate demand as some homogenous fluid."[36]

On the other hand, he may underestimate the flexibility of resources employed in specialized military production, which is only a fraction of military expenditures and real resources allocated to the military effort. In addition to direct substitution between resources employed for specialized military equipment and alternative civilian uses, there may also be considerable flexibility through indirect substitution of resources even in the short run. Any significant release of resources through disarmament measures would not result in a one-to-one pairing of bomber and school construction but would entail shifts in demand and substitutions of resources throughout the entire economy.[37] In the long run, of course, beyond the immediate problems of conversion, a very high degree of resource flexibility can be assumed. More basically, such resource-oriented criticism of opportunity costs stated in terms of budgetary alternatives mistakes their simplicity for naivete. They are evidently addressed to governmental decision-makers and are intended as expressions of budgetary rather than societal opportunity costs in terms of real economic resources.[38]

Performance opportunity costs focus more on the dynamic effects of military expenditures on the functioning of the economy rather than on specific resources consumed. Military expenditures, it is argued, entail lost economic growth or lost jobs, in comparison with alternative civilian expenditure patterns. Marion Anderson, for example, has argued that military expenditures do not in fact create jobs when compared with alternative civilian expenditures. In this view the opportunity costs of military expenditures in lost growth, lost employment, lost exports, and their aggregate drain on the economy may be considerably greater than the resource costs of military expenditures.

Military Keynesianism and Opportunity Costs

An important perspective on the economic impact of military expenditures stresses not supply but demand and sees the problems of the U.S. economy in terms of chronic tendencies toward the underutilization of economic resources. In this view, associated with Keynesian macroeconomic analysis, military expenditures may, in a slack economy, increase the utilization rate of existing capacity and even stimulate higher growth rates. Thus the costs of military spending to society may be offset, in part or in total, by the expansionary effects of the resulting increase in aggregate demand. Thus, it is argued, the U.S. rearmament for World War Two reemployed a major portion of capital, labor and other resources which were unused or underutilized because of the Great Depression. Although New Deal economic policies and the expansion of civilian demand had begun to show some positive effects, full employment and sustained economic growth, was not achieved until the initiation of the military buildup.[39] Similarly, many leftist critics of American capitalism have argued that the relatively high and historically unique period of sustained economic growth after World War

Two is in good part the result of the regulative and stimulative impact of military expenditure on the U.S. economy.[40]

This positive assessment of military Keynesianism compares, in a specific situation of underutilized resources, government military expenditures without reference to possible alternative civilian expenditure patterns. To the extent that military expenditures employ otherwise underutilized or idle economic resources, their marginal opportunity costs may be low in comparison with idle resources. However, performance opportunity costs, in contrast to resource costs, can only be defined in terms of some probable or hypothetical alternative civilian use, and marginal opportunity costs that postulate no alternative civilian expenditure represent a tendentious scenario.

From an opportunity costs perspective, military expenditures are wasted resources from the point of view of the civilian economy. Alternative civilian expenditure patterns would have an equal or greater stimulative effect on aggregate demand. Demand management in a Keynesian sense may also be accomplished by other means than the expansion of government purchases of goods and services, as both U.S. and Western postwar economic history indicates. Finally, military Keynesianism represents more than a discrete allocation of current consumption to military purposes. Productive resources of the economy are reallocated to the military sector, with resultant long-term effects on the structure of the economy.

Applying these three conceptions of opportunity costs to the military expenditures yields somewhat different results. The budgetary perspective equates the opportunity costs of the national military effort with budget outlays that might otherwise have been used for civilian purposes. The resource perspective, on the other hand, understands the opportunity costs of military expenditures in terms of the value of the real resources employed in the light of alternative civilian uses. Performance opportunity costs— growth, employment, and inflation effects—represent a somewhat different and more comprehensive dimension of the analysis of the economic and social consequences of military spending.

Performance opportunity costs are the result of both the budgetary and resource constraints entailed by the national military effort, though not reducible to these. They represent the most important dimension of the opportunity costs of the national military effort, but are also the most difficult to specify. This perspective depends not only on the budgetary and resource restraints imposed by the national military effort but on such additional factors as the characteristics and state of the national economy; the impact of military expenditures and specific resource allocations on growth, employment, inflation, and international competitiveness; the context of government economic policy; and the nature of alternative civilian patterns of expenditure posited in terms of which opportunity costs are assessed. In short, it requires us to think about alternative futures.

Notes

1. *Economic and Social Consequences of the Arms Race and Military Expenditures* (New York: United Nations, 1983); *Study on the Relationship Between Disarmament and Development* (New York: United Nations, 1982) and earlier reports in this series.

2. Both the Stockholm International Peace Research Institute, (SIPRI) and the International Peace Research Institute, Oslo, have devoted considerable attention to such issues. A recent bibliography, *Economic and Social Consequences of the Arms Race and of Military Expenditures, 1977–1981: A Selected Bibliography of English Language Publications,* has been assembled by the Dag Hammarskjold Library of the United States (New York, September 1981). See also the references cited in this book.

3. Arnold Kanter, "That '3 Percent' for Defense," *Washington Post* (December 27, 1978), p. 19.

4. This conception of military expenditures is the basis of an opportunity cost approach to assessing the military burden. See the UN studies cited in note 1 and Seymour Melman, *The Permanent War Economy* (New York: Simon & Schuster, 1974), chapter 1, for example. It was also the conception of military expenditures in classical political economy: see Adam Smith, *An Inquiry into the Nature and Causes of the Wealth of Nations* (Edinburgh, 1976), book 5, chapter 1. It remained the predominant view of the economics of military spending down to the postwar period. See for example, F.W. Hirst, *The Political Economy of War* (London, 1914) and A.C. Pigou, *The Political Economy of War* (London, 1921). The Cold War also led to the development by economists and policymakers of a much more positive assessment of military expenditures that can be termed military Keynesianism." The genesis of this new perspective was discussed in chapter 1 of this book. For an overview of military expenditures in economic thought, see Gavin Kennedy, *The Economics of Defense* (London: Farber & Farber, 1974), chapter 1.

5. An additional large share of government outlays consist of transfer payments, such as social security and interest payments.

6. Perhaps most consistently by Seymour Melman in *Our Depleted Society* (New York: Dell, 1965), *Pentagon Capitalism* (New York: McGraw-Hill, 1970), and the *Permanent War Economy.*

7. See, for example, Ernest Mandel, *Marxist Economic Theory* (New York: Monthly Review Press, 1969).

8. Gavin Kennedy employs this perspective in *The Economics of Defense;* see especially chapter 2.

9. Comment by Mancur Olson in *The Measurement of Economic and*

Social Performance, ed. Milton Moss (New York: National Bureau of Economic Research, 1973), p. 405.

10. Adam Smith, *Wealth of Nations,* "On the Expense of Defense."

11. *Traite d'economie politique,* 1803, book 2, chapter 7, section 2, quoted in Kennedy, *The Economics of Defense,* p. 32.

12. See, for example, A.C. Pigou, *Political Economy of War,* (London, 1921) and F.W. Hirst, *The Political Economy of War* (London, 1914, 1916). For an overview, see Kennedy, *Economics of Defense,* chapter 1.

13. Calculated from *Budget of the United States Government, Fiscal Year 1981* (Washington, D.C.: GPO, 1980), p. 566.

14. For an overview of concepts and problems in national income analysis see Wilfred Beckerman, *An Introduction to National Income Analysis,* 2d ed. (London: Weidenfeld and Nicolson, 1976).

15. F. Thomas Juster, "A Framework for the Measurement of Economic and Social Performance," in Moss, *Measurement of Economic and Social Performance,* p. 48.

16. William D. Nordhaus and James Tobin, "Is Growth Obsolete?" in Moss, ibid., p. 515.

17. Comments by Juster in Moss, ibid., p. 108. Other significant categories of government expenditures may merit a similar classification. Nordhaus and Tobin maintain that expenditures for environmental protection, for example, are similarly an economic cost and not an addition to economic welfare as in the current GNP accounting. Police expenditures may also be considered an expense rather than an addition to national product. Although government military purchases are not in this respect unique, they are by far the largest such item accounting for about two-thirds of U.S. government purchases of goods and services.

18. For a description, see "Budget System and Concepts" in *Budget of the United States Government, Fiscal Year 1983* (Washington, D.C.: GPO, 1982), part 7.

19. For an explanation of definitions 1 and 2 see idid.; on definition 3, see *Budget of the United States, 1979, Special Analyses,* section 1:13, for the relationship between budget outlays and GNP categories; for definition 4, see *SIPRI Yearbook: World Armaments and Disarmament* (London: Taylor and Francis, 1980), p. 34.

20. This discussion relies on Lawrence J. Korb, "The FY 1980–84 Defense Program: Issues and Trends," *AEI Foreign Policy and Defense Review,* 5:4 (1980), p. 9.

21. Ibid. The retirement rolls are projected to increase by about 200,000 people over the next five years; although retirement pay is automatically adjusted to reflect changes in the consumer price index (CPI), current

retirees will draw larger payments because of the sharp increases in military pay scales under the volunteer army.

22. The *Defense Monitor,* 8:7 (June 1979), quotes two Carter administration officials caught in the act of tailoring their descriptions of military spending to fit different audiences. First:

> Defense has not grown and is not growing at the expense of other federal programs. . . Since (1967) . . . Defense has shrunk to about its pre-Vietnam levels. Measured in constant 1972 dollars, Defense obligational authority is today 1.1 percent below that of 1964 (Secretary of Defense Harold Brown, testifying before the House and Senate Budget Committees, February 21, 1979).

Second:

> I am happy to report to you that under President Carter defense resources and forces have risen steadily. We have increased the real level of resources actually devoted to defense to recover from a number of years of decreasing DOD budgets. . . . under President Carter's leadership, we have set a course of steady real growth (Edward R. Jayne, Associate Director, Office of Management and Budget, addressing the American Defense Preparedness Association, March 8, 1979).

The West German government reported three different figures for its military expenditures in a single year, varying from 36 to 52 billion DM in 1979. The lower figure was communicated to the German public while the higher figure was reported to NATO at a time when the German government was under pressure to increase its contribution to the alliance. See Michael Brzoska, Peter Lock, and Herbert Wulf, "An Assessment of Sources and Statistics of Military Expenditure and Arms Transfer Data," (New York: United Nations report prepared for the Group of Governmental Experts on the Relationship between Disarmament and Development, 1980), p. 7.

23. For a critique of official presentations of data on military spending, see "Measuring the Military Burden," *Defense Monitor,* 7:7 (June 1979); and "The Impact of Reagan's Rearmament," Council on Economic Priorities, *Newsletter,* May 1981.

24. See *National Defense Budget Estimates for FY 1983,* chapter II, pp. 79–80.

25. For an excellent discussion, see Ron Huisken, *The Meaning and Measurement of Military Expenditure,* SIPRI Research Report 10 (Stockholm: SIPRI, 1973), pp. 13–15.

26. For the latest UN study with this orientation see *Reduction of Military Budgets, International Reporting of Military Expenditures* (New York: United Nations, 1981).

27. For this type of argumentation see James Cypher, "Capitalist Planning and Military Expenditures," *Review of Radical Political Economy* vol. 6 (1974), pp. 1–19; Thomas Cusack and Miroslav Nincic, "The Political Economy of US Military Spending," *Journal of Peace Research,* 16:2 (1979), p. 112; Michael Reich, "Does the U.S. Economy Require Military Spending?" *American Economic Review,* vol. 62, pp. 296–303.

28. Cypher, "Capitalist Planning," p. 2 and appendix, pp. 16–19.

29. See U.S. Department of Commerce, Bureau of Economic Analysis, *The National Income and Product Accounts of the United States,* 1929–76 Statistical Tables (Washington, D.C.: GPO, 1981), table 3:16.

30. Emile Benoit, "The Monetary and the Real Costs of National Defense," *American Economic Review,* 58:2 (1968), pp. 398–416.

31. Adam Smith, *Wealth of Nations.*

32. David Greenwood, *Budgeting for Defense* (London: Royal United Service Institute for Defense Studies, 1972), p. 7.

33. "The Chance for Peace," in *Department of State Bulletin,* April 27, 1953, quoted by Ron Smith, "The Resource Cost of Military Expenditure," in Mary Kaldor and others, *Democratic Socialism and the Cost of Defense* (London: Croom & Helm, 1979) pp. 263–264.

34. *World Military and Social Expenditures, 1981* (Leesburg, VA.: World Priorities, 1981). Published annually.

35. Ron Smith, "The Resource Cost of Military Expenditure," in Kaldor, *Democratic Socialism and the Cost of Defense,* p. 264.

36. Ibid.

37. Charles Hitch and Roland McKean, *Economics of Defense in the Nuclear Age* (Cambridge, Mass.: Harvard University Press, 1960), pp. 22–24.

38. Although Ron Smith (see note 35) introduces resource cost analysis as a critique of opportunity costs in terms of budgetary expenditures it seems clear from subsequent remarks that it is supplementary rather than an alternative:

> The distinction made in the list above between *substitution in production and expenditure* is important. The former emphasizes the *technical specificity of the factors that produce the output*—to what extent they can be used to produce different types of goods. The latter emphasizes *the social and political trade-offs* which determine the extent to which consumers, government and electorate are willing, *at the margin,* to replace one commodity by another in their total final demand."

39. See chapter 1; for example, the quotation from Keynes in note 1.

40. The classic source of this argument is Paul Baran and Paul Sweezy, *Monopoly Capital* (New York: Monthly Review Press, 1966).

3 The Military Use of Resources

The national defense function as defined by the U.S. budget is the most frequently used definition of military expenditure. In addition to DOD Military expenditures, this narrow definition includes DOE military-related nuclear activities, the costs of maintaining strategic stockpiles, the Selective Service System, and emergency planning (see chapter 2). This chapter presents a broader and more realistic definition of military spending and examines its implications for the U.S. economy and society.

Other Military-Related Expenditures

Critics charge that the U.S. budget seriously understates the costs of the U.S. military effort. They argue that it neglects such items as foreign military assistance, much of foreign economic aid, Veterans Administration expenditures, NASA military-related spending, retirement pay for federal civilian employees in military-related work, and interest payments on the portion of the national debt attributable to past and present military expenditures. Cypher, for example, argues that foreign military assistance to friendly governments on concessional terms also represents a military or national defense expenditure.[1]

The NATO and U.S. national income account definitions do include military assistance. Even the U.S. Arms Control and Disarmament Agency (ACDA) uses the NATO rather than the U.S. budget definition in *World Military Expenditure and Arms Transfers.* In this case the actual expenditures involved are currently minor (about $1 billion in the 1980 budget), because U.S. arms transfers have shifted in recent years from grants to sales of military equipment. An additional $500 million in payments due was waived in the Foreign Military Sales Financing Program.[2]

Another point of contention is foreign economic assistance in the international affairs budget. Foreign economic assistance is coordinated quite closely with the foreign politico-military policy aims of the United States. In 1980, $1.9 billion of this $7.3 billion in outlays was actually included with military assistance in the category of "international security assistance" under international affairs in the budget. Israel and Egypt, which are military allies, have received more U.S. bilateral foreign aid in recent years than other countries. The NATO definition also includes such assistance as U.S. military expenditure. A recent Pentagon study of military burden-sharing within NATO includes foreign aid used as security assistance in calculating members' NATO contribution.[3] In 1953 and 1954 the federal budget actually included all foreign aid as military assistance. Political-military concerns rather than humanism have been the predominant rationale for foreign economic assistance among U.S. policy-makers. Cypher argues that approximately 50 percent of the international affairs budget category, which includes both foreign economic and military assistance, should be considered military expenditure. This estimate appears to be reasonable; of the total 1980 outlay of $5.2 billion, therefore, $2.6 billion would be attributable to national defense.

NASA expenditures are another disputed item. The U.S. military spent $5.3 billion on its space programs in 1979, slightly more than NASA. Critics charge that NASA itself, despite its civilian garb, has a largely military function and orientation.[4] For example, the customers for the space shuttle's first commercial flights are primarily military. However, Cypher's 100 percent allocation of NASA expenditures to the military may well overstate the closeness of the relationship between NASA and the military. A more conservative 50 percent yields $2.6 billion in 1980 NASA military-related outlays.

Interest on the public debt is one of the largest items in the U.S. federal budget after national defense and transfer payments, amounting to $73 billion in 1980. Much of this debt was acquired to meet wartime and peacetime military expenditures. Cypher allocates a full 75 percent of such interest to military expenditures—an additional $56.1 billion in national defense-related outlays for 1980. This argument is convincing because the financing costs of government activities are certainly part of its real costs; the conventional treatment of such expenditures as nondefense expenditures is questionable.

Expenditures for veterans' benefits are included in a separate budget category, apparently on the logic that they do not constitute payment for current services. Clearly, VA benefits compensate military personnel for previous services. The question of when to include such costs in the military budget is open to debate, but total exclusion is arbitrary. Why retirement pensions of military personnel are included in the national defense budget, whereas VA benefits are excluded, remains obscure. These expenditures are quite large in relation to the defense budget; adding VA expenditures puts an additional $21.1 billion in military spending in 1980.

The national defense definition also fails to include retirement pay for DOD civilian employees, which is included in the budget under income security. Such civilian pensions are clearly a nonwage cost of military employment. Retirement pay for all federal civilian employees was $14.7 billion in 1980. Of the 1,882,300 civilian employees, about 1 million worked either directly for DOD (880,000) or for the Veterans Administration (193,100). If 50 percent of these costs are allocated to national defense, an additional $7.4 billion was spent on the military in 1980.

The usual U.S. government data on the economic burden of the military effort also neglects two private sector elements. Foreign military sales—as opposed to grants—are not included in any of the four official definitions of military expenditure in chapter 2. Such sales reached $10 billion in 1980 (including $1.8 billion in commercial exports licensed under the Arms Control Export Act). These sales are cleared directly through the U.S. government, although the ultimate consumer is a foreign state permitted to purchase U.S.-made military equipment. Some companies sell more hardware, such as combat aircraft, to other countries than to the U.S. military; foreign purchases of U.S. military hardware amount to approximately 40 percent of U.S. government purchases—an astounding figure that indicates the importance of these sales to U.S. military-industrial producers.[5] Similarly, these producers' expenditures for investment in plant and equipment in a given year are not included in the narrow definition of military spending.

Murray Weidenbaum and others argue that national income accounts figures on military spending are inadequate to examine the effect of military demand on the American economy because these expenditures are entered in the national income accounts only at the stage of actual delivery of military equipment and final payment. Budget outlays record progress payments over several years only after military production has begun.

According to Weidenbaum, the more useful data series available for an economic analysis is "obligations incurred." Although the stimulus effect, in terms of capital formation and production in the private economy, begins as soon as the U.S. government contracts for purchases, such nongovernmental expenditures for military purposes are recorded either as inventory accumulation or as investment expenditures for plant and equipment, and registered only with a time lag in actual budget outlays or in national income account defense purchases. This distinction is important for the timing of the impact of military expenditures, although obligations incurred are ultimately reflected in budget outlays.[6]

Table 3–1 compares the narrow definition of military expenditure (see chapter 2) with the broader definition that incorporates the military-related expenditures described in this section. Such additions greatly increase total U.S. military expenditures. In 1980 the national defense total increases by 74 percent—from the official $135.9 billion to 237.7 billion. The definition of the scope of military expenditure is thus clearly more than a merely technical question.

Table 3-1
Military Expenditure Conventionally and Broadly Defined
(billions of dollars)

Fiscal Year	National Defense	Other Military-Related Spending								Total Combined Military Expenditure
		Foreign Military Assistance (100%)	NASA (50%)	Veteran Benefits (100%)	Civil Service Retirement (50%)	Foreign Economic Assistance (50%)	Interest on Public Debt (75%)	Foreign Military Sales (100%)	Total	
1972	76.6	.7	1.6	10.7	1.9	1.6	16.5	1.94	34.9	111.5
1973	74.5	.8	1.5	12.0	2.3	1.2	18.1	1.87	37.8	112.3
1974	77.8	1.3	1.5	13.4	2.8	1.4	22.0	3.66	46.1	123.9
1975	85.6	2.0	1.5	16.6	3.5	1.8	24.5	4.05	54.0	139.6
1976	89.4	1.9	1.7	18.4	4.1	1.7	27.8	7.20	62.8	152.2
1977	97.5	2.0	1.8	18.0	4.8	2.0	31.4	8.54	68.5	166.0
1978	105.2	2.0	1.8	19.0	5.3	2.3	36.5	9.09	76.0	181.2
1979	117.7	1.9	1.9	19.9	6.2	2.4	44.9	9.04	86.2	203.9
1980	135.9	2.8	2.2	21.2	7.4	2.8	56.1	9.30	101.8	237.7

Sources: Budget of the United States Government, 1982 (Washington, D.C.: Government Printing Office, 1981) and Foreign Military Sales and Military Assistance Facts (Washington, D.C.: DOD, 1981). National defense, military assistance, veterans benefits, civil service retirement, foreign economic assistance, and interest on public debt correspond to U.S. budget codes 050, 152, 700, 602, 151, and 901 respectively. NASA space activities are budget codes 253, 254, and 255. Military assistance includes off-budget outlays. Foreign military sales represent deliveries plus commercial exports under the Arms Export Control Act.

The Military Burden

As discussed in chapter 2, such financial data on military expenditure, whether narrowly or broadly defined, represents a very mixed assortment of items. In this section, I consider which military and military-related expenditure items are relevant to military resource usage. Chapter 2 distinguished between the societal resource burden and the governmental budgetary burden of the national military effort, as well as between the current burden and that attributable to past military effort—for example, VA benefits or interest payments on past war debt. This section undertakes to develop that analysis further, determining whether specific expenditures represent resource burden in GNP terms, budgetary burden, or both and whether they represent expenditures for current or for past military effort. Certain nongovernmental resource usage in GNP categories is also considered. Appendix A includes a more detailed explanation of the individual items included in the estimates.

The results of this analysis are summarized in table 3–2. Total military costs (current and past), the (societal) resource burden and the (budgetary) financial burden of the U.S. military effort considerably exceed the official national defense budget definition. With respect to the societal resource burden (that is, monetary value of goods and services allocated to the military effort), the official NIPA defense purchases figure for 1980 of $126.1 billion is exceeded by about 50 percent. Similarly, the budgetary burden of the nation's military effort far exceeds the official national defense budget figure of $135.9 billion, which increases to $228.4 billion.

Estimating the Military Burden

The military burden is conventionally expressed in terms of military expenditure as a percentage of the gross national product. The revised estimate of U.S. military spending developed in the first section of this chapter—the numerator in the military burden equation—is significantly higher than that in official statistics. Selecting and defining the proper denominator is equally difficult. The military expenditure-GNP index is a crude, imprecise tool that may understate the actual burden of military expenditures on an economy. Seymour Melman, for example, argues that GNP is too broad a concept and the correct measure is the ratio of military spending to the total fixed capital formation in the economy. According to Melman, although the U.S. military budget amounted to 4.9 percent of GNP in 1977, it comprised 46 percent of fixed capital formation. In Japan and West Germany, the corresponding proportion of fixed capital formation was 3.7 percent and 18 percent respectively.[7]

Table 3-2
Components of the Military Burden, FY 1980
(billions of dollars)

	Resource Burden	Budegetary Burden
Current Military Effort		
Defense purchases (including military assistance)[a]	126.8	126.8
NASA (50%)	2.2	2.2
Foreign economic assistance (50%)	2.8	2.8
Civilian and military retirement and VA benefits (accrual basis)[b]	40.5	—
Industry adjustment[c][d]	7.5	—
Foreign military sales[e]	(9.3)	—
Military share of interest payments on current deficit (about 50%)[f]	—	3.4
Past Military Effort		
VA benefits, purchases[g]	5.3	21.2
Military retirement	—	11.9
DOD civilian retirement	—	7.4
Military share of interest on past debt (about 75%)[f]	—	52.7
Total	185.1 (194.4)	228.4

Source: Calculated from outlays for FY 1980 reported in Executive Office of the President, Office of Management and Budget, *Budget of the United States Government, FY 1982* (Washington, D.C.: Government Printing Office, 1981).

[a]National defense outlays minus military retirement pay plus military assistance.

[b]Estimated at current budget costs of present military and civilian retirement and veterans benefits.

[c]The industry adjustments for work in progress for both U.S. and foreign purchases is important for year-to-year variations but not the long-term total. In periods of declining military purchases, current outlays will exceed obligations incurred and the adjustment will be negative.

[d]Estimated on the basis of the difference between DOD outlays and obligations incurred in FY 1980.

[e]Foreign military sales are a somewhat anomalous element. Although they represent the allocation of significant U.S. industrial resources for military purposes, they are paid for by the ultimate foreign purchaser, not by the United States. Hence, the societal resource burden of the U.S. military effort is to this extent a gross rather than a net concept.

[f]Interest payments on federal debt amounted to $74.8 billion in 1980, and total debt in 1980 equaled $915 billion. Military allocated share was calculated as indicated on basis of the share of military expenditures in total federal funds expenditures. Current 1980 debt costs are estimated, assuming an 11.5 percent interest rate. Obviously this estimating procedure is crude and intended merely to suggest rough orders of magnitude.

[g]Purchases of goods and services estimated at 25 percent of Veterans Administration budget outlays on basis of NIPA data published by the Department of Commerce.

The dynamic implications of the military burden for an economy, including the effects on its rate of growth and competitive disadvantages, are perhaps more accurately indicated by an index such as Melman proposes than by GNP. Somewhat analogous to an individual firm, an economy has only a determinate profit or surplus in a year over and above its reproduction costs. The military burden of 5 to 7 percent of GNP comes off the top of this disposable surplus, thus diverting funds that might have gone for increased productive investment. Melman's approach presents military expenditure in terms of its opportunity costs for fixed capital formation in the economy. Nevertheless, if our aim is to express military spending as a resource burden in a societal sense, then Melman's description of military spending as a percentage of fixed capital formation is inappropriate. GNP is a more appropriate base for a crude indicator of the general economic burden of military expenditure. Utilizing our revised calculation of $185.1 billion to estimate the military component of GNP or military product, the ratio of gross military product to total GNP was 7.3 percent in FY 1980, or quite significantly higher than the official figure of 5.3 percent. If the higher budgetary burden of $228.4 billion is used, which is more comparable to the official statistic, the military burden is in fact about 8.8 percent.

Another major issue is whether the budgetary burden of military expenditure should be expressed as a percentage of all federal spending in the unified budget (that is, federal funds plus trust funds) or only as a percentage of federal funds expenditures. Federal funds consist largely of general fund receipts that are not earmarked by law for specific purposes; trust funds are receipts and expenditures for carrying out specific purposes and programs, which are unavailable for the general purposes of government. Social Security expenditures account for the bulk of trust fund expenditures. The federal deficit originates in the federal funds accounts rather than in the largely self-financing trust funds. Whichever numerator is used, the broader definition of the budgetary burden of the U.S. military effort will of course yield percentages significantly higher than the official figures based on the national defense component of the U.S. budget. Thus for FY 1980 the official national defense share of U.S. government expenditures was 23.6 percent of the total budget and 32.4 percent of federal funds expenditures. According to our critical higher estimate of military spending the corresponding figures are 39.3 percent and 54.1 percent respectively.

Real Resources Utilized for Military Purposes

Financial data alone do not indicate the resources absorbed by the military effort—labor, industrial capacity, raw materials, R&D and even land. This more concrete form of social accounting of the impact of the arms race avoids some of the pitfalls of purely financial data and of GNP accounting. Moreover, it provides a more vivid picture of the resource opportunity costs in terms of actual resources. It also is a basis for evaluating either the conversion problems attendant upon successful disarmament or, conversely, the strains likely to be associated with increased military spending.

Military-Related Employment

Estimates of military-related production and employment in the United States and other countries depend on the definition of military spending. Nevertheless, despite the use of a narrow or a more expansive definition of the scope of military expenditure, it is useful to distinguish between different categories of military-related employment to assess the employment consequences of the arms race and of possible disarmament measures.[8]

Members of the Armed Forces.   In the United States, uniformed military personnel make up the bulk of armed forces employment and have almost exclusively military tasks. In countries where the armed forces carry out essentially civilian functions, these figures should be adjusted downward. For example, the U.S. Army Corps of Engineers is responsible for civilian flood control and river and harbor construction projects. Paramilitary forces are a significant factor in some other countries, which may require some upward adjustment to the number of military personnel. Special border police, coastal patrols, and civil defense units may also have military functions even when not administratively subordinate to the national military establishment. The U.S. Coast Guard and Border Patrol, for example, are administered by the Departments of Transportation and Interior respectively, but have at least residual military functions. Because none of these examples employ significant numbers, for all practical purposes armed forces employment in this country can be equated with the number of uniformed military personnel of the Department of Defense.

Civil Service Personnel.   The U.S. government employs many civilian personnel in military-related tasks, including DOD civilian employees as well as those of other departments, depending on the definition of military expenditure. These civilian employees are employed in administrative or technical capacities to maintain and operate the military establishment and related functions.

Direct and Indirect Industry Employment.   Direct employment refers to employment generated in firms and industries in producing goods and services to meet military final demand; indirect employment is that generated in those firms and industries which provide intermediate goods and services as subcontractors and suppliers in the production chain. The analytic basis of the indirect and direct employment concept is input-output modeling of the interrelationship of all industries in the economy. It is a powerful tool for economic analysis of the impact of defense spending. Civilians employed in military-industrial establishments operated by the government are included in this category. In some market economies, military-industrial production is largely in the public sector; even in the United States, the production of atomic weapons, much conventional ordnance, and a significant share of repair work on major weapon systems is performed in government facilities.

Multiplier Effect Employment. In contrast to indirect employment resulting from the production of intermediate goods and services for military final demand, multiplier effect employment results from the further diffusion of the stimulus of capital and labor income from direct and indirect military demand throughout the economy. The distinction between indirectly generated employment in the sense on intermediate output and multiplier effect employment generated by military expenditure is frequently not clearly observed.

Estimates of the defense multiplier fall in the range of 1.5 to 2.0.[9] If the defense multiplier were equal to 2.0, for every job created directly and indirectly by military spending in an input-output sense one additional job is created through the multiplier effect of military spending. Under a more conservative estimate of 1.5, then for every two jobs created directly or indirectly by military final demand one additional job is created. Table 3–3 summarizes estimates of such employment.

These estimates are based on the narrow DOD definition of military expenditure and do not include all military-related employment. The VA

Table 3–3
U.S. Military-Related Employment, 1983

Armed services	2,189,000
DOD civilian	1,035,000
Industry employment (direct and indirect)	2,862,000
Total government and industry employment	6,086,000
Multiplier employment (1.5–2.0)	3–6,000,000
Total military-related employment	9–12,000,000

Source: Office of the Assistant Secretary of Defense (Comptroller), *National Defense Budget Estimates for FY 1983* (March 1982), table 7–7.

and NASA and the employment impact of their industry purchases are the most important agencies omitted. In 1983 they employed 216,800 and 22,000 persons respectively and had budget outlays of $24.3 and $6.5 billion. Many people are also employed in industry to meet military demand under the Foreign Military Sales program, officially estimated at 350,000 in 1976.[10] Probably 1 million persons were employed directly or indirectly in such activities in 1983, which raises the totals of military-related employment to about 7 million for total government and industry employment and 10.5 to 14 million including employment effects throughout the economy. The number of people working for the military, directly or indirectly, is about 6.8 percent of total employment; 10.2 to 13.6 percent of employed persons are engaged in military-generated employment.

Military-Industrial Production

Military final demand includes both specialized and nonspecialized goods. Similarly, subcontractors and industrial suppliers can be classified as specialized and nonspecialized.

Reported military procurement outlays were $29 billion in 1980, while shipments of defense products by manufacturing industries amounted to $48.2 billion in the same year. In DOD budget usage, "procurement" is a narrow category that approximates but probably underestimates specialized military production; "defense shipments" include all military final demand in manufacturing. Production for military use is estimated to be approximately 10 percent of all manufacturing shipments, concentrated in certain key industries and localities.[11]

Table 3–4 gives the distribution by industrial sector of industry shipments to the Department of Defense from ninety-two selected industries. The average percentage of military sales for all manufacturing industries is 7.9 percent; it is much higher in many key industries, especially ordnance, radio and TV communications equipment, aircraft (including engines and parts), shipbuilding, and guided missiles. Because the chart data is confined to DOD shipments, and direct employment of prime contractors and subcontractors, it in fact underestimates military-related production and employment in industry: NASA, DOE nuclear programs, and other military-related U.S. government purchases are excluded, as are 235,600 employees in DOD industrial facilities and foreign military sales.

Military demand is highly concentrated in relatively few larger firms. The top 25 military prime contractors accounted for 45.2 percent of the value of DOD contracts and the top 100 firms accounted for 65.9 percent of DOD contract awards in 1980. Many of these firms are largely or wholly dependent on military business.[12] Military-related production and employ-

Table 3-4
U.S. Military Production and Employment by Industrial Sector, 1980

Code	Industry	Value of Shipments ($ billion)		Percentage		Total Employment	Defense-Related Employment
		Total	DOD	DOD	Total		
	92 selected industries	613.8	48.2	7.9	100	6,072,600	743,600
28	Chemicals and allied products	20.4	0.3	1.4	0.6	123,600	6,100
29	Petroleum and coal products	178.1	2.2	1.2	4.6	116,600	1,600
30	Rubber and miscellaneous plastic products	8.4	0.2	2.1	0.4	151,000	3,800
33	Primary metals industries	40.6	0.6	1.5	1.3	341,900	8,500
34	Fabricated metal products	49.9	2.8	5.6	5.8	703,000	50,100
3463	Nonferrous forgings	0.9	0.2	21.4	—	7,200	1,400
3482 3483 3484 3489	Ordnance	4.3	1.7	39.2	3.5	82,600	32,400
35	Machinery, except electrical	104.8	2.7	2.6	5.6	1,382,600	39,100
36	Electrical and electronic equipment	96.2	12.6	13.1	26.1	1,628,300	227,500
3662	Radio and TV communications equipment	24.9	10.8	43.6	22.5	419,800	183,300
37	Transportation equipment	72.0	24.8	34.5	51.5	941,600	372,700
3721 3724 3728	Aircraft	43.9	14.6	29.8	30.2	577,800	202,900
3731	Shipbuilding and repairing	9.1	3.3	36.2	6.8	170,000	65,800
3761	Guided missiles, space vehicles	7.4	4.8	64.2	9.9	93,400	73,100
38	Instruments and related products	39.1	1.5	3.9	3.2	600,100	25,500
3811	Engineering and scientific instruments	3.0	0.3	10.0	0.6	49,700	5,300

Source: U.S. Department of Commerce, Current Industrial Reports, *Shipments to Federal Government Agencies, 1980* (Washington, D.C.: Government Printing Office, 1981).

Table 3-5
Concentration of Defense Employment in Industry by Metropolitan Areas, 1980

Number of Employees	Number of Metropolitan Areas
Under 1,000	48
1,000–2,000	12
2,000–5,000	38
5,000–10,000	15
10,000–25,000	10
25,000–50,000	7
50,000–100,000	0
Over 100,000	1
None reported[a]	158

Source: U.S. Department of Commerce, Bureau of the Census, Current Industrial Reports, *Shipments to Federal Government Agencies,* 1980, table 5, my calculations. Metropolitan areas are standard metropolitan statistical areas (SMSA) as defined by the Department of Commerce. They include both private industry and DOD industrial facilities.
[a]Estimates include only DOD defense employment and only direct employment by prime contractors and subcontractors.

ment is concentrated in certain localities and regions, which increases its impact. In addition, DOD military and civilian personnel are heavily concentrated in relatively few major military bases and administrative centers. Table 3-5 summarizes the distribution of defense employment in industry by metropolitan areas showing heavy concentration in very few areas. The top eight areas of concentration are: Boston, 35,300; Nassau-Suffolk, N.Y., 30,900; Philadelphia, 26,900; Chicago, 27,800; St. Louis, 27,300; Anaheim, 28,700; Los Angeles, 136,100; San Jose, 30,900. They account for 343,900 or 35 percent of DOD-related industry employment.

These figures illustrate the geographic concentration of such employment but, for the reasons given above, represent conservative estimates of total military-related industry employment. They do not, of course, include uniformed and civilian personnel at military bases.

Certain occupational groups are particularly concentrated in military-industrial employment and the rate of union membership among production workers in military industry is considerably higher than the U.S. average for all industry, reflecting largely the concentration of such employment in larger firms and in construction. In the early 1970s, an estimated one out of five engineers, including about 50 percent of aeronautical engineers and 20 percent of electrical engineers, were engaged in defense work.

Among scientists, one out of four physicists and one out of five mathematicians were similarly employed. Among skilled workers, defense work employs an estimated one-sixth of all machinists and one-fifth of all sheet metal workers.[13] The implications of these patterns for the economic and social impact of military expenditures will be examined further in chapter 5.

Raw Materials

The U.S. military is also a major user of increasingly scarce nonrenewable raw materials, as the volume of U.S. military expenditures and the scale of U.S. military industrial production suggests. At the same time there has been an emphasis on qualitative improvements—increasingly more sophisticated and expensive weaponry—rather than numbers. As a corollary, each generation of weapon systems has quantitatively declined. This qualitative advance implies that the relative importance of iron and steel in military consumption has declined while that of aluminum, titanium and other relatively scarce minerals has increased. For example, approximately 25 percent of the weight of advanced U.S. combat aircraft (the F-14 and F-15) is titanium, whereas only 8 to 10 percent of the weight of models produced in the 1950s (the F-8 and F-105) was titanium.[14] Recent estimates of average military share in total U.S. consumption of thirty-two non-fuel minerals between 1969 and 1972 is given in table 3-6. The U.S. military is also a major consumer of oil, amounting to some 8 percent of total annual U.S. consumption.

Land Use

The U.S. military takes up a far from negligible space. Its land resource use amounts to 41,742 square miles, including 3,374 square miles of territory in foreign countries. More than 70 percent of this land area is located in California, Arizona, Nevada, New Mexico, Alaska, and Utah—an area approximately equal to the size of Ohio. Although much of this area is desert land used to test nuclear weapons, missiles, and air combat systems, military requirements do compete directly with civilian demand for industrial, residential, agricultural, or recreational uses, in addition to the environmental concerns such usage raises.

The land use requirements of the military have increased as the range and speed of weapons have increased. The Army now considers that at least 324 square kilometers are necessary for exercises involving an armored division and 664 square kilometers are desirable. The Air Force requires even larger areas, given the speed of modern aircraft and the need to test air-to-

Table 3-6
Military Consumption of 32 Nonfuel Minerals, 1969-1972

Mineral	Average Military Share of Total U.S. Consumption (%)
Titanium	40.0
Germanium	26.8
Thallium	24.5
Garnet	21.8
Thorium	15.8
Cobalt	15.5
Copper	15.5
Silicon	10.9
Cadmium	10.8
Mica	10.8
Beryllium	10.5
Lead	10.0
Molybdenum	9.8
Zinc	9.3
Tantalum	9.0
Antimony	8.8
Iron	8.5
Tungsten	8.5
Tin	7.5
Lithium	7.3
Fluorspar	6.8
Mercury	6.8
Graphite	6.3
Platinum	6.2
Silver	6.0
Aluminum	5.8
Columbium	5.8
Yttrium	4.5
Asbestos	3.5

Source: Data compiled by Ron Huisken for UN Centre for Disarmament. Derived from E.E. Hughes and others, *Strategic Resources and National Security: An Initial Assessment* (Menlo Park: Stanford Research Institute, 1975) and, for titanium, from U.S. Congress, *Twenty-First Annual Report of the Activities of the Joint Committee on Defense Production* (Washington, D.C.: Government Printing Office, 1972), p. 16.

surface munitions. The Carter administration's proposal for land mobile deployment of the MX missile in Utah and Nevada, which would have required an estimated area of 6,000 square miles for the initial deployment of 200 missiles, is indicative of growth potential in military requirements.

Land is also to a certain extent a nonrenewable resource. Military training areas and firing ranges are subjected to often irreversible environmental destruction, and craters and unexploded ammunition represent long-term hazards to subsequent alternative uses.[15] Defense Secretary Weinberger has indicated to Congress that land used by the U.S. military is valued at approximately $30 billion. On the whole, however, land resource use by the military is mitigated by sheer size and relative low population density in the United States. For example, military land allocations are valued at over $80 billion in the more densely populated Federal Republic of Germany.[16]

Guns vs. Butter: Tradeoffs in the U.S. Budget

It is sometimes assumed that there is a simple tradeoff between military and civilian expenditures, particularly social welfare expenditures, within the U.S. budget-making process. It is reasonable to expect that conflicts between civilian and military allocations of national resources would be particularly manifest at this point of decision: guns or butter? Although the conflict is acute within the federal budget, there is no evidence for a simple tradeoff (that is, an inverse relationship) between military and civilian or military and social welfare expenditures.

Russett uses regression analysis to examine tradeoffs between military spending and other GNP components, including government civilian spending.[17] He found, for the 1939–1958 period, a statistically significant negative correlation between military expenditure and federal civil purchases; that is, a $159,000 reduction in civil expenditures for each $1 million increase in military spending ($r^2 = .38$). On the whole, the relationship is relatively weak and falls far short of a simple substitution effect between military and civilian expenditures.[18] In a more recent study of the relationship between military spending and federal spending on health and education over the 1941–1977 period Russett again failed to find any general pattern of tradeoffs. Tradeoffs occurred in only fourteen of the thirty-nine years and usually when military spending declined. The clear tradeoffs that characterize the Reagan administration appear to be the exception rather than the rule.[19]

Although military expenditure occurs at the expense of actual or potential civilian product, this tradeoff does not necessarily take place between military and civilian spending. The situation is too complex, and there are other alternative tradeoffs. Military expenditure may also be at the expense of current private consumption, private investment (through tax increases), or government civil programs, or even shift costs toward the future (through external debt or deficit financing) or some combination. Nevertheless, military and civilian expenditures do practically compete in the budget allocation process, particularly at national governmental level where military expenditure is determined; moreover, tax increases entail political costs, while deficit financing may entail economic costs for the economy (such as inflation). There is no reason to expect a simple substitution effect but tradeoffs are a likely outcome under some circumstances.

A recent study examining the guns or butter thesis for the United States, Britain, France, and West Germany concluded that the European countries tended to opt for guns and butter, but the U.S. record shows a significant substitution effect during the 1949–1978 period.[20] This substitution effect was attributed to several characteristics: the more cyclical character of U.S. military expenditures, its frequent involvement in wars, and the relative underdevelopment of the U.S. welfare state, which in Europe makes social welfare expenditures more resistant to downward pressure. The econometric model used in this study is considerably more complex than that in Russett's earlier regression analysis. Its model of the governmental allocation process incorporates relatively sophisticated variables that take into account changing domestic economic variables, with their related impact on government revenues and social welfare expenditures, internal political variables, and the external environment (tensions, wars). It is evidence for a complex rather than a simple substitution between military and social welfare expenditures in the U.S. federal budget.

The Making of the Pentagon Budget

Studies of the U.S. and DOD budget-making processes shed some light on the complexities of the actual allocation process and are a needed compliment to macrostatistical studies. Although established military priorities carry great weight and tend, like other government programs, to be self-perpetuating, military program requirements as perceived by the Department of Defense clearly do not automatically determine military budget allocations. Rather the practice of postwar administrations shows a strong top-down political-level determination of the budgetary process in which defense spending is only one—albeit large and special—part.

Typically, overall levels of defense spending are worked out between the White House, DOD, and OMB levels in light of conflicting domestic needs and the overall requirements of government fiscal policy:

> At any given point in time political and economic limits on defense expenditures exist. The question of whether budget limits drive strategy and force posture, or the reverse, is an empty one when it is recognized that an effective defense strategy must reflect domestic priorities and economic stabilization policy as well as strictly national security considerations.[21]

John Crecine, an expert on the defense resource allocation process as an organizational and bureaucratic phenomenon, has summarized defense budgeting in the context of federal budgeting as a fundamental situation of insufficient resources to satisfy all claims. He describes this heuristically as the Great Identity in Budget Planning:

$$(\text{Total Federal Revenues}) + (\text{Deficit}\ (+)\ \text{or Surplus}\ (-)) =$$

$$(\text{DOD Expenditures}) + (\text{Non-Defense Expenditures})$$

This identity holds both in the planning stage and when government resources are being expanded, for all values of "T." The total size of federal budget has social and political meaning. The "deficit" has important economic policy implications and a political significance in its own right. The division of resources between the defense and non-defense items is important for any political administration.[22]

Crecine points out it is very difficult to vary one of these policy instruments and its associated policy objectives and simultaneously meet the demands of the other three. There are furthermore "significant organizational and bureaucratic constraints" on defense and nondefense spending because both these also represent ongoing organizations and programs and their respective vested interests.

The exact procedures and the precedence given to defense spending requirements as perceived by the professional military has varied considerably among administrations. At one extreme, the budgetary process in the Truman administration before the Korean escalation gave priority to domestic needs, and the sum available for defense was determined by subtracting the cost of domestic programs from anticipated revenues. The first step was the imposition of a ceiling on DOD expenditures—a fixed one-third of the federal budget until the outbreak of the Korean war.[23] Eisenhower imposed a similar, much higher ceiling. Once the overall defense budgetary ceiling was determined, the Secretaries of Defense in the Truman and Eisenhower administrations would allocate the total amount among the three services.[24] Both administrations put strong restraints on defense expenditures as a result of a traditional view of public finance that was wary of high levels of military spending; they sought to limit government spending, and, in particular, avoid deficits.[25]

During the Kennedy-Johnson period, the emphasis under Secretary of Defense McNamara was on overall coordination and planning of the national military effort through the introduction of the planning, programming, and budgeting system (PPBS), which concentrated control over military program decisions in the Office of the Defense Secretary. While it was declared policy that no budget ceilings were imposed and that the country would spend whatever was necessary for defense, overall ceilings were in fact imposed. As Korb dryly notes:

> It was more than a mere coincidence that what this country could afford for defense from FY 1963 through FY 1966, before the Vietnam buildup, came within one percent of $46 billion each year and that the Army, Navy and Air Force shares of the budget were a fairly constant 27, 32, and 41 percent respectively.[26]

In the post-McNamara period, Nixon's Secretary of Defense Melvin Laird reverted to the practice of imposing explicit budgetary ceilings in return for a restoration of the initiative of military services in designing their own forces, in contrast to the greater centralization in the McNamara years. This practice was followed throughout the Nixon-Ford years.[27] Under Carter, strict fiscal controls were again the rule, with the services required to develop budget proposals for three possible budgets (minimal, maintenance of forces, and enhanced) that would specify their own priorities. In contrast, the Reagan administration appears to be less restrained by fiscal policy concerns about deficits than any other postwar administration and to give greatest precedence to military expenditures.

The predominance of budgetary targets (that is, that U.S. military spending should reach the estimates of U.S.S.R. spending by 1986) in Reagan administration pronouncements suggests a high degree of politicization of defense budgeting, if now in an upward direction.[28] Recent budget proposals represent political posturing and a signal for domestic and foreign policy quite apart from specific military programs. The confrontation with Congress over the FY 1984 budget reflects the mounting political pressures on the administration to curtail its planned military expenditures because of the need for fiscal restraint, other competing domestic priorities, and doubts about both the wisdom and the pace of the Reagan administration's vast weapons acquisition programs. The impact of the Reagan military buildup on the Federal budget allocations and the economy as a whole is considered in chapter 8.

Notes

1. J. Cypher, "Capitalist Planning and Military Expenditure," *Review of Radical Political Economics,* vol. 6 (1974), pp. 1–19.

2. The Foreign Military Sales Financing Program has largely replaced the earlier Military Assistance Program of arms grants. This program provides low-interest loans (repayment is frequently waived), and loan guarantees for military purchases. Budget outlays were $1.95 billion in 1980. The grant component of such financial assistance is difficult to determine;

$500 million is included in the category "payment waived" for FY 1980. DOD, Security Assistance Agency, *Foreign Military Sales and Military Assistance Facts* (December 1980), p. 14.

3. *International Herald Tribune* (April 23, 1981), p. 1.

4. According to DOD's plans in late 1983, 15 of the planned 44 space shuttle flights until 1986 will have exclusively military missions; 114 of the 234 flights planned until 1994 are to be used for military purposes. *Tagesspiegel* (June 24, 1982), p. 3. See also "Military Race in Space," *Defense Monitor,* 9:9 (1980).

5. For an overview see Jacques Gansler, *The Defense Industry,* (Cambridge, Mass.: MIT Press, 1980), chapter 8.

6. Murray Weidenbaum, *The Economics of Peacetime Defense* (New York: Praeger, 1974), pp. 13–14. See also Weidenbaum: "The Economic Impact of the Government Spending Process," *University of Houston Business Review,* vol. 8 (Spring 1961), pp. 4–47.

7. *The Nation* (May 9, 1981), pp. 568–569.

8. For a conceptualization of the employment effects of military spending, see *Study on the Relationship between Disarmament and Development* (New York: United Nations, 1982), chapter 3; and Chris Pite, "Employment and Defense," *Statistical News,* no. 51 (November 1980).

9. The estimates are from *Study on the Relationship Between Disarmament and Development.* The source for the 1.5 multiplier is U.S. Department of Defense, Office of the Assistant Secretary, *National Defense Budget Estimates for FY 1979,* p. 102; for the 2.0 multiplier, M.H. Best and W. Connolly, *The Political Economy* (Lexington, Mass.: D.C. Heath, 1976), pp. 55–56.

10. Congressional Budget Office, *The Effects of Foreign Military Sales on the Economy* (Washington, D.C.: Government Printing Office, 1976).

11. See *Study on the Relationship Between Disarmament and Development,* chapter 3. The 1980 data are from *National Defense Budget Estimates for FY 1983,* table 6–7, and table 3–4 in this chapter.

12. Department of Defense, Office of the Secretary of Defense (Directorate for Information, Operations, and Reports), *100 Companies Receiving the Largest Dollar Volume of Prime Contract Awards, Fiscal Year 1980* (annual). For an analysis with data on contractor dependency on DOD, see "The Defense Department's Top 100," Council on Economic Priorities *Newsletter* (November 1980).

13. Richard Dempsey and Douglas Schmude, "Occupational Impact of Defense Expenditures," *Monthly Labor Review* (December 1971), pp. 12–15. These figures represent conservative estimates. They are based on a narrow definition of military purchases. Furthermore, they rely on the average occupational mix for these industries, whereas military-industrial production employs an above-average proportion of scientists, engineers, and skilled workers.

14. *Study on the Relationship between Disarmament and Development,* paragraph 136.

15. Ibid., pp. 58–59; Malvern Lumsden, "The Military Use of a Scarce Resource: The Case of Land" (Stockholm, 1980). U.S. data can be found in Office of the Secretary of Defense, Washington Headquarters Services (DIOR), *Real and Personal Property of the DOD* (annual).

16. *FY 1983 Report of the Secretary of Defense* (Washington, D.C.: Government Printing Office, 1982), p. 3–21.

17. Bruce Russett, *What Price Vigilance* (New Haven, Conn.: Yale University Press, 1970), p. 140.

18. In an even earlier study, Pryor found a statistically significant but quite small substitution effect between military and U.S. federal civilian expenditures in the 1956–1962 period (excluding transfer payments). Frederick L. Pryor, *Public Expenditures in Communist and Capitalist Nations* (London: Allen and Unwin, 1968), p. 124.

19. Bruce Russett, "Defense Expenditures and National Well-Being," *American Political Science Review,* 76:4 (December 1982), pp. 767–777.

20. Richard Eichenberg, William Domke, and Catherine Kelleher, "Patterns of Western Resource Allocation: Security and Welfare," *Publication Series of the International Institute for Comparative Social Research* (Berlin: Science Center, 1980).

21. John P. Crecine, "Defense Budgeting: Organizational Adaptation to Environmental Constraints," RAND Corporation RM 6121 P-R- (1970), quoted in Aaron Wildavsky, *Politics of the Budgetary Process,* 3d ed. (Boston: Little, Brown, 1979), p. xvii.

22. John Crecine and Gregory Fischer, "On Resource Allocation Processes in the U.S. Department of Defense," *Political Science Annual,* vol. 4 (1973), p. 189.

23. For an overview see Lawrence J. Korb, "The Budget Process in the Department of Defense, 1947–77; The Strengths and Weaknesses of Three Systems," *Public Administration Review* (July/August 1977), pp. 334–346. For more detailed studies of this early period see the studies in Warren Schilling, ed., *Strategy, Politics, Defense Budgets* (New York: Columbia University Press, 1962); and Samuel Huntington, *The Common Defense* (New York: Columbia University Press, 1961).

The assumption of the need for a balanced budget together with the priority given to domestic programs severely restrained military expenditures until the outbreak of the Korean conflict. Then, budgetary ceilings on military expenditures were eliminated until spending stabilized at their much higher cold war levels. Wildavsky, *Politics of the Budgetary Process,* preface and p. 11.

24. Korb, "The Budget Process," p. 335.

25. Ibid.; Huntington, *Common Defense.*

26. Korb, "The Budget Process," p. 338. On the other hand, the Bureau of the Budget was not authorized to cut DOD (McNamara) budget submissions without White House approval, and any determination of overall ceilings took place at the highest levels of government.

27. Ibid.

28. Secretary Weinberger, for example, has repeatedly emphasized such overall budgetary targets, with accompanying charts, in testimony before Congress and in other public statements.

4 Military Expenditure and Economic Growth

Opinion is divided about the relationship between military expenditure and economic growth. There is no generally accepted theory of economic growth in terms of which military spending can be evaluated. Moreover, military spending itself is very heterogeneous, including expenditures for personnel, R&D, procurement, construction, operations, and maintenance, each of which may have quite different economic effects. Military spending is only one variable in a complex economic situation, and its impact on the economy varies with the general state of the economy, the financing of such expenditures, and the impact of other government programs.

Global Comparisons of the Military Burden

It is difficult to make any strong inferences about the relationship of military expenditure to economic growth on the basis of available macrodata. For the United States as well as for most other Western market economies, military expenditure, while rising in absolute terms, has declined as a percentage of GNP since the Korean war period when U.S. spending reached a postwar peak of about 13 percent of GNP. The general pattern is that of declining rates of growth within each set of national data and declining rates of increase in industrial productivity, particularly after the 1973–1974 recession. At the same time military expenditure as a percentage of GNP has also declined, particularly in the United States, although the overall trend was interrupted first by the Vietnam buildup and again by Reagan. Certainly much more than the rate of military expenditure determines the rate of economic growth. The economic crisis in the early 1970s may well mark the end of an era of historically unprecedented GNP growth rates and expansion of international trade.[1] This long wave of economic expansion carried both large military spenders, such as the United States, and countries such as Japan with remarkably low rates of military expenditure.

Cross-national macrostatistical studies show a definite relationship between a lower military burden and higher rates of economic growth, most strikingly in Japan and the Federal Republic of Germany. Such cross-national comparisons control effectively for common trends in the economic development of the Western world in the postwar period. There may, however, be factors in the experience of individual nations other than the military burden that explain such differences. In a recent study, Ron Smith has examined the relationship between growth rate and military expenditure in fifteen Western industrial nations.[2] To remove cyclical variations, the variables were averaged for the 1960–1970 period. The relationship between average growth rate and average share of military expenditure in GNP for the fifteen countries was strongly negative (−0.54) and significant at the 95 percent level, confirming the impression given by the cross-national data in table 4–1.[3]

In U.S. timeseries data, military expenditure increases with economic growth, as do all government expenditures. To correct the effects of serial correlation in timeseries data, analyses of the relationship between military expenditure and growth have typically examined the relationship between growth rates and military expenditure or rates of change in military expenditure. Caputo examined U.S. timeseries data on the relationship between

Table 4–1
The Military Burden and Economic Performance of Selected OECD Countries, 1960–1979
(annual averages)

	Military Expenditure (% GDP)[a]	Investment (% GDP)[b]	Growth (% GDP)[c]	Productivity (% Change)[d]
United States	7.4	17.6	3.6	2.6
Great Britain	5.4	18.4	2.5	2.9
France	4.6	22.7	4.8	5.5
Federal Republic of Germany	3.9	24.1	3.9	5.4
Italy	2.9	20.8	4.5	6.1
Canada	2.7	22.9	4.8	3.9
Japan	0.9	32.7	8.5	8.1

Sources: *SIPRI Yearbook 1981* (London: Taylor and Francis, 1981), p. 166; see also *Yearbooks* for earlier years; United Nations, *Yearbook of National Account Statistics, 1979,* vol. 2 (New York: United Nations, 1980), pp. 30, 42, 44–49; OECD, *National Accounts of OECD Countries,* vol. 1 (Paris: OECD, 1981), pp. 24–71; Congressional Budget Office, *The Productivity Problem* (Washington, D.C.: Government Printing Office, 1981), p. 1137. Derived from Robert DeGrasse, Jr. and others, *The Costs and Consequences of Reagan's Military Buildup* (New York: Council on Economic Priorities, 1982), table AI, pp. 50–52.

[a]Average percent of gross domestic product devoted to military spending.
[b]Average percent of gross domestic product devoted to fixed capital formation.
[c]Average real growth in domestic product.
[d]Rate of change of productivity in manufacturing.

the rate of increase in defense expenditure and the rate of increase in national income for the 1950–1970 period.[4] He found the two to be highly interrelated ($r = +0.80$, significant at the 0.01 level).

Using a somewhat different procedure, Cusack and Nincic found a strong positive relationship between the real rate of increase in GNP and real increases in U.S. military spending between 1946 and 1978, leading them to conclude that military expenditure has been employed to stimulate economic growth in the United States ($r = +0.52$).[5] On the other hand, Nardinelli and Ackerman performed a somewhat different analysis with surprising results.[6] Instead of using total GNP data, they distinguish between GNP and net GNP (GNP minus defense expenditures). Implicitly, they examine the relationship between military expenditure and civilian economic growth. A simple regression analysis of percentage change in defense expenditures on percentage change in net real GNP for the 1905–1973 period shows a statistically significant but weak relationship between the two variables.[7] However, the analysis for subperiods shows a strong negative effect of military expenditure on civilian economic growth for the 1946–1973 period ($-.082$, $r^2 = .44$).

Such analyses of year-to-year fluctuations using timeseries data focus the analysis on short-term and marginal impacts of changes in military expenditure on economic growth. They show that military spending can be and has been used as an instrument of economic policy.

Military Expenditure and the Components of Economic Growth

To go beyond such an unsatisfactory macrostatistical approach to the relationship between military spending and economic growth, it is necessary to examine the impact of military resource allocation on the components of economic growth. Three factors seem to be particularly important: growth in capital stock, which is dependent on the rate of savings and investment; expansion of the labor force and upgrading of labor force skills, which is dependent upon population growth and education and training; and growth in productivity, which is dependent on technical progress and innovation.[8] The main elements of an argument as to how military expenditure may function to impede economic growth are summarized here:

Investment. To the extent that the military burden depresses the share of investment, it can be expected to have a negative effect on economic growth by impeding the renewal and expansion of existing capital stock as well as the rate at which technical progress and innovation are spread throughout the economy. This slowdown can occur through several mechanisms, including the following.

1. Military expenditure may, insofar as it is financed by borrowing from the public, directly decrease civilian demand if purchases of goods and services are decreased to buy bonds; or it may crowd out private civilian investment by the demand it makes on money markets, driving up interest rates and increasing the cost of capital to other borrowers.[9] Conversely, insofar as such expenditure is financed out of increased taxes on business or individuals, it deters investment in or shifts demand from the civilian economy to public military consumption and the private industries that produce for it.

2. Supply bottlenecks may develop that constrain civilian investment. Military procurement purchases are particularly directed at industries that produce key capital goods. Moreover, the episodic character of military procurement purchases means that they are frequently a source of disproportions in industry; even at a high average level of military spending, there is considerable fluctuation in the composition of military industrial demand.[10]

Research and Development. The military burden on the economy can also affect economic growth negatively by dampening the growth of productivity in the civilian economy. Growth in an advanced economy like the United States is generally considered to be particularly dependent on growth in productivity through technical progress based on research and development. However, much of the U.S. investment in R&D is diverted into channels that are relatively nonproductive for the civilian economy.

Labor. In very tight labor markets or at high levels of military mobilization, military use of available labor resources can lead to acute constraints on growth. Even at the present peacetime levels, military-related employment is approximately 7 million or roughly 6 percent of the total U.S. labor force. Although this level of military employment leads to some specific critical shortages among types of skilled workers, the current general slackness of the U.S. labor market means that military manpower demands are not a significant constraint on U.S. economic growth.

This chapter focuses on the direction and magnitude of the influence of military expenditure on two critical growth resources: investment and research and development. Employment effects of military spending are discussed in chapter 5.

Military Expenditure and Investment

U.S. Timeseries Studies

Considerable evidence indicates that military spending has a negative impact on investment and economic growth. The allocation of a large share of national resources to the military effort takes place at the expense of other potential resource uses. The effect on investment can be investigated from U.S. timeseries data and cross-nationally in terms of relative changes in the shares of consumption (C), investment (I), government purchases (G), and exports (E) in the national income accounts. Russett has computed the various kinds of public and private expenditures as percentages of GNP and regressed them against military expenditure as a proportion of GNP for the 1939–1968 period.[11] This period includes World War Two, Korea, and Vietnam. Table 4–2 shows that increases in military expenditure as a percentage of GNP take place not only at the expense of personal consumption but also to a significant degree at the expense of investment in producers' durable equipment and housing. Thus a $1 billion increase in military spending would result in a decline of $293 million in total fixed investment and $110 million in producers' durable equipment.

Russett's analysis focuses on the historical pattern of tradeoffs for marginal increases or decreases in military expenditure in one nation. Assuming a marginal productivity of capital of 20 to 25 percent—that is, that an additional dollar of investment in any single year will produce 20 to 25 cents of annual additional production in perpetuity—an extra $1 billion for defense expenditures would reduce investment by $292 million and production by $65 million a year in perpetuity.[12]

Russett's analysis has been criticized for including World War Two data in his timeseries and for failing to distinguish between the possibly

Table 4–2
Estimates of the Opportunity Costs of Military Spending, 1959–1968

Item	Variance Explained (%)	Regression Coefficient
Fixed investment	72	−.292
Nonresidential structures	62	−.068
Producers' durable equipment	71	−.110
Residential structures	60	−.114
Personal consumption	84	−.420
Durable goods	78	−.163
Services	55	−.187
Exports	67	−.097
Imports	19	−.025
Federal civil purchases	38	−.048

Source: Bruce M. Russett, *What Price Vigilance? The Burdens of National Defense* (New Haven, Conn.: Yale University Press, 1970), table 5.1, p. 140. Reprinted with permission.

Note: Both variance and regression were statistically significant at the 0.001 level in all entries except imports. The regression coefficient gives the amount of variance in the dependent variable for each dollar change in military expenditure.

quite different pattern of tradeoffs for military expenditure in different subperiods. Although the United States devoted over 30 percent of GNP to the Second World War effort at its peak, only 13 percent of GNP was consumed during the Korean war and 9 percent during the Vietnam war buildup. Levels were significantly lower during the intervening peacetime years. Moreover, government policies for financing the military effort differed during these three mobilization periods.

Hollenhorst and Ault have modified Russett's analysis to take these subperiods into account (see table 4–3). The most important finding is the great difference in the patterns of tradeoffs in the different periods. Only World War Two shows a strong negative impact of military expenditure on investment, whereas the Vietnam war buildup shows a positive relationship between increased military expenditure and investment in producers' durable equipment. For the Korean war and peacetime periods the only significant relationships are positive ones for nonresidential structures.[13]

Kenneth Boulding has examined historical data on the composition of gross capacity product (GCP) in the United States between 1929 and 1969 (see table 4–4).[14] GCP is GNP adjusted to include "unrealized product" resulting from unemployment or idle resources in the economy. Except for the inclusion of unrealized product, Boulding's analysis of GNP components is similar to Russett's, but his timeseries is longer and his focus is not year-to-year variations but structural change in the American economy over the period between 1929, when military expenditure amounted to only 0.6 percent, and 1969 when it amounted to 8.2 percent of GCP.

His principal conclusion is that military expenditure has grown within the structure of the U.S. economy almost entirely at the expense of personal consumption expenditures, which have declined since 1929 from 72.6 percent to 59.8 percent of GCP, accounting for almost all of the 14.3 percent increase in government civilian and military spending. In contrast, gross private domestic investment expenditures showed only a slight decline and the share of fixed producers' durable equipment actually increased from 5.3 percent to 6.8 percent of GCP.[15] Boulding's structural analysis of change in the economy before and after the rise of a permanent arms economy supports Russett's critics, who maintain that his overall timeseries data give too much weight to the dramatic movements in the economy during the World War Two mobilization and find stronger and more significant negative relationships to personal consumption expenditures.

Russett's type of analysis has also been criticized because it is static, that is, it focuses on the correlation between the military share of GNP and other GNP components such as investment without taking into consideration GNP growth. If military expenditure stimulates economic growth, as some maintain, then the relative decline in the investment share of GNP

Table 4–3

Opportunity Costs of Military Spending, 1939–1968: Alternative Estimates for Selected Subperiods

GNP Component	Regression Coefficients			
	Peacetime	World War Two	Korean War	Vietnam War
Fixed investment	—	−.223	—	—
Nonresidential structures	.110	−.041	.069	—
Producers' durable equipment	—	−.089	—	.115
Residential structures	—	−.093	—	−.110
Personal consumption	−.813	−.490	—	−1.152
Durable goods	—	−.129	—	—
Nondurable goods	−.883	−.210	−.566	−1.426
Services	—	—	−.254	—
Exports	—	—	—	—
Imports	.110	.001	—	.199
Federal civil purchases	−.168	−.065	—	—

Source: Jerry Hollenhorst and Gary Ault, "An Alternative Answer to: Who Pays for Defense?" *American Political Science Review,* 65:3 (1971), p. 761. Reprinted with permission.

Note: Where no regression coefficient is shown, no significant relationship exists at the .05 level of confidence (two-tailed *t* test).

Table 4–4

Composition of the Gross Capacity Product, 1929 and 1969
(% GCP)

	1929	1969	Change
GNP	97.0%	96.8%	−0.2%
Unrealized product	3.0	3.2	+0.2%
Civilian government purchases			
Federal	0.6	2.4	+1.8%
State and local	6.8	11.7	+4.9%
Total	7.4	14.1	+6.7%
National defense	0.6	8.2	+7.6%
Total government	8.0	22.3	+14.3%
Gross private domestic investment	15.2	14.5	−0.7%
Personal consumption expenditures	72.6	59.8	−12.8%
Net exports of goods and services	1.1	0.2	−0.9%

Source: Kenneth Boulding, "The Impact of the Defense Industry on the Structure of the American Economy," in *The Economic Consequences of Reduced Military Spending,* ed. Bernard Udis (Lexington, Mass.: Lexington Books, 1973), p. 228. Reprinted with permission.

may not actually be at the expense of investment and civilian economic growth in absolute terms. Certainly the Second World War and the post-war period of unprecedented U.S. prosperity demonstrate that a high level of military expenditure is not incompatible with relatively high rates of growth.

Comparative Studies

Cross-national studies may be better suited than timeseries data to evaluate the impact of military spending on the growth of the U.S. economy in comparison with other industrialized market economies. Cross-national studies of OECD countries by Smith show a strong negative relationship between military expenditure and investment.[16] There is a strong negative association between average military expenditure as a share of gross domestic product (GDP) and investment share in GDP (−0.73, significant at the 95 percent level). Smith's use of a two-variable model—growth and military share of GDP—strengthens this conclusion. Using this model, he further examines timeseries data for individual countries, all of which yield negative coefficients in the 0. to 1.0 range, however with relatively weak statistical significance levels and wide variations in the amount of variation accounted for:[17]

> This result, that there is a resource tradeoff between the shares of output devoted to military expenditures and investment between nations in the advanced capitalist world, seems to be a robust cross-section result which is not inconsistent with time-series evidence for most countries.[18]

Subsequent work by Ron Smith and Dan Smith using a more complex econometric model have strengthened the case for a negative impact of military expenditure on growth through a negative effect on investment. In the empirical model the rate of growth depends on growth in capital stock, which is a function of the share of investment in GNP; rate of growth in the labor force, which is a function of population growth; and the rate of growth in total factor productivity, which is a function of R&D expenditures. The estimates indicate that military expenditure has a positive effect on growth through increased R&D expenditures and spinoff. This effect, however, is more than outweighed by the negative effect of military expenditure on growth through displacement of investment. Approximate estimates are given of a negative effect of −0.28 and a positive effect of +0.15, leading Smith and Smith to conclude that for OECD countries military expenditure reduces the growth rate.[19]

This study and others tend to explain the tradeoff between military expenditure and investment with the argument that consumption is difficult to curb and therefore, military expenditure is competitive with investment. However, this argument is not self-evident. For the United States at least, Boulding shows that historically the rise in military and other public expenditures as a share of output has been at the expense of private consumption. Insofar as the argument is social-psychological, it would seem to imply that to depress the level of consumption is difficult (outside of wartime or other national crises), but not that the share of consumption in output should be constant. Rather it would imply that it is easier to increase military expenditure absolutely in times of rapid economic growth but more difficult in times of relative economic stagnation.[20]

The lack of structural tradeoff in the U.S. economy between increased military expenditure and investment (table 4–4) does not necessarily contradict the cross-national analyses for the postwar period that show a strong negative relationship between the military burden and investment, or the rather weaker evidence for such a tradeoff in the other studies of U.S. time-series data.[21] Although, as Boulding maintains, U.S. investment has not declined in comparison to the historical share of investment in GNP and until recently growth rates per capita or per civilian employee have been at or above their historical averages, both the rate of investment as well as the rate of growth in other OECD countries has been much above their prewar historical averages and higher than U.S. rates (see table 4–1).

Investment and Growth Bottlenecks

Defense procurement purchases can impede investment and growth in civilian industry as a result of bottlenecks in capital goods industries where defense purchases compete with civilian investment demand. As shown in chapter 3, DOD defense purchases are highly concentrated in a few industries, particularly electrical and electronic equipment (13.1 percent); radio and TV communications equipment (43.6 percent); aircraft (29.8 percent); shipbuilding (36.2 percent); missiles and space vehicles (64.2 percent); and engineering and scientific instruments (10 percent of all shipments respectively in 1980; see table 3–4). Unfortunately, more detailed breakdowns beyond broad industrial categories, which would make it possible to specify precisely the bottleneck effect of DOD purchases, are not available at the end of 1983. The Office of the Secretary of Defense has reportedly begun to develop a detailed economic impact model to guide policymakers in the future.[22]

Some more impressionistic accounts describe the current strains on the defense industrial base after a long period of declining demand in the post-Vietnam era.[23] Gansler, for example, argues that an analysis of the specific structure and condition of the defense industry is necessary to understand the macroeconomic effects of the current rapid increase in military expenditures.[24] Although there are many underutilized plants and employees in the defense sector (defense procurement fell over 50 percent in constant dollars from the Vietnam-war peak until defense procurement purchases began to climb again in 1976), there has been a drastic deterioration of the defense-industrial base, particularly at the level of key parts suppliers.

Increased demand for commercial aircraft competes directly with defense production for engineers, skilled labor, the use of production machinery, and many scarce parts. (Gansler reports an estimated shortage of 30,000 engineers in the Los Angeles area alone in 1980).[25] As a result, lead times for acquisition of critical aircraft components had increased to months and in some cases years (table 4–5 summarizes some of these data). Existing bottlenecks in labor, parts, and production machinery are so great that, according to Gansler, "it is highly unlikely that greatly increased defense funds, spent on the present products and with the present contractors, would not yield significantly more military equipment but would only raise the prices."[26]

In this case, the most immediate civilian competitor is the aircraft industry—perhaps the most extreme example of the bottleneck effect of military industrial production. However, similar negative impacts occur at the microeconomic level in other advanced industrial sectors of the U.S.

Table 4–5
Lead Times for Selected Aircraft Components
(weeks)

	December 1975	December 1977	August 1979
Titanium	50–55	40–46	99–105
Hydraulic fittings	36–38	32–34	80–84[a]
Aluminum and steel	48–50	34–40	78–89
Titanium sheets and plates	12–18	14–20	76–77
Hinges	50–52	56–60	72–90[a]
Aluminum extrusions (sheets, plates)	12–16	18–26	68–73
Electrical connectors	16–24	20–28	47
Castings, large	30–32	38–40	46–62
Bearings	16–20	20–26	46–55
Cobalt/molysteel bar	12–18	24–30	44–50[a]
Fasteners	6–8	6–8	39–54

Source: Air Force and Joint Logistics Commanders Data (July 1979). Reported in Jacques Gansler, *Defense Industry* (Cambridge, Mass.: MIT Press, 1980), table 2.9, p. 66.
[a]April 1979 data.

economy in which military demand is concentrated. In every case the actual effect depends both on the state of civilian demand for these products and industrial resources as well as on fluctuations in military demand. There are some signs, for example, that the bottlenecks in aircraft production described by Gansler at the beginning of the 1980s have decreased as a result of the following deep economic recession, which particularly affected the commercial aviation industry.

In this respect, the extreme volatility of military procurement demand, in addition to its absolute levels, should be recognized as a cause of periodic bottlenecks in military-industrial production as well as in industrial sectors where military-industrial demand for economic resources competes with civilian demand. In addition to this overall volatility, specific military programs often severely strain industrial resources. The best recent example was the proposed, and since rejected, plan of the Carter administration for land-based mobile deployment of the MX missile, which was estimated to have required 40 percent of U.S. cement production for three years.

Military Expenditure and Productivity

The U.S. Productivity Crisis

Second, military expenditure is thought to have a negative impact on economic growth through its consequences for the growth of productivity. There is now widespread agreement that there is a productivity crisis in the United States. Table 4–6 shows trends in productivity growth for the United States and eight principal OECD trading partners. In comparison to its own long-term and more recent postwar rates of growth, growth in productivity in recent years shows a marked decline in the U.S. time-series data, and this relative decline is even more marked in comparison to its OECD trading partners. For the entire postwar period these countries have experienced historically unprecedented growth rates spurred by similarly unprecedented rates of growth in productivity. Their rates far exceeded the historical average for the United States as well as their own prewar averages. Although showing a downward trend in recent years, these countries (except the United Kingdom) have still maintained rates of increase in productivity considerably above that of the United States.

The U.S. decline has been a decrease in both the productivity of capital and the growth of labor productivity. That is, not only has the rate of growth in GNP per civilian employed person declined but also the ratio of the growth rate in GNP to the rate of growth rate in fixed nonresidential investment; there is less payoff in growth for a given investment rate than in the past. In fact, U.S. private nonresidential investment, although signif-

Table 4-6
Output per Employed Person in Selected OECD Countries
(annual average rate of change, percent per year)

	1955–1960	1960–1964	1964–1969	1969–1973	1973–1977
Austria	4.2	4.6	5.1	6.1	2.9
Belgium	2.1	4.1	3.6	4.3	2.2[a]
France	4.9	5.1	5.2	5.1	2.4
Germany	5.0	4.8	4.9	4.2	3.2
Italy	4.6	6.3	6.2	4.8	1.0[a]
Japan	7.3	10.3	8.8	8.1	2.7
Netherlands	3.6	3.4	4.9	4.5	2.7
United Kingdom	1.8	2.3	2.6	2.9	0.4
United States	1.0	3.1	1.9	1.5	0.3

Source: OECD, *Technical Change and Economic Policy* (Paris: OECD, 1980), table 13, p. 69.
[a] 1973–1976 only.

icantly lower than other Western market economies, has shown no secular decline in recent years as a percentage of GNP. The rate of growth of U.S. nonresidential fixed investment has actually improved relative to European rates because of a slackening of the earlier very high postwar investment rates in these countries. Nevertheless, the productivity gap has continued to increase.[27] The explanation for the productivity decline in the U.S. in both its historical and comparative dimensions must be sought elsewhere.

There is little agreement among economists on the reasons for declining productivity and the gap between the performance of the U.S. economy and that of other Western capitalist nations. A number of explanations or partial explanations have been advanced: the decline in R&D expenditures since the 1960s; the trend toward a service-oriented economy; the effect of health, safety, and environmental regulations on growth; the increase of younger workers and women in the work force; the alienation and lack of motivation among workers; and lower levels of capacity utilization because of sluggish growth.[28]

Lester Thurow, for example, argues that declining R&D expenditures can not be the cause since the fall in productivity growth started in 1965 before the decrease in R&D expenditures, which in any case would only have affected productivity with a considerable time lag.[29] Furthermore, U.S. investment in plant and equipment has not been falling but was actually higher in the 1973–1978 period (10.1 percent of GNP) than in the 1948–1965 period (9.5 percent), when productivity growth was highest. Thurow argues that about 30 percent of the decline in productivity growth can be attributed to slower growth and greater idle capacity; another 40 percent can be explained by shifts in the economy toward sectors in which productivity is lower; the shift away from agriculture, which for a long period enhanced average productivity in the economy, has now ended; and the current shift toward the service sector in particular is now retarding productivity growth. The balance of the decline can, he argues, be traced to three industries—mining, utilities, and construction—for reasons peculiar to these industries.

In a recent study of the slowdown in productivity growth, Norsworthy, Harper, and Kunze found that such determinants as the capital-labor ratio; intersectoral shifts in capital; pollution abatement capital expenses; the changing age, sex, and educational composition of the labor force; inter-industry shifts in the labor force; and the ratio of hours worked to hours paid could only account for a very small fraction of the productivity growth decline.[30] Earlier, E.F. Denison argued that the factors usually mentioned as possible determinants of the decline in productivity growth do not ade-quately explain the drops that occur after about 1965 and 1973.[31] However, he argues that the productivity drop between the 1965–1969 and 1969–1973 periods is attributable to lower rates of utilization. The further and more general decline in the 1973–1978 period is a "mystery," essentially unex-plained either by lower rates of utilization or other specific determinants. None of these discussions consider the possible effects of military use of R&D resources.

Military R&D vs. Growth-Oriented R&D

Critics of the economic impact of military spending emphasize the impor-tance of R&D for the growth of productivity in a modern economy and the extent to which the U.S. military effort has diverted a large share of R&D into economically relatively unproductive military uses. Although the United States devotes a relatively large share of its national product to R&D, the share devoted to growth-oriented civilian R&D is signif-icantly lower, declining, and now surpassed by most of its Western trading partners.

One of the distinctive characteristics of military industrial production is its R&D intensity. According to SIPRI calculations, military R&D amounted to 43 percent of the value of production of military equipment in 1975, while in the civilian manufacturing sector R&D expenditures amounted to only 2.3 percent of the value of manufacturing output. According to this measure, average military product is twenty times more R&D-intensive than average civilian manufacturing product[32] and certainly the ratio is even higher in military-related space research.

The implications of this fact for the overall U.S. economy and the allocation of U.S. R&D resources can be seen from an index of growth-oriented R&D constructed by Solo for the 1950s.[33] Growth-oriented R&D excludes military and space R&D, expenditures for medical research, and a portion of company-financed R&D (estimated at 30 percent of military and space agency R&D) considered to be military and space-oriented. The resulting index shows growth-oriented R&D as essentially stagnant as a share of national income (1953 = 100, 1960 = 97), while the residual of predominantly military-space R&D skyrockets (1950 = 100, 1960 = 233). Obviously, the R&D boom of the 1950s and 1960s was highly selective and established a continuing pattern.

Boretsky has constructed a similar index of civilian-equivalent R&D for the 1960s.[34] He shows that the United States ranked ahead of only Canada and Italy in growth-oriented R&D as a percentage of GNP. OECD data on the 1960s and 1970s show that, although the United States has been the perennial leader in share of GDP devoted to R&D expenditure, declining slightly from 2.90 percent in 1963 to 2.30 percent in 1975, it now lags behind the Netherlands, Japan, and West Germany in the share of GDP devoted to civilian R&D (table 4–7). If space R&D were subtracted, the United States would rank even lower.

The U.S. R&D expenditure boom in the postwar period was not necessarily an addition to inventive and innovative activity but in part merely a new way of organizing such activity. According to Robert Solo:

> Through the advent of R&D, those who were, or who might have been, restless, probing industrialists, innovating entrepreneurs, or inventors tinkering in their shops became, instead, engineers on project teams, heads of research divisions, scientists in laboratories, or subcontractors with the task of developing a component for a complex weapons system.[35]

As evidence, he notes the U.S. decline in patents per capita at the same time as R&D expenditure has grown. This paradoxical result is, he argues, exactly what one would expect, because individualized and market-directed creative activity results in more patents; in institutionalized team research, individual reward no longer depends on patent protection. The shift to R&D is not only a shift in the organizational form of inventive and creative brainpower but also a shift in its focus. Earlier unorganized and individualized inventive activity was almost exclusively oriented toward nonmilitary industry, while the postwar R&D phenomenon has been heavily oriented toward military and space research.[36]

R&D Personnel

There are no complete figures on public and private research scientists and engineers involved in military and military-related space research. Published

Table 4-7
Defense and Civilian R&D Expenditures in Selected OECD Countries
(% GDP)

	1963	1967	1971	1975
United States				
Total	2.90	2.90	2.60	2.30
Defense	1.37	1.10	0.80	0.64
Other	1.53	1.80	1.80	1.66
Germany[a]				
Total	1.40	1.70	2.10	2.10
Defense	0.14	0.21	0.16	0.14
Other	1.26	1.49	1.94	1.96
United Kingdom[a]				
Total	2.30	2.30	2.10[b]	2.10
Defense	0.79	0.61	0.53	0.62
Other	1.51	1.69	(1.57)	1.48
France				
Total	1.60	2.20	1.90	1.80
Defense	0.43	0.55	0.33	0.35
Other	1.17	1.65	1.57	1.45
Japan				
Total	1.30	1.30	1.60	1.70
Defense	0.01	0.02	—	0.01
Other	1.29	1.28	—	1.69
Canada				
Total	1.00	1.20	1.20	1.00
Defense	0.09	0.09	0.06	0.04
Other	0.91	1.11	1.14	0.96
Italy				
Total	0.60	0.70	0.90	0.90
Defense	0.01	0.02	0.02	0.02
Other	0.59	0.68	0.88	0.88

Source: *Technical Change & Economic Policy,* (OECD, Paris, 1980)-Table 1. Reprinted with permission.
[a]Germany and United Kingdom, 1964.
[b]1970.

surveys show that approximately three-fourths of research scientists and engineers with federal support were funded by the Department of Defense, NASA, and the Atomic Energy Commission.[37] In Dumas's recent estimate, one-third of all full-time U.S. research scientists and engineers are employed in military (including space) research; this number is fairly close to the consensus approximation.[38] This figure is astounding, but the actual negative impact on civilian R&D capabilities is probably even greater than the percentage implies. The enormous government investment in military and space research has given a tremendous prestige and institutional priority to military-oriented R&D, it is plausibly argued, drawing a disproportionate share of the brightest and most creative scientists and engineers. Even if government demand for military and space research increased the total volume of research, and thus did not occur entirely at the expense of funds for civilian-oriented research, this qualitative distortion of the orientation of the U.S. scientific community surely has a significant impact.

Sectoral Distribution of R&D

The allocation of one-third of U.S. R&D resources to the military effort also affects the level and distribution of R&D resources in the economy. In terms of opportunity costs, civilian growth-oriented R&D might have been 50 percent higher and the distribution of R&D among industrial sectors less heavily weighted in favor of the military-oriented aerospace and electronics industries than it is now. The fact that many countries with lower overall R&D outlays as a share of GDP have higher levels of civilian R&D expenditures indicates that at least a partial tradeoff between military and civilian R&D occurs.

Table 4–8, which shows the sectoral distribution of R&D in manufacturing for several OECD countries, confirms this expectation. About 85 percent of U.S. government-financed research in manufacturing is concentrated in the aerospace and electronics industries. Other industries are, in comparison with their share in industry-financed research, largely or totally neglected by government military-oriented R&D largesse. Countries with low military-oriented R&D expenditures, such as Japan, which has no significant defense-oriented R&D, show quite different patterns of sectoral distribution of government-financed and total R&D. Japanese civilian electronics, chemical, and "other transport" (auto) sectors receive the largest share of government-financed R&D inputs. The share of total R&D going to basic metals, chemical, and other manufacturing industries is also significantly larger than in the United States.

The argument that military expenditure has a negative effect on economic growth because it diverts scarce R&D resources hinges on the assumed relationship of two seemingly incontrovertible facts: the relative decline in U.S. productivity growth and the disproportionately heavy U.S. investment of R&D resources in military and space-related technology at the expense of growth-oriented technology.[39] The productivity growth decline in the U.S. timeseries data and relative to Western Europe and Japan is a complex phenomenon and no monocausal explanation is plausible. Boretsky suggests that, in addition to the disproportionate share of R&D resources devoted to the military, lower rates of investment in plant and equipment and a

Table 4-8
Sectoral Distribution of R&D Expenditure in Manufacturing in Selected OECD Countries
(percent)

		France			Germany			Japan			United Kingdom			United States		
		Industry-Financed	Government-Financed	Total	Industry-Financed	Government-Financed	Total	Industry-Financed	Government-Financed	Total	Industry-Financed	Government-Financed	Total	Industry-Financed	Government-Financed	Total
Electrical/	1967	22.7	25.6	24.6	25.2	25.8	25.9	24.4	33.0	24.5	22.3	27.9	24.1	20.0	28.8	24.4
Electronics	1975	27.0	35.7	31.7	30.0	31.0	29.9	26.0	32.3	26.1	20.5	34.5	26.0	20.9	30.4	21.8
Chemical	1967	27.4	3.7	19.0	33.2	4.3	28.5	27.1	11.0	27.0	21.0	1.1	14.7	21.0	2.8	11.8
	1975	26.1	2.9	19.2	35.0	2.3	29.1	22.4	2.9	22.1	29.5	1.9	19.7	21.4	3.2	14.6
Machinery	1967	7.7	2.4	5.6	12.2	37.1	16.2	10.7	22.0	10.8	14.4	7.4	11.8	17.3	6.4	11.8
	1975	7.0	1.4	5.2	13.0	20.7	13.9	9.9	7.4	9.8	11.3	1.9	7.9	21.8	6.7	18.7
Air and Space	1967	8.0	66.1	28.8	0.9	24.9	5.0	0.0	0.0	0	7.1	61.0	25.3	14.5	56.8	35.8
	1975	6.6	57.8	20.2	2.0	40.9	9.5	0.0	0.0	0	5.0	58.8	23.9	8.3	54.7	24.4
Other transport	1967	13.7	0.5	8.6	14.9	1.3	12.6	12.5	22.0	12.5	12.4	1.3	8.5	12.6	4.5	8.6
	1975	15.9	0.5	11.1	14.0	0.5	11.6	18.3	50.0	18.9	12.3	2.2	8.6	13.9	4.1	10.4
Basic metals	1967	6.1	1.3	4.4	9.8	0.3	8.4	10.6	6.0	10.6	7.1	0.7	5.0	4.9	0.3	2.6
	1975	5.4	0.7	4.1	3.0	2.1	3.1	9.5	4.4	9.4	5.9	0.2	3.8	4.5	0.3	3.2
Chemical-linked	1967	10.1	0.2	6.1	2.4	0.3	2.1	7.7	0.0	7.7	9.9	0.3	6.7	5.1	0.3	2.7
	1975	8.9	0.5	6.2	2.0	1.3	2.0	6.4	1.5	6.3	10.8	0.3	7.1	4.4	0.5	3.6
Other manufac-turing	1967	4.3	0.2	2.9	1.4	0.5	1.3	7.0	6.0	6.9	5.8	0.3	3.9	4.6	0.1	2.3
	1975	3.2	0.5	2.3	1.0	1	0.9	7.5	1.5	7.4	4.7	0.2	3.0	4.8	0.1	3.3
Total manufac-turing	1967	100	100	100	100	100	100	100	100	100	100	100	100	100	100	100
	1975	100	100	100	100	100	100	100	100	100	100	100	100	100	100	100

Source: *Technical Change and Economic Policy* (Paris: OECD, 1980, table 2, p. 31. Reprinted with permission.

worldwide "one-sided diffusion of U.S. advanced technology" are also to blame.[40] There are other possible explanatory factors as mentioned earlier. The evidence at the level of macro data on productivity and the military share of R&D expenditures is necessarily circumstantial. However, the importance of R&D inputs for productivity growth and the R&D intensity of military-industrial production, strongly support the argument that the overall impact of military-industrial production on productivity growth is negative. Although the direction of the impact is evident, its magnitude can not be estimated but seems significant. Certainly, if all R&D resources were devoted to the military effort—to state an extreme hypothetical case—the impact would be disastrous. If, on the other hand, the military share is only one-third of R&D resources, the impact is less but the negative implications for civilian productivity and growth seem clear.

Civilian Spinoffs of Military R&D

Proponents of military-oriented R&D stress the key role of these high-technology industries in stimulating American economic growth and the benefits of such military-space research for the civilian economy. The heavy concentration of military R&D in the aerospace and electronics sectors is said to have had significant civilian spinoffs—for example, U.S. world leadership in civilian aircraft and electronic components. These claims are difficult to assess. Much if not most military and space research has little value for civilian industrial or other uses:

> a considerable part of space and military R&D efforts are devoted (1) to the preparation of research proposals and other presentations; (2) to the design, engineering, and testing of prototype weapons, space instruments, and space vehicles; (3) to the delicate modifications of instruments, mechanisms, and materials in the unique variation required for unique tasks; and (4) to the planning, scheduling, and integration of component developments into a complex space and weapons system. None of these are likely to have any general value or be of conceivable relevance to the advance of the civilian technology.[41]

For example, in 1982 $20 billion of obligation authority was requested for the DOD or 48 percent of all government R&D funding. DOE and NASA requested an additional $12.2 billion, a significant proportion of which must be considered defense-related. Table 4–9 gives a breakdown of DOD funding obligations for 1982. Only the $3.8 billion (19.9 percent of the total) for "technology base" and "advanced technology development" seems likely to have spinoff potential. These categories include research in electronics, materials research, environmental research, computer science, information sciences, behavioral research, and research on lasers and par-

Table 4–9
U.S. Defense Department R&D, 1982
($ millions)

Activity	
Research, development, test, and evaluation	
Technology base	2,998
Advanced technology development	796
Strategic programs	4,093
Tactical programs	6,955
Intelligence and communications	1,958
Programwide management and support	2,618
Other appropriations	615
Total	20,033
Total basic research (included above)	(704)
R&D facilities	280
Total	20,312

Source: *Budget of the U.S. Government, 1982, Special Analyses* (Washington, D.C.: Government Printing Office, 1981), p. 317. Data are for budget authority requested.

ticle beams. Strategic programs R&D is devoted to full-scale development of the MX missile as well as continued work on ballistic missile technology, ballistic missile defense, space defense systems, second-generation cruise missiles, and a new manned bomber among other projects, none of which seem to have much potential for civilian applications.

The largest single component of DOD R&D funding is for tactical programs, including such items as avionics for precise delivery of munitions at night, ground and air-launched cruise missiles, the C-X transport aircraft, a Navy antisubmarine helicopter, undersea surveillance systems, a larger gun for the Army's M-1 tank, new antitank missiles, and so on. Again, while spinoffs are possible and do occur, the bulk of this research is highly specialized. DOD R&D funding hardly represents major support of the needs of U.S. civilian industry.

Two aspects of the relationship between military-space and industrial technologies further undermine the argument for the spin-offs or spillover benefits of such R&D: the increasing divergence of military and civilian technologies and the institutional secrecy surrounding military research that inhibits its diffusion and application to civilian purposes. The increasingly exotic character of contemporary military technology makes it less relevant for civilian applications, implying that any spinoff benefits for the civilian economy may in fact be diminishing. Mary Kaldor has used the term "baroque technology" to characterize the type of technical change now predominant in the military-industrial sector: "'Baroque' technical change

involves incremental improvements to a given set of performance characteristics through, often radical, changes in hardware.''[42] The development
of baroque weaponry entails "more and more effort . . . to achieve ever
smaller improvements in military capability." The resulting weapon systems are "expensive, overelaborate, and less and less useful." Each generation of aircraft, for example, has entailed a quantum leap in costs; modern
fighters cost 100 times more than in World War Two. The sophistication
and technical complexity to achieve enhanced performance have the paradoxical result that military aircraft break down more often and require
much more maintenance and more frequent repairs than commercial aircraft (see table 4–10).[43]

Furthermore, the benefits of military R&D have not been evenhanded.
Civilian aircraft and electronics have gained at the expense of other sectors.
However, even in these two industries the case for military-industrial primed
innovation and growth is not unambiguously positive. Since 1945, only
Boeing has been successful in commercial aircraft production. The development of the 727 in the early 1960s was a response to Boeing's failure to
secure two major military contracts. Kaldor argues perceptively that in
addition to indirect support from military and space R&D, "social partiality" (such as the new network of airports and the volume of U.S. commercial air traffic) was a key prerequisite for the U.S.'s dominant world

Table 4–10
Fighter Aircraft Readiness Indicators

Aircraft	Complexity	Not Mission Capable (%)	Mean Flight Hours Between Failures	Maintenance Events Per Sortie	Maintenance Manhours Per Sortie
Air Force					
A-10	Low	32.6	1.2	1.6	18.4
A-7D	Medium	38.6	0.9	1.9	23.8
F-4E	Medium	34.1	0.4	3.6	38.0
F-15	High	44.3	0.5	2.8	33.6
F-111F	High	36.9	0.3	9.2	74.7
F-111D	High	65.6	0.2	10.2	98.4
Navy					
A-4M	Low	27.7	0.7	2.4	28.5
AV-8A	Low	39.7	0.4	3.0	43.5
A-7E	Medium	36.7	0.4	3.7	53.0
F-4J	Medium	34.2	0.3	5.9	82.7
A-6E	High	39.3	0.3	4.8	71.3
F-14A	High	47.1	0.3	6.0	97.8

Source: *Aviation Week and Space Technology* (October 6, 1980). Courtesy *Aviation Week and
Space Technology.*

market position in civilian aviation, just as in the past a similar social partiality fostered the development of the U.S. auto industry.[44]

The military market has been the central factor in the development of the U.S. electronics industry and its world market preeminence. The United States developed the three major components—the transistor, the integrated circuit, and the microprocessor—that revolutionized the postwar electronics industry. While the invention of the transistor and the integrated circuit were both financed by private funds, the military market provided an initial outlet at a time when unit costs were too high for commercial markets. Experience gained in military production then made possible a reduction of unit costs and successful commercialization. Although the actual invention of the microprocessor was a response to a request by a Japanese calculator company, it was certainly a product of the R&D climate fostered by U.S. military demand in the 1950s.[45]

In Kaldor's opinion, the initial boost given the development of the electronics industry by military-industrial demand and the innovative climate of military R&D may belong to the past: "As the electronics industry reaches the middle phases of its development when product technology gives way to process technology and when innovation slows down the U.S. may lose its leading positions."[46] Japan already is the leading producer of consumer electronics and is expanding its position in industrial products, most notably numerically controlled machine tools. It is now challenging the U.S. position in electronic componentry.

The decline of American competitiveness, even in electronics, and the success of Japanese products despite their relatively low level of innovative research has been attributed to the Japanese emphasis on process technology, which reduces the production costs and improves the quality of civilian products, in contrast to the U.S. preoccupation with product technology. Kaldor argues that this emphasis in U.S. electronics R&D, which has received massive military funding, is a consequence of its involvement in the design of baroque weaponry. Kaldor's analysis thus suggests a very surprising result. Even in the aircraft and electronics industries, where the sheer volume of military-financed R&D and military demand has made them preeminent, the military orientation of these industries may be impeding their current and future commercial prospects.[47]

Solo has also argued that the growing divergence of military technology from civilian technology has not only made it less relevant to civilian needs but, for institutional reasons, also made transfer between the two technologies more difficult. Military technology has become more specialized in terms of its concentration in relatively few firms and in government research facilities. R&D work in this government-sponsored environment is not only technically specialized but also quite different from market-oriented R&D. As a result, military-space R&D personnel have correspondingly more specialized careers and find it difficult to transfer to civilian-oriented industrial research and vice versa.[48]

Furthermore, national security considerations limit the free flow of information, which is a systematic obstacle to the transfer of information not only to potential enemies but also to civilian industry. Even within these constraints, the government has made few efforts to facilitate the transfer of military-supported R&D to civilian purposes through accessibility and information retrieval systems.[49]

Notes

1. Arthur Lewis, "The Slowing Down of the Engine of Growth," *American Economic Review,* vol. 7 (1980), pp. 555–564.

2. R.P. Smith, "Military Expenditure and Capitalism," *Cambridge Journal of Economics* (1977), no. 1, pp. 61–76.

3. Ibid., p. 71. However, this correlation was no longer statistically significant when Japan was removed from the sample. Faini and others also examined the relationship between growth rate in GDP and changes in military expenditures as a percentage of GDP for a group of fourteen developed market economies for the 1952–1968 period, using a more complex econometric model. They report a slight positive relationship between growth and the military burden ($+0.0019$, $r^2 = .23$); however, their model employs an adjustment for a country's "intrinsic" growth rate, which means that it in effect compares the short-term stimulative effect of changes in military expenditure and not growth rates; Richard Faini, Patricia Annez, and Lance Taylor, "Defense Spending, Economic Structure and Growth: Evidence Among Countries Over Time" (Report to the Group of Governmental Experts on the Relationship between Disarmament and Development, United Nations, Centre for Disarmament, 1980).

4. David Caputo, "New Perspectives on the Public Policy Implications of Defense and Welfare Expenditures in Four Modern Democracies," *Policy Science,* vol. 6 (1975), pp. 423–446, 437.

5. Miroslav Nincic and Thomas Cusack, "The Political Economy of U.S. Military Spending," *Journal of Peace Research,* 16:2 (1979), p. 106.

6. Clark Nardinelli and Gary Ackerman, "Defense Expenditures and the Survival of American Capitalism," *Armed Forces and Society,* 13:1 (1976), pp. 13–16.

7. Ibid.; see table 2, p. 15.

8. On the sources of economic growth see, for example, Samuel Kuznets, *Economic Growth of Nations* (Cambridge: Harvard University Press, 1971) and Edward F. Denison, *Why Growth Rates Differ* (Washington, D.C.: Brookings, 1967). For a more recent study focusing on declining

U.S. economic growth, see Denison, *Accounting for Slowing Economic Growth* (Washington, D.C.: Brookings, 1979). For an effort to relate some of these general considerations to military spending see Ron Huisken, "Armaments and Development" (Report prepared for the Independent Commission on Disarmament and Security, New York, 1981).

9. The phenomenon of "crowding out" is used to explain the failure of expansionary fiscal policy to stimulate overall economic growth. See "Crowding Out and Its Critics," *Review,* Federal Reserve Bank of St. Louis (December 1975).

Another possibility is monetizing the debt by Federal Reserve purchases of treasury obligations on the open market. "In effect, the FR is indirectly financing the government deficit through an expansion of the money supply." Wallace Peterson, *Income, Employment and Economic Growth,* 4th ed. (New York: Norton, 1979), p. 271.

10. On this aspect see in particular Jacques Gansler, *The Defense Industry* (Cambridge, Mass.: MIT Press 1980), chapter 1.

11. Bruce Russett, *What Price Vigilance?* (New Haven, Conn.: Yale University Press, 1970) and "Who Pays for Defense?" *American Political Science Review,* vol. 63 (1969), pp. 412–426.

12. Ibid., p. 418.

13. Neither analysis makes any effort to adjust for differences between the civilian and the military product or civilian and military investment that may have a significant effect. If there is no strong evidence in the timeseries data that investment in capital stock declines generally with increases in military expenditure, certainly growth of civilian investment can be expected to show a relative decline. Nardinelli and Ackerman, "Defense Expenditures," pp. 13–16.

Russett's data for year-to-year correlation of changes is also subject to technical problems that have been noted in the literature, particularly the fact that budget obligations rather than budget expenditures may be a better index of the economic impact of military expenditure. See the discussion in chapter 2.

14. Kenneth Boulding, "The Impact of Defense Spending on the U.S. Economy", in Bernard Udis, ed., *The Economic Consequences of Reduced Military Spending* (Lexington, Mass.: Lexington Books, 1973), pp. 225–252.

15. Ibid., table 4, p. 230.

16. R.P. Smith, "Military Expenditure and Capitalism."

17. Ibid., p. 72. But with relatively weak levels of statistical significance and large differences in the amount of variation accounted for. Gross domestic product is GNP minus gross product originating outside the country.

18. Ibid., p. 73.

19. Dan Smith and Ron Smith, "Military Expenditures, Resources and Development," Report prepared for the Group of Governmental Experts on the Relationship between Disarmament and Development (manuscript, New York, 1980).

Russett also examined timeseries data for Canada (1947–1964), the United Kingdom (1947–1965), and France (1950–1965); See note 11. Although both UK and French data showed negative coefficients for fixed investment and military expenditures, that for Canada was positive.

20. Ron Smith, "The Resource Cost of Military Expenditure," in Mary Kaldor and others, *Democratic Socialism and the Cost of Defense* (London: Croom & Helm, 1979), p. 267. It has also been suggested that tradeoffs between military expenditure and investment are especially likely to occur when they represent tradeoffs in the government budget—that is, when a large proportion of investment is public investment.

21. R.P. Smith, "Military Expenditure and Capitalism," and Dan Smith and Ron Smith, "Military Expenditures." See also Ronald P. Smith, "Military Expenditures and Investment in OECD Countries, 1954–1973," *Journal of Comparative Economics* 4 (1980), pp. 19–32.

22. Briefly described by DOD economist David Blond in his preface to the "Summary Report" of the DOD symposium on "the Impact of Higher Levels of Defense Spending" (Office of the Secretary of Defense, October 1980).

23. For example, U.S. Congress, House Committee on the Armed Services, "The Ailing Defense Industrial Base: Unready for Crisis," Report for the Defense Industrial Base Panel (Washington, D.C.: Government Printing Office, 1980); and Defense Science Board, *1980 Summer Study Task Force on Industrial Responsiveness* (Washington, D.C.: Office of the Assistant Secretary of Defense for Research and Engineering, January 1981).

24. Gansler, *Defense of Industry;* see chapter 1 of this book for an overview of his thesis.

25. Ibid., p. 286.

26. Ibid., p. 15.

27. Michael Boretsky, "Trends in U.S. Technology: A Political Economist's View," *American Scientist* (January/February 1975). See especially table 4, p. 312.

28. For a discussion of factors involved see Denison, *Accounting for Slower Economic Growth.*

29. Lester Thurow, *The Zero Sum Society* (New York: Basic Books, 1980), pp. 85 ff.

30. J.R. Norsworthy, Michael Harper, and Kent Kunze, "The Slowdown in Productivity Growth: Analysis of Some Contributing Factors," *Brookings Papers on Economic Activity,* 2 (1979), pp. 387–419, table 11.

31. Denison, *Accounting for Slower Economic Growth.*

32. *World Armaments and Disarmament: SIPRI Yearbook 1979* (London: Taylor and Francis, 1980), table 1.1.

33. Robert Solo, "Gearing Military R&D to Economic Growth," *Harvard Business Review* (November–December 1962), pp. 52–53.

34. Boretsky, "Trends in U.S. Technology," table 7, p. 316.

35. Solo, "Gearing Military R&D," p. 53.

36. Ibid.

37. Lloyd J. Dumas, "The Impact of the Military Budget on the Domestic Economy," *Current Research on Peace and Violence,* vol. 2 (1980), p. 74. Based on National Science Foundation surveys.

38. Ibid.

39. Boretsky, "Trends in U.S. Technology," has made this argument most forcefully and Dumas, "Impact of the Military Budget," has presented additional evidence.

40. Boretsky, "Trends in U.S. Technology," p. 316.

41. Solo, "Gearing Military R&D," p. 54.

42. Mary Kaldor, "The Role of Military Technology in Industrial Development," Report to the Group of Government Experts on the Relationship between Disarmament and Development (New York, 1980, manuscript), p. 1. The following discussion of the relationship between military and civilian technology is based on her analysis. It also appears in her recent book, *The Baroque Arsenal* (New York: Hill and Wang, 1981), chapters 1 and 3.

43. Ibid., pp. 11–12.

44. Ibid., p. 37.

45. Ibid., p. 39.

46. Ibid.

47. Ibid., p. 40.

48. Solo, "Gearing Military R&D."

49. Ibid., and Sherman Gee, "Military-Civilian Technology Transfer: Progress and Prospects," *Defense Management Journal* (April 1975), pp. 46–51.

5 Military Expenditure and Employment

Military expenditure creates employment. As noted in chapter 3, military-related employment in the U.S. arms economy is quite large. Between 9 and 12 million people are employed as members of the armed forces, DOD civilian personnel, and directly or indirectly in industry, including multiplier effect employment. This estimate is rather conservative because it is based on the fairly narrow official definition of military-related spending.

Although the costs and dangers of the arms race are lamented, military-related employment is clearly its political and economic silver lining. The confidence of U.S. policy elites in the ability of the economy to perform without the arms economy has grown since the 1940s and 1950s, but military-related employment is still a powerful vested interest. Defense firms and the military services, for example, make data on the local employment benefits of any major new weapon system or military program conspicuously available to Congress and the public. Corporate lobbyists and their Pentagon and Congressional allies understand the appeal of such employment to the many people and localities that significantly depend on military-related work.

Employment Opportunity Costs of Military Spending

Anderson's Views

The conventional wisdom that military expenditure creates employment has been increasingly challenged in the literature on such spending's economic and social effects. In *The Empty Pork Barrel,* Marion Anderson recently turned the argument completely around and argued that, "Contrary to popular and long held beliefs, a high level of military spending creates unemployment."[1] This seemingly paradoxical conclusion is derived from a civilian opportunity costs perspective that, when stated less polemically, is highly persuasive. The main thesis propounded by Anderson and other authors is that, while military expenditure, like any government expendi-

89

ture, does create employment, other alternative civilian expenditure patterns would create as much or more employment.

Anderson finds that for the 1968–1972 period (when military expenditures averaged about $80 billion) the net annual loss was about 840,000 jobs. According to a 1982 update, there was a net loss of over 1 million jobs a year in the late 1970s. This is by far the boldest hypothesis on the employment effects of military spending. Anderson's results depend on a calculation for each state of the number of jobs created by military expenditure and the number of jobs foregone that would have resulted from an alternative civilian allocation of resources. Although the general thesis—that alternative civilian expenditures would create as many or more jobs—is certainly cogent, the estimates of the employment or disemployment effects of military expenditure is inevitably subject to large margins of error.[2]

Anderson estimates military-related employment for each sector of each state's economy based on a calculation of the dollar amount of value added attributable to military prime contracts. This estimate is then multiplied by the ratio of payroll to total value added in that sector, yielding an estimate of the total payroll in the sector generated by military prime contracts. This last figure is then in turn divided by the average wage in industry created by military spending.

This methodology is employed to estimate the number of jobs generated by military spending in durable goods, nondurable goods, residential construction, and nonresidential construction. In addition the average total number of civilian and military personnel stationed in the state was calculated from official data. Anderson's estimates cover military and civilian personnel and direct and indirect employment, but not multiplier-effect employment.

However, the estimates of foregone civilian employment are somewhat more speculative. Russett's estimates of the opportunity costs of military spending (see table 4–2) are used to estimate the number of jobs that would be created by an alternative civilian pattern of expenditures. As discussed earlier, Russett's regression analysis showed uniformly negative relationships between military expenditures and all other GNP components. Anderson multiplied military outlays by Russett's negative coefficients for durable goods and five other sectors of GNP—nondurables, residential construction, nonresidential construction, services, and state and local government consumption—to estimate by sector the foregone value added. This figure is in turn multiplied by the state's share of total national value added in durables, yielding an estimate of the value added in durables foregone in each state. The wage share of total value added foregone and the number of jobs foregone is calculated as described above for military expenditure. The estimates yielded by these procedures are summarized in table 5–1.

Table 5–1

Employment Effects of Military Expenditures, 1977–1978
(average annual)

	Civilian Jobs Foregone	Military Jobs Created	Net Employment Effect
Durable goods	− 537,050	612,800	75,750
Nondurable goods	− 229,650	45,400	− 184,250
Residential construction	− 380,650	125,100	− 255,550
Nonresidential construction	− 226,450	7,500	− 218,950
Services	− 1,563,400		− 1,563,400
State and local government	− 1,063,550		− 1,063,550
Uniformed and nonuniformed military personnel		2,194,500	+ 2,194,500
			− 1,015,500

Source: Marion Anderson, *The Empty Pork Barrel* (Lansing, Mich.: Employment Research Associates, 1982), table 7. Reprinted with permission of Employment Research Associates, 400 S. Washington Ave., Lansing, Michigan.

Again, there are serious shortcomings in the construction of the estimates for military jobs created and civilian jobs foregone. First, the estimates of military employment include only employment in the fifty states, thus omitting DOD military and civilian personnel stationed in Washington, D.C., and abroad. Thus the estimate of 2,194,500 DOD military and civilian personnel is rather low. Official data gives the total of such DOD employment as slightly in excess of 3,000,000.

Second, the omission of any estimate for states or nationally of military purchases of services is conspicuous. Third, the method of estimating military-industrial employment assumes that all value added takes place in the industrial sector of the prime contractor and at average payroll percentage of value added and average wage for the sector. These assumptions overstate military-industrial employment because skill levels and pay levels are higher for specialized military production. Moreover, indirect employment (subcontractors, suppliers, and their suppliers) in part occurs in sectors other than that of the prime contractor, creating a considerable error factor in calculating the job creation effect of military purchases.

The total estimate of 790,800 jobs created by military-industrial production is uncommonly low.[4] Anderson estimates total military employment at 2,985,300 jobs, whereas narrow DOD official estimates for 1978 indicated 4,854,000 jobs.[5]

The estimates of alternative civilian employment are also subject to problems. The use of Russett's coefficients as a basis of the estimates is particularly troubling. If Russett's opportunity cost coefficients for military spending have any validity, it would seem to be for marginal changes in military spending. In fact, the Anderson study postulates a shift of all military spending to alternative civilian job opportunities. Russett's coefficients in fact confuse two issues and introduce unnecessary controversy into the estimates of alternative jobs. In fact, we do not know what the alternative civilian patterns would look like in the event of general and complete disarmament. Most policy discussion is confined to marginal allocation decisions in the federal budget. Russett's coefficients merely represent past experience that includes wide variations in shorter subperiods. It would be simpler and preferable simply to postulate Russett's or some other alternative civilian expenditure pattern as a scenario and then to estimate employment effects—the standard methodology in other studies estimating employment effects of alternative civilian expenditure patterns based on input-output models of the economy.

In general, Anderson's case for greater job creation through civilian spending is based on an unequal comparison. The level of spending postulated in the civilian scenario is significantly higher than that for military spending. Morgan calculates that in the original 1975 study, the implicit estimates for civilian spending foregone are $8.4 billion higher than the military expenditure total included in the job creation comparison.[6] This gap may in part be a result of unequal counting (for example, the omission of the service sector category of spending and job creation from the military total), but is primarily the fault of the scenario's focus on spending in the fifty states and exclusion of military expenditures and job creation in Washington and abroad. The balance of the higher estimate of civilian jobs may be attributed to sectoral shifts in the alternative scenario toward more labor-intensive production—for example, from durables to services. Anderson suggests this argument in the 1982 edition, but does not examine it in detail.

On the whole, *The Empty Pork Barrel* is a largely heuristic exercise. Its value is in illustrating the job opportunity costs of military resource allocations for the economy as a whole and for individual states, even though it uses rough estimation procedures.

Bezdek's Analysis

In another major study, Roger Bezdek has used a complex policy simulation model of the U.S. economy to analyze the effects of variations in defense spending on the economy.[7] Bezdek's interindustry (86 industries) input-output model also includes data on the regional distribution of economic activity, employment, and skills. The model was developed within the Department of Commerce to simulate manpower effects of compensated shifts in defense spending. Compensated means in this case that the changes in military spending are offset by corresponding increases or decreases in nonmilitary government spending such that total GNP and the public private composition of GNP remain unchanged.

Rather than assuming that tradeoffs between military spending and other economic sectors conform to any particular pattern, Bezdek bases his analysis on three hypothetical scenarios. He first projects the 1980 U.S. economy in terms of a baseline scenario of yearly 2.5 percent increases in defense spending from 1975 to 1980. Then, holding all other basic economic aggregates constant (GNP, personal consumption, net exports), he analyzes the impact on employment of two alternative scenarios for government expenditures. The first entails a 30 percent decrease in military expenditures and corresponding increases in expenditures for health, education, welfare and other civilian programs. The second scenario entails a 30 percent increase in military expenditures with corresponding decreases in social expenditures. In each scenario military and civilian programs to be reduced or increased are specified.

The model converts these alternative spending patterns into impact on output and employment in different industries, which is further broken down in terms of regional and occupational impacts. The 30 percent defense spending increase scenario results in a net loss of 1.3 percent in output and employment in terms of the baseline scenario, whereas the 30 percent civilian spending increase results in a 2.1 percent gain in employment and output. The major reason for these results is that "defense purchases are concentrated in relatively capital-intensive industries while the domestic programs distribute their output requirements to relatively more labor-intensive industries."[8]

Bezdek's study confirms Anderson's findings of the beneficial effects on employment when resources are shifted from military to civilian uses. Indeed, Bezdek's conclusions are even stronger—showing a greater increase in employment in industry resulting from a 30 percent reduction in military expenditures than Anderson showed for a shift of all military expenditures to civilian uses. The detailed industry input-output model yields a methodologically more consistent and more convincing analysis of present military versus alternative civilian expenditure patterns than the more eclectic methodology of the Anderson study. However, Bezdek focuses on employment in industry and apparently assumes that, because government expenditures remain constant with the compensated shift in military expenditures, government employment levels will also remain constant (in the face of a 40 percent cut in military personnel costs as specified).

The Bezdek scenarios are quite specific. Cuts are specified for particular military programs and compensating increases in civilian program areas are itemized. This level of detail is a significant improvement—required by the input-output technique of analysis—over general statements about the supposed employment effect of unspecified changes in military expenditures. Obviously, the actual economic effects depend on the exact nature of the cuts or increases. Like civilian expenditures, military expenditures have very heterogeneous employment effects.

Dresch's Model

A third major study, conducted by Dresch and Goldberg for the United Nations, models the impact of a hypothetical 20 percent reduction in U.S. military expenditures on the U.S. economy.[9] In the Dresch study, IDIOM, an interindustry, national-regional policy evaluation model, has its theoretic origins in the development of differential incidence analysis within public finance theory: "The most important single insight of modern incidence theory is that the effects of government policies can only be assessed with reference to some base, i.e., the configuration of the economy under some alternative public policy."[10] This approach is equivalent to calculating the opportunity costs of military expenditures in terms of other possible patterns of resource allocation (see chapter 2).

Dresch and Goldberg's income determination component is a simple Keynesian multiplier model with exogenous or predetermined final demands that operate via the multiplier to determine level of income and output. However, IDIOM departs from the simple Keynesian model in that the exogenous final demands are specified as final purchases from individual producing sectors, with intermediate purchases from other sectors and capital and labor coefficients for the sectors represented by an input-output model. The model is designed to assess the effects of policy alternatives that can be represented by changes in government expenditures, taxes, or transfer payments. The national model is supplemented by a regional model. The model incorporates an 83-order input-output matrix designed to represent the U.S. economy in 1970.

In the UN study, the model analyzed a 20 percent reduction of U.S. military spending in 1970, or $15.2 billion out of a total budget of $75 billion. Such reduction had two possible forms: either a general across-the-board cut of 20 percent of all military programs (*GD*) or a cut concentrated in strategic weapons programs (*SD*), which would amount to 95 percent of all such expenditures in 1970. Five alternative types of compensating expenditures are considered: U.S. exports to developing countries (*EDC*); U.S. machinery and transportation equipment exports (*ME*); personal consumption (*PC*); social and educational services (*SS*); and private fixed investment (*FI*). That is, the model examines ten different scenarios for reductions in military spending and compensatory expenditures. The employment effects of military spending versus alternative patterns of civilian expenditure can be seen only indirectly in the study in terms of the amount of compensating expenditure required under each to hold total employment constant.

Dresch and Goldberg's findings (see table 5–2) indicate that the employment opportunity costs of military spending are greater in only two of ten disarmament scenarios. Both involve the reallocation of military spending to social and educational services. The positive employment benefits in these two scenarios seem to be a consequence of the net reduction in imports as well as of the greater labor intensity of social and educational services. In the other scenarios, the differential employment effects of military spending (not specialized military industrial production) are positive rather than negative. Both civilian alternatives *ME* and *FI* are relatively capital-intensive and the lack of differential employment benefits over military spending is not surprising. Civilian alternative expenditure scenario *EDC* is not described in sufficient detail to judge.

Perhaps the most surprising result of Dresch and Goldberg's study is that personal consumption (*PC*) in the form of transfer payments to low-income groups does not show a positive employment differential. The differential employment impact of military expenditure programs is indicated by the consistently higher disemployment effect of general disarmament (*GD*) versus strategic disarmament (*SD*). In every alternative civilian expenditure scenario, a higher level of spending is required to compensate for the employment effects of a general 20 percent reduction in military spending than for a 20 percent reduction concentrated in the area of strategic weapons programs. Such programs are on the average more capital-intensive both in terms of government military expenditures and in terms of the requisite military-industrial production.

Employment Opportunity Costs of Specific Weapon Systems

The studies described in the previous section consider the opportunity costs for the general economy as a whole of changes in military expenditures. Other studies focus on the employment and other related effects of specific procurement programs, such as the MX missile or the B-1 bomber. Although proponents of a new weapon system customarily tout the employment and other benefits it would bring to particular localities and the gen-

Table 5-2
Summary Effects of a Compensated 20 Percent Defense Contraction
(% net change in 1970 values)

	Reduction/Compensation Scenarios									
	GD/EDC	*SD/EDC*	*GD/ME*	*SD/ME*	*GD/PC*	*SD/PC*	*GD/SS*	*SD/SS*	*GD/FI*	*SD/FI*
Net Change										
Total employment	0.0	0.0	0.0	0.0	0.0	0.0	0.0	0.0	0.0	0.0
Total labor earnings	-0.1	-0.2	0.1	0.1	-0.7	-0.7	-0.0	-0.0	-0.0	-0.1
Net capital income	1.5	1.2	0.7	0.9	1.8	1.5	0.0	-0.2	1.0	0.7
GDP	0.5	0.3	0.5	0.3	0.2	0.1	-0.0	-0.1	0.4	0.3
Imports	0.8	0.2	1.0	0.4	0.6	-1.1	-1.9	-2.3	-0.2	-0.7
Compensating expenditure ($ billions)	$19.371	$18.089	$19.018	$17.760	$17.908	$16.78	$13.813	$12.899	$18.291	$17.081
% 1970 Defense reduction	127.9	119.4	125.5	117.2	118.2	110.4	91.2	85.1	120.7	112.7
% 1970 Compensating expenditure	166.1	155.1	106.4	99.3	22.5[a]	21.0[a]	14.3	13.3	13.8	12.9

Source: Stephen Dresch and Robert Goldberg, "IDIOM: An Inter-Industry, National-Regional Policy Evaluating Model," *Annals of Economic and Social Measurement*, no. 2/3 (1973). Reprinted with permission.

Key: EDC—exports to developing countries, ME—machinery and transportation equipment exports, PC—personal consumption, SS—social and educational services, FI—fixed investment, GD—20 percent general defense reductions, SD—20 percent strategic defense reduction.

[a]Percentage of transfer income.

eral economy, more critical studies now also include examinations of the employment opportunity costs of these systems.

The MX Missile

In a new study of the MX missile, David Gold criticizes the Air Force's own economic analysis of the full-scale engineering development of the MX missile for failing to compare the employment impact of the missile program with other alternative uses of the same funds.[11] Using input-output data on the U.S. economy, Gold, Paine, and Shields determined the value and distribution of inputs required to produce $1 billion of output for guided missiles in comparison with a similar output in new public utility construction, intercity railroad construction, intracity railroad construction, residential construction, and solar energy equipment. Data on direct and indirect interindustry inputs when combined with industry employment coefficients make it possible to compare the direct and indirect employment effects of a given dollar amount of output in missile production with five other alternative government purchases from industry. The resulting employment effects are listed in table 5-3.

The five alternative civilian expenditure programs have employment effects equal or greater than that of the MX missile program. In three alternatives—mass transportation equipment, public utility construction, and housing—the job creation potential of the alternatives is decidedly greater.[12]

Table 5-3
Employment Impact of Alternative Uses of $1 Billion of New Final Demand
(numbers of jobs per $1 billion—1972 dollars)

Alternatives	Direct Plus Indirect Employment	Direct Employment	Indirect Employment
Guided missile	53,248	25,055	28,193
Mass transit equipment	77,356	32,889	44,467
Public utility construction	65,859	32,173	33,686
Railroad equipment	54,220	20,260	33,960
Housing	68,657	31,016	37,641
Solar energy/energy conservation	65,079	+	+
Solar energy	57,235	+	+

Source: David Gold, Christopher Paine, and Gail Shields, *Misguided Expenditure, An Analysis of the Proposed MX Missile System,* (New York: Council on Economic Priorities, 1981), table 5. Reprinted with permission.

Surprisingly, guided missile production is found to have the lowest percentage of manufacturing inputs (60 percent) and the lowest percentage of capital goods manufacturing inputs (14 percent) of all the alternatives considered. This result is interesting for two reasons. First, it is frequently argued that military procurement programs create fewer jobs because they are concentrated in relatively capital-intensive manufacturing sectors, in contrast to more labor-intensive social programs. Second, military procurement is often regarded as particularly opportune and important for its stimulative impact on key capital goods industries. These findings suggest that these common assumptions are no longer true in highly specialized military aerospace production.

However, in the context of the actual production of such highly advanced weaponry, these findings are less surprising. In specialized military production, general R&D costs and administrative overhead are markedly higher than in such civilian sectors as the Gold study proposed as alternatives. After all, the Reagan administration, for example, plans to produce only 100 technologically highly sophisticated, expensive, and deadly MX weapons. Gold, Paine, and Shield's reliance on input-output industry averages for the guided missile industry as a whole, may actually overestimate MX-related employment.

B-1 Bomber

In another study, Chase Econometrics has examined, under contract to the prime contractor Rockwell International, the economic impacts of the B-1 bomber program.[13] The Chase study compared the effects of B-1 bomber expenditures with a tax cut and with a welfare program of the same amount. Both the tax cut and the welfare transfer would create as many or more jobs than the B-1 program. That is, Chase's own forecasting model predicts nationwide employment increases of 291,000 jobs between 1975 and 1984 with the B-1 program; 290,000 with a tax cut; and 287,000 jobs with a welfare transfer program.

In a second analysis using an input-output model, Chase compared the employment effects of the B-1 program with a tax cut, a housing program, and a public works program of the same magnitude. The housing expenditure alternative would create 70,000 more jobs and the public works program 60,000 more jobs than the B-1 program. Bezdek similarly concluded that the B-1 bomber program would create fewer jobs than many other types of alternative civilian expenditure (see table 5–4).[14]

In general, there is a strong case for the thesis that military expenditures entail employment opportunity costs. Military expenditures create jobs but alternative civilian expenditures create more jobs all things being equal.

Table 5-4
Labor Requirements Generated by B-1 Bomber and by Alternative Federal Expenditures

Program	Jobs
B-1	58,591
Education	118,191
Social Security	108,196
Welfare payments	99,406
Conservation and recreation	88,415
Highway construction	84,933
Public housing	84,524
Mass transit construction	83,536
Sanitation	78,954
Law enforcement	74,601
Army Corps of Engineers	69,384

Source: Gordon Adams, *The B-1 Bomber: An Analysis of Its Strategic Utility, Cost, Constituency, and Economic Impact* (New York: Council on Economic Priorities, 1976), table 10, p. 21. Reprinted with permission.

However, the existence and magnitude of the employment opportunity costs depend on the particular type of expenditures involved in each case.

The most frequent explanation of the positive employment effects of a shift from military to civilian production is that military production is concentrated in more capital-intensive industries, particularly the durable goods manufacturing sector, than civilian production. This explanation seems to assume that reallocating military expenditures typically shifts the sectoral distribution toward the nondurable goods, construction, and service sectors. This argument, however true in the past, may be a misleading picture of contemporary specialized military-industrial production.

Greater labor intensity can be said to explain employment opportunity costs of military expenditure only if labor intensity is defined as employment intensity—the number of persons employed directly and indirectly as expressed in employment per $1 billion of final demand. That is, the number of jobs created in an industry is not only a function of total labor costs as a percentage of value added but also a negative function of the average wage level.

In nonspecialized military industrial production, where the product is very close to or the same as the products sold to civilian industry (such as office equipment or automobiles), the employment intensity of expenditures may be enhanced in the traditional sense by shifting demand to other more labor-intensive sectors. On the other hand, the heterogeneity of military expenditures means that this argument is not applicable, for example, to military personnel expenditures, which are more labor- and employment-intensive than any civilian alternative, particularly during periods of military draft. The employment opportunity costs of military spending are highest in the case of specialized military-industrial production.

As described in the previous section, the development and production of high-tech weaponry is increasingly labor intensive. However, the higher labor-cost component is apparently more than offset by the high pay of this extremely qualified labor force. Overall DOD R&D costs have been 35 to 40 percent of procurement outlays in recent years, fifteen to twenty times the average ratio for civilian products. The percentage for individual programs such as the B-1 bomber and MX missile is even higher. Typically, 30 to 50 percent of the work force in the aerospace industry are scientists and engineers, and the administrative and managerial component of the work force is increasingly high. In the guided missile industry, to take an extreme example, only 27.8 percent of the work force are production employees, compared to an average figure of 88 percent for U.S. industry as a whole.[15] As a result military spending for such programs creates relatively fewer jobs than most civilian alternatives.

Industrial, Regional, and Occupational Effects

In addition to the opportunity costs of military expenditures for employment, military spending has differing impacts on the industrial, geographic, and occupational distribution of employment, which in turn is important for the political economy of the arms race and disarmament. A number of studies have investigated these redistributive impacts of military vis-à-vis alternative civilian spending.

Impact on Industries

Leontief and others employed an input-output model of the U.S. economy in 1958 to study the industrial and regional impact of a hypothetical 20 percent across-the-board reduction in military spending combined with a compensating proportional increase in nonmilitary final demand throughout the economy.[16] Of the 56 industries considered, 10 experienced net declines in employment, and 46 showed net increases after the postulated reduction in military spending. Although the positive impact on employment is highly dispersed over a large number of industries, the negative impact of a 20 percent decrease in military spending is highly concentrated in four sectors: the aircraft sector had a 16.05 percent employment decline;

ordnance, a 15.42 percent drop; R&D, 13.26 percent; and electronics, 5.40 percent.

In contrast to Leontief, Bezdek found that the number of gainers and losers by industry in the 30 percent increase/decrease in military spending scenarios examined were approximately equal (see table 5-5).[17] When defense spending decreases, 41 industries showed a net loss and 38 experience a net gain in employment; when military expenditures increase, 40 industries show a gain in employment and 39 a loss. A 30 percent compensated decrease in military expenditures showed not only big losers, such as aircraft (−9.2 percent) and ordnance (−16.5 percent) but also big gainers such as medical, educational and nonprofit organizations (11.7 percent); drugs, cleaning, and toilette preparations (7.3 percent); and new construction (14.6 percent), among others. Bezdek's disarmament scenario would shift production away from manufacturing toward services, with 35 manufacturing industries showing a reduction in employment and only 16 gains.

Bezdek's two major alternative scenarios reflect a hypothetical compensated shift within public expenditures between military and domestic social programs, whereas the Leontief study assumed an across-the-board cut in military expenditures and a proportionate increase in all public and private nonmilitary output. Their findings are not comparable by industry because both are sensitive not only to the existing distribution of military output but also to the specific scenarios postulated.

Table 5-5
Effect of Compensated Increases and Decreases in Military Spending on Forecast 1980 Industry Output and Employment
(% change)

Industry[a]	Change in Military Expenditure
	Compensated 30% Decrease
Aircraft and parts	−16.5
Ordnance and accessories	−9.2
Stone and clay mining and quarrying	−8.3
Construction, mining, and oil field machinery	−5.1
Lumber and wood products, except containers	+5.2
Primary nonferrous metals manufacturing	+5.8
Primary iron and steel manufacturing	+5.9
Drugs, cleaning, and toilet preparations	+7.3
Medical, educational, and nonprofit organizations	+11.7
New construction	+14.6
All industries	+2.1

Table 5-5 continued

Industry[a]	Change in Military Expenditure
	Compensated 30% Increase
Aircraft and parts	+ 17.8
Ordnance and accessories	+ 16.6
Iron and ferroalloy ores mining	+ 10.5
Other transportation equipment	+ 9.0
Material-handling machinery and equipment	+ 7.5
Nonferrous metal ores mining	+ 6.9
Office, computing, and accounting machines	+ 6.8
Electric industrial equipment and apparatus	+ 6.7
General industrial machinery and equipment	+ 6.7
Radio, television, and communications equipment	+ 6.3
Electronic components and accessories	+ 6.3
Stone and clay mining and quarrying	+ 6.2
Metal-working machinery and equipment	+ 6.2
Scientific and controlling instruments	+ 6.0
Special industry machinery and equipment	+ 5.8
Tobacco manufactures	− 5.1
Lumber and wood products, except containers	− 6.4
New construction	− 13.2
All industries	− 1.3

Source: Roger Bezdek, "The 1980 Economic Impact—Regional and Occupational—of Compensated Shifts in Defense Spending," *Journal of Regional Science,* 15:2 (1975), table 3. Reprinted with permission.

[a]Impact greater than ± 5 percent.

Regional Effects

Military expenditures and possible shifts to alternative civilian programs also have important regional effects on employment. Table 5-6 shows the regional distribution of U.S. military-related employment in private industry, DOD-owned industrial facilities, and for uniformed and civilian personnel stationed in the United States. It is regionally concentrated in the Southeast (24.3 percent), Southwest (11.6 percent), and West Coast (24.6 percent)[19]

Leontief and others investigated the regional effects of a 20 percent across-the-board cut in military expenditures. He found that in 1965 output would have shifted by only 1.16 percent if military final demand were cut by 20 percent. The impact is greatest in California, with a decrease in output of 2.39 percent and an increase of 0.54 percent, for a net change of − 1.85 percent. Regions comprising twelve states show gross loss of output and employment in excess of 2 percent. Leontief's results appear somewhat low in light of the fact that national defense expenditures were 7.5 percent of GNP even in this pre-Vietnam escalation period.[20]

Table 5-6
Regional Distribution of Domestic Military Employment, 1980

Region	Private Industry	R&D Facilities	Military Personnel	Total	% of Total
New England (Maine, New Hampshire, Vermont, Massachusetts, Rhode Island, Connecticut)	115,500	12,800	59,500	187,800	5.9
Middle Atlantic (New York, New Jersey, Pennsylvania)	98,500	33,000	140,200	271,700	8.6
East North Central (Ohio, Indiana, Illinois, Michigan, Wisconsin)	78,700	12,500	150,400	241,600	7.6
West North Central (Minnesota, Iowa, Missouri, North Dakota, South Dakota, Nebraska, Kansas)	57,000	—	114,650	171,650	5.4
South Atlantic (Delaware, Maryland, District of Columbia, Virginia, West Virginia, North Carolina, South Carolina, Georgia, Florida)	80,400	60,500	630,000	770,900	24.3
East South Central (Kentucky, Tennessee, Alabama, Mississippi)	12,400	14,000	147,650	174,050	5.5
West South Central (Arkansas, Louisiana, Oklahoma, Texas)	48,000	22,200	297,000	367,000	11.6
Mountain (Montana, Idaho, Wyoming, Colorado, New Mexico, Arizona, Utah, Nevada)	25,600	10,000	173,250	208,850	6.6
Pacific (Washington, Oregon, California, Alaska, Hawaii)	227,300	70,700	482,350	780,350	24.6
Total	743,600	235,600	2,194,500	3,173,700	100

Source: U.S. Department of Commerce, Bureau of the Census, Current Industrial Reports, *Shipments to Federal Government Agencies, 1980* (Washington, D.C.: Government Printing Office, 1981), tables 5 and 7; Marion Anderson, *The Empty Pork Barrel* (Lansing, Mich.: Employment Research Associates, 1982), appendix A (for 1977–1978), includes both uniformed and nonuniformed military personnel.

Bezdek also finds that the West, Southwest, and Southeast register the greatest net losses in employment when military spending is cut (see table 5-7).[21] However, Bezdek finds the net loss in employment is not more than 1.2 percent in any region, despite the larger cut he postulates (30 percent versus Leontief's 20 percent). That is, the losses in employment are more

Table 5-7
Estimated 1980 Regional Employment Before and After Compensated Increases and Decreases in Defense Expenditures[a]
(thousands)

Region	Status Quo Forecasts[b]	Defense Expenditure Decrease		Defense Expenditure Increase	
		Total Employ-ment[c]	Percent Change[d]	Total Employ-ment[e]	Percent Change[f]
New England (Maine, Vermont, New Hampshire, Massachusetts, Connecticut, Rhode Island)	5,616	5,690	+ 0.8	5,634	− 0.2
New York	8,701	9,078	+ 4.3	8,422	− 3.2
Middle Atlantic (Pennsylvania, New Jersey)	8,764	9,223	+ 5.5	8,462	− 3.4
Eastern Midwest (Michigan, Ohio)	9,094	9,504	+ 5.2	8,850	− 3.0
Central Midwest (Illinois, Indiana, Wisconsin)	9,819	10,298	+ 4.9	9,518	− 3.1
West North Central (North Dakota, South Dakota, Minnesota, Nebraska, Iowa, Kansas, Missouri)	7,503	7,760	+ 3.4	7,375	− 1.7
Upper South Atlantic (West Virginia, Maryland, Delaware, Virginia, Washington, D.C.)	5,340	5,455	− 2.2	5,291	− 0.9
Lower South Atlantic (North Carolina, South Carolina, Georgia, Florida)	8,964	8,903	− 0.7	8,955	− 0.1
East South Central (Kentucky, Tennessee, Mississippi, Alabama)	5,697	5,737	+ 0.7	5,682	− 0.3
West South Central (Oklahoma, Arkansas, Louisiana)	3,557	3,591	+ 0.1	3,508	− 1.4
Texas	5,136	5,105	− 0.6	5,149	+ 0.3
Mountain (Idaho, Montana, Wyoming, Nevada, Utah, Colorado, Arizona, New Mexico)	4,306	4,252	− 1.2	4,350	+ 1.0
Pacific Northwest (Washington, Oregon)	2,541	2,528	− 0.5	2,557	+ 0.6
California	11,004	10,891	− 1.0	11,096	+ 0.8

Source: Roger Bezdek, "The 1980 Economic Impact—Regional and Occupational—of Compensated Shifts in Defense Spending," *Journal of Regional Science,* 15:2 (1975), p. 193. Reprinted with permission.

[a]Regional estimates exclude Alaska and Hawaii.

dispersed, while the net increases in employment are very much larger than in the Leontief study, with the two largest gainers, the Middle Atlantic and Eastern Midwest regions, showing increases of 5.5 percent and 5.2 percent in employment, respectively. Such shifts may be the result in part of changes in the database, but the most likely explanation is a different methodology for estimating employment effects based on numbers of jobs (Bezdek) rather than labor earnings (Leontief). Apparently, the Leontief study underestimates the number of jobs created by alternative expenditure patterns because of intcrindustry pay differentials. Furthermore, Bezdek's scenarios not only postulates a 50 percent greater shift in expenditure but are also selective—in contrast to the across-the-board cuts postulated by Leontief—and therefore may be expected to have a more differential regional impact. Unfortunately, Bezdek did not replicate the Leontief scenario among his model estimates.

Dresch and Goldberg, who proposed ten alternative scenarios for a 20 percent cut in military spending and alternative civilian expenditures, show again the South, Southwest, and West-coast regions to be the most consistent losers in employment across the range of scenarios, with considerable variation.[22] Anderson also shows a similar pattern of regional loss and gain in employment.[23]

Occupational Effects

Given the concentration of military-industrial production in relatively few industries, the impact of shifts in expenditure from military to civilian production can be expected to be very significant on particular occupational groups. The data reported for changes in employment levels, even when a shift from military expenditures would increase civilian-related production employment, are net employment figures. Bezdek's data on occupational job displacement indicate that "massive gross job change and displacements and changes in the requirements for specific occupations would probably occur."[24]

Table 5–8 lists occupational shifts in jobs that would be affected by a 30 percent cut in military expenditures in the Central Midwest region (Illinois, Indiana, Wisconsin). This area would have a net gain of 4.9 percent in overall employment levels, but quite different effects on specific jobs.

---

[b]Employment estimates based on a "most likely" set of economic and social assumptions.

[c]Net regional employment after a compensated 30 percent reduction in defense expenditures.

[d]Percentage change in regional employment computed using status quo employment as the base.

[e]Net regional employment after a compensated 30 percent increase in defense expenditures.

[f]Percentage change in regional employment computed using status quo employment as the base.

Table 5-8
Effects of Changes in Defense Expenditures on 1980 Requirements for Selected Occupations (Illinois, Indiana, and Wisconsin)

30 Percent Decrease		30 Percent Increase	
Occupation	Percent	Occupation	Percent
Positive Change[a]		Positive Change[b]	
Hospital attendants	18.2	Mathematicians	9.1
Medical technicians	18.0	Aeronautical engineers	8.6
Physicians and dentists	17.7	Metalworking assemblers	8.1
Professional nurses	17.1	Machinists	7.8
Social and welfare workers	16.8	Toolmakers and diemakers	7.2
Protective service workers	15.9	Industrial engineers	6.6
Miscellaneous social scientists	14.9	Metalmolders (except	
Biological scientists	14.1	coremakers)	6.5
Plasterers	12.8	Mechanical engineers	6.4
Roofers and slaters	12.7	Electrical engineers	6.1
Civil engineers	10.9	Metal and wood patternmakers	6.0
Stenographers, typists, and		Welders and flamecutters	5.8
secretaries	9.6	Rollers and roll hands	5.7
Chemists	9.6	Biological scientists	5.5
Elementary and secondary			
school teachers	9.5		
Agricultural scientists	9.0		
Negative Change[a]		Negative Change[b]	
Metalworking assemblers	−8.4	Medical technicians	−16.8
Metalworking inspectors	−8.0	Physicians and dentists	−16.6
Machine tool operators	−7.9	Professional nurses	−16.0
Toolmakers and diemakers	−7.6	Plasterers	−14.8
Semiskilled textile occupations	−7.4	Biological scientists	−12.6
Machinists	−7.1	Pharmacists	−11.1
Aeronautical engineers	−7.0	Cements and concrete finishers	−9.9
Heat treaters and annealers	−6.5	Elementary and secondary	
Electroplaters and		school teachers	−9.0
electroplaters' helpers	−6.4	Dieticians and nutritionists	−8.4
Industrial engineers	−6.2	Chemists	−8.1
Metal and wood pattern makers	−6.0	Log and lumber inspectors	−7.6
Welders and flamecutters	−5.8	Excavating and grading machine	
Mechanical engineers	−5.8	operators	−7.2
Airplane mechanics and		Carpenters	−7.0
repairmen	−5.6	College teachers	−6.1
Jewelers and watchmakers	−5.5	Psychologists	−5.8

Source: Roger Bezdek, "The 1980 Economic Impact—Regional and Occupational—of Compensated Shifts in Defense Spending," *Journal of Regional Science,* 15:2 (1975), table 5. Reprinted with permission.

[a]Net changes in requirements corresponding to a 30 percent decrease in defense expenditures offset by increases in spending for public nondefense programs.

[b]Net changes in requirements corresponding to a 30 percent increase in defense expenditures offset by decreases in spending for public nondefense programs.

The first column shows the percentage increase in selected occupations resulting from the cut in military spending and reallocation of expenditures to government, civilian, social, and educational programs. The second column indicates decreases in selected occupations heavily affected by cuts in military spending in the region.

The overall gain in employment, when viewed at the micro level depicted by such occupational data, is not an unmixed blessing. On the one hand, some affected occupations suffer sharp declines—such as machinists, metal workers, and aeronautical engineers. On the other, labor shortages and inflationary tendencies are foreseen in many occupations if public non-military spending were to increase. The alternative social expenditures in the Bezdek scenario affect many highly skilled craftsmen and professional workers whose skills are not easily transferable from military to civilian production. Bezdek thus indicates severe labor market strains resulting from even moderate disarmament measures with a favorable macroeconomic impact on a region. To ease such adjustments, policymakers should plan either a tax reduction, which would diffuse increased civilian demand more evenly throughout the economy and avoid an overrapid expansion in certain specialized occupations, or conversion planning, which would relate the alternative civilian expenditures more closely to the skills of the occupational groups and production facilities most affected by the decreases in military expenditures.

Dresch and Goldberg have also published data on the occupational impacts of disarmament measures.[25] The level of aggregation of these data does not permit a micropicture of the occupational shifts comparable to that of Bezdek; however, the diversity of Dresch and Goldberg's scenarios (two types of decrease in military spending with five types of compensating expansion of civilian demand) illustrates the range of choice of public policy in controlling the distribution of the negative and positive impacts of demand for specialized labor. The impact of disarmament measures on employment in "metal crafts" ranges from +6.5 percent to −2.2 percent, depending on the composition of public expenditures. In the higher range, the scenario postulates a compensating increase in machinery and transportation equipment output; in the lower range, the compensating expenditure increases go to social and educational services. Demand for other types of craft and professional workers shows a similar sensitivity.

The methodology of *The Empty Pork Barrel* was extended in a later study, *The Impact of Military Spending on the Machinists Union.*[26] Because machinists are concentrated in certain industries, particularly in the durable goods sector, the type of jobs foregone is as important as the absolute number. Using Russett's opportunity cost coefficients, Anderson concludes that 118,000 machinist jobs are foregone by military expenditures while only 88,000 jobs are created. It would seem more prudent to give a range of alternative scenarios for the reallocation of current military spending rather than relying so heavily on the scenario implicit in Russett's coefficients.

As Dresch and Goldberg's data make clear, the actual impact on a specific occupational group is highly sensitive to the actual scenario postulated for reductions in military spending and alternative civilian expenditures. Moreover, as the Bezdek data illustrate, some types of alternative civilian expenditures for social and educational services can dramatically reduce the employment of some occupational groups (for example, the International Association of Machinists). Anderson's analysis is misleading insofar as it implies that the interests of IAM workers is merely to push for reallocation of resources from military to civilian uses. At the microlevel severe dislocation would take place even when there is a net gain in employment—which depends in fact on the disarmament scenario and may or may not occur. IAM members also have an interest in conversion planning. In general, the more specific the military expenditure reduction scenario and the more specific the alternative civilian expenditures scenario is, the more dramatic the impact on specific localities, industries, and occupational groups.[27]

Labor Force Effects

The number of jobs created is only one aspect of the labor market situation. Direct and indirect military-related employment can also affect the size of the labor force in such a way as to partially offset positive effects such job creation may have on overall employment. During World War Two, the military draft resulted in a sharp increase in the U.S. labor force participation rate. Some, particularly younger, military personnel would have not otherwise been in the labor force. And the drafting of other older males often meant a reduction in family earnings and sometimes a reduction in births which led wives and other dependents to enter the labor force.[28] This effect is most evident during the mobilization for major world wars but also manifests itself in limited war or cold war periods like that prevailing in the United States since 1950.

Notes

1. Marion Anderson, *The Empty Pork Barrel: Unemployment and the Pentagon Budget* (Lansing, Mich.: Public Interest Research Group, 1975), entered in the *Congressional Record* (June 4, 1975), S 9666–9672. The report has been updated several times, the latest in 1982; however, the argument has remained substantially unchanged.

2. This is perhaps not sufficiently stressed in Anderson's data for individual states or for the national totals.

3. The exact methodology can be found in appendixes to each edition of *The Empty Pork Barrel.*

4. DOD reports a figure of 1,775,000 for defense-related employment in fiscal year 1978. Office of the Assistant Secretary of Defense (Comptroller), *National Defense Budget Estimates for Fiscal Year 1983,* March 1982, p. 83. This estimate corresponds quite closely to and appears to be based upon Bureau of Labor Statistics manpower factors for the employment impact of government expenditures. U.S. Department of Labor, Bureau of Labor Statistics, *Factbook for Estimating the Manpower Needs of Federal Programs* (Washington, D.C.: Government Printing Office, Bulletin 1832, 1975).

5. Ibid. In his critique of the original Anderson study, Morgan maintains that there is a technical error in the estimates that results in a significant underestimation of military-related industry employment. William F. Morgan, "Unemployment and the Pentagon Budget: Is There Anything in the Empty Pork Barrel?" (Alexandria, Va.: Center for Naval Analyses, 1976), pp. 6–8.

6. Ibid., p. 6.

7. Roger Bezdek, "The 1980 Economic Impact—Regional and Occupational—of Compensated Shifts in Defense Spending," *Journal of Regional Science,* 15:2 (1975), pp. 183–197. Bezdek elaborates in more detail in *Long-Range Forecasting of Manpower Requirements* (New York: IEE Press, 1974). Bezdek's empirical results by industry are reproduced in table 5.

8. Bezdek, "The 1980 Economic Impact," p. 190.

9. Stephen Dresch and Robert Goldberg, "IDIOM: An Inter-Industry, National-Regional Policy-Evaluating Model," *Annals of Economic and Social Measurement,* 2/3 (1973), pp. 323–341.

10. Ibid., p. 323.

11. *Misguided Expenditure, An Analysis of the Proposed MX Missile System* (New York: Committee on Economic Priorities, 1982).

12. A possible caveat to Gold, Paine, and Shields' analysis of employment opportunity costs (ibid.): the input-output data on which Gold relies include R&D costs as well as procurement (actual production). His employment comparison are thus valid for the MX program as a whole, but underestimate the employment created by expenditures for actual procurement of the MX missile—the present stage of policy decision in terms of which an opportunity analysis would be relevant. The research and development costs of the MX missile program are largely sunk costs. This fact not only enhances the prospects of the program in a bureaucratic-political sense but also minimizes its opportunity costs at the point of actual decision.

13. Chase Econometrics Associates, *Economic Impact of the B-1 Program on the U.S. Economy* (Bala Cynwyd, Pa., 1975).

14. B-1 labor power requirements are simulated via the aircraft procurement vector in his model. Similarly, DeGrasse has calculated that the projected $34 billion cost of the proposed MX missile could be used to fund a ten-year program subsidizing energy efficiency measures that could cut oil imports by 23 to 54 percent (depending on the measures) and create 115,000 jobs. Robert deGrasse, Jr., "Shifting MX Expenditures to Energy Efficiency: Memo on the National Security Implications of Alternative Energy Development" (New York: Council on Economic Priorities, 1980, manuscript.

15. Jacques Gansler, *The Defense Industry* (Cambridge, Mass.: MIT Press, 1980), pp. 53, 101–103. This distinction between employment intensity and labor intensity is sometimes ignored in assessing employment impacts of military spending. Thus Leontief and others, using 1958 input-output data, studied the implications of a 20 percent across-the-board cut in military purchases of goods and services; they found that the military product mix has a higher labor cost content than the average civilian product mix. That is, $1 million in military goods and services would require 21 percent more in total wage and salaries paid for all labor engaged directly or indirectly than would $1 million of nonmilitary output. Thus the study assumes that "it would take $7.6 billion of additional civilian demand to compensate the cancellation of $6.3 billion worth of military spending." The authors clearly seem to equate total labor costs with the level of employment, which assumes that average pay is the same for both military and civilian production. Wassily Leontief and others, "The Economic Impact—Industrial and Regional—of An Arms Cut," *Review of Economics and Statistics,* 47:3 (1965), pp. 217–241.

16. Ibid.

17. Bezdek, "The 1980 Economic Impact," pp. 190–191.

18. Mancur Olson, *The Logic of Collective Action* (Cambridge, Mass.: Harvard University Press, 1965).

19. Leontief and others, "The Economic Impact—Industrial and Regional—of an Arms Cut,"

20. Ibid., p. 223.

21. Bezdek, "The 1980 Economic Impact."

22. Dresch and Goldberg, "IDIOM," table 4–7.

23. Anderson, *The Empty Pork Barrel.*

24. Bezdek, "The 1980 Economic Impact," p. 192.

25. Dresch and Goldberg, "IDIOM," table 4–3—Occupational Effect of a Compensated 20% Defense Contraction, 1970.

26. Lansing, Mich.: Employment Research Associates, 1979. A subsequent study by Marion Anderson employs the same methodology; see *Bombs or Bread, Black Employment and the Pentagon Budget,* (Lansing,

Mich.: Employment Research Associates, 1982). It is subject to the same comments as the machinists union study and the *Empty Pork Barrel* (note 1).

27. See, for example, Gordon Adams, *The B-1 Bomber: An Analysis of its Strategic Utility, Cost, Constituency, and Economic Impact* (New York: Council on Economic Priorities, 1976).

28. See E.F. Denison, *Accounting for U.S. Economic Growth: 1929–1969* (Washington, D.C.: Brookings, 1974). He cites as his source Clarence Long, *The Labor Force and Changing Income and Employment* (Princeton, N.J.: Princeton University Press, 1959).

6

Military Expenditure and Inflation

Inflation has been an endemic economic problem in the United States and other market economies since World War Two; it has been particularly acute since the beginning of the 1970s. The causes of inflation and, in particular, the recent acute inflation are controversial; it would certainly be a mistake to regard the high level of military expenditures during this period as its principal cause. Nevertheless, military expenditures, which averaged 8.2 percent of GNP and about 50 percent of government expenditures from 1951 to 1981, play a significant role.

Military-Related Inflation

Three main types of inflation are usually identified in the economic and public policy literature according to their respective causes: demand-pull inflation, cost-push inflation, and monetary inflation. This chapter examines in turn the role of military expenditures in each type of inflation. The relationship between military spending and inflation is particularly complex, and our goal here can only be to elucidate the possible relationships. In light of the available historical and empirical evidence, it is possible to make a prudent assessment of the significance of military expenditures for inflation in the postwar era.

Demand-Pull Inflation

Demand-pull inflation is caused by excess demand for goods and services—that is, demand which exceeds the existing productive capacity and labor resources of the economy. Military expenditure is a cause of demand-pull inflation insofar as it contributes to excess demand. If there are significant unemployed economic resources, then—all else being equal—additional military spending will stimulate increased output (that is, economic growth) and not be inflationary. On the other hand, if the existing productive capacity of the economy is being fully utilized, additional military expenditures will generate demand-pull inflation unless government implements offsetting measures to curtail civilian demand.[1]

113

In a certain tautological sense, military expenditure always contributes to inflation when there is demand-pull inflation in the economy because it constitutes a large component of total demand. More particularly, sharp increases in military expenditure are often the critical factor in setting off an inflationary burst. For example, economists now generally agree that the Vietnam escalation from 1965 to 1968 was a clear case of demand-pull inflation generated in the first instance by increased military spending:

> Given a civilian economy that had just reached capacity operation before the Vietnam War began, the war created classic excess-demand inflation. The military, for example, needed millions of boots. Orders were placed, and this forced up the price of civilian's shoes as military boots competed for scarce leather and shoemaking capacity. Employers started competing for workers, and wages rose. All across the economy prices started to rise as demands exceeded production capacities.[2]

Although Keynesian macroeconomic theory focuses on the relationship between government fiscal and monetary policy and the level of aggregate demand in the economy as a whole, government purchases of military-industrial products are in fact concentrated in relatively few industries (aircraft, missiles, electronics, munitions, shipbuilding, and tracked vehicles) through which military demand sets off a ripple effect throughout the entire economy (see chapter 3). Therefore, demand-pull inflation can occur in these sectors due to excess military-related demand, even when productive capacity in other sectors of the economy is considerably underutilized.

Gansler recently emphasized this microeconomic perspective on military expenditures and their inflationary potential.[3] He argues that an analyses of the effects of increased military expenditure which is limited to the macroeconomic level may overlook the most important fact, the current state of the U.S. defense industry: "it is necessary to look at the specific structure and condition of the defense industry in order to see what the economic effects of such increased defense expenditures are likely to be."[4] Gansler calls attention to such factors as the long-term contraction of the U.S. military industrial base in the post-Vietnam period, particularly at the level of key subcontractors and parts suppliers; the upsurge in defense production in the late 1970s; and increased demand for commercial aircraft at the beginning of the 1980s, which competes with defense production for engineers, skilled labor, the use of certain production machinery, and critical parts.[5] Gansler concludes that:

> it was highly likely that greatly increased defense funds, spent on the present products with the present contractors, would not yield significantly more military equipment but would only raise prices. The existing bottlenecks of labor parts, and production machinery would not be removed, and the few firms doing the business on increased demand would simply pay more for the scarce parts and labor and charge the government for the equipment produced.[6]

Similarly, David Gold argues on the basis of input-output analysis of guided missile production, that the MX missile is likely to be more inflationary than other alternative civilian expenditures because "the industries providing inputs into guided missiles are operating at higher levels of capacity utilization than is the case for the other five spending patterns."[7]

Monetary Inflation

Monetary inflation is caused by increases in the supply of money and credit in the economy without corresponding growth in output. Monetarists, whose influence is strong within the Reagan administration, argue that too much money chasing too few goods is the most important or even the only cause of inflation. In a monetarist perspective, the public policy prescription for dealing with inflation should be to tighten the money supply by printing less and restricting credit. Pure monetarists would argue that variations in the supply of money affect only the inflation component of nominal GNP but not output or GNP in real terms. In the monetarist view deficit spending is, insofar as it leads to an expansion of the money supply, inherently inflationary. While even Keynesian economists would concede that monetary inflation is a real phenomenon, they differ rather with respect to the conceptual framework for understanding the phenomenon of inflation, the appropriate responses of government policy and the tradeoffs entailed between output and inflation.[8]

Military expenditure contributes to monetary inflation insofar as it is a large component of the U.S. federal budget and hence a significant source of federal deficits. However, it is not federal budget deficits that cause monetary inflation, but rather financing such deficits by expanding the money supply.

The individual links in this causal chain illustrate the relationship between military spending and monetary inflation. The share of federal budget deficits which can be attributed to military expenditures can be equated to the share of military expenditures in the federal budget. However, determining the actual military share of the budget is difficult (see chapters 2 and 3). Not only do definitions of military spending differ, but there is also disagreement about whether the administrative budget or the unified budget, which includes social security and other trust fund expenditures, is the appropriate point of reference. Table 6-1 provides alternative estimates of military expenditures as a percentage of the U.S. budget for the 1950–1980 period.

To estimate the military-related share of the budget deficit, it seems more reasonable to use the administrative budget. The trust fund expenditures in the unified budget are earmarked for almost exclusively social welfare purposes. In the past, trust fund accounts have never run a deficit and

Table 6-1
National Defense Expenditures as a Percentage of the U.S. Budget and Source of Budget Deficits, 1950-1980
(conventional and alternative estimates)

Fiscal Year	National defense expenditures as percentage of all budget outlays	National defense expenditures as percentage of federal funds outlays	National defense-related expenditures as percentage of federal funds outlays
1950	29.1	31.3	74.5
1955	58.1	61.6	77.9
1960	49.0	60.2	79.0
1965	40.1	50.1	73.9
1970	40.0	50.3	67.8
1975	26.2	35.7	53.9
1980	23.6	32.4	50.5

Source: Calculated on the basis of data given in table 7-1, "Federal Outlays, FY 1945-1983," *National Defense Budget Estimates for FY 1983,* Office of the Assistant Secretary of Defense (Comptroller), March 1982; federal funds data (excluding trust funds) from the annual *Economic Report of the President* (Washington, D.C.: Government Printing Office, 1982), table B-72; *Statistical Abstract of the United States* (Washington, D.C.: Government Printing Office, 1981), table 417, p. 245. For 1950 and 1955, "federal funds" is equated with "total budget expenditures," that is, without "total trust account expenditures" as reported in *Statistical Abstract of the United States, 1957,* table 437, p. 363.

Note: National defense expenditures refers to the national defense function as reported in the U.S. budget. National defense-related expenditures include veterans benefits and services, space, and international affairs expenditures, as well as 75 percent of net interest payments on the U.S. public debt for an alternative high estimate of budgetary burden of past and current military operations.

no general revenue funds have been used to finance the social security system. The historical purpose of the social security trust fund accounting system has been to brake expanding expenditures by tying them to the necessary tax revenues. Certainly, most critics would welcome a system for financing military expenditures through a trust fund, which would require a "national defense tax" to be specifically deducted from each paycheck and an upward adjustment in the tax rate to cover any increase in military spending.

The second link between military expenditures and monetary inflation is the financing of government deficits by expanding the money supply. Military expenditure may, of course, be financed through taxes rather than by deficit financing. Even government deficit financing may not be inflationary, in the sense of increasing the money supply, if the debt is financed by the sale of government securities to private consumers and investors.

Table 6–2
Monetization of the Federal Debt
($ billions)

Fiscal Year	Gross Federal Debt	Debt held by Federal Reserve (%)	Money Supply (% Change)[b]
1954	270.8	9.2	
1955	274.4	8.6	
1956	272.8	8.7	
1957	272.4	8.4	
1958	279.7	9.1	
1959	287.8	9.0	
1960	290.9	9.1	0.7
1961	292.9	9.3	3.2
1962	302.3	9.8	1.8
1963	310.8	10.3	3.7
1964	316.8	11.0	4.6
1965	323.2	12.1	4.7
1966	329.5	12.8	2.5
1967	341.3	13.7	6.6
1968[a]	369.8	14.1	7.7
1969	367.1	14.7	3.2
1970	382.6	15.1	5.3
1971	409.5	16.0	6.5
1972	437.3	16.3	9.3
1973[c]	468.4	16.1	5.5
1974	486.2	16.6	4.4
1975	544.1	15.6	5.0
1976	631.9	15.0	6.6
1977	709.1	14.8	8.1
1978	780.4	14.8	8.3
1979	833.8	13.9	7.2
1980	914.3	13.2	6.4

Source: Executive Office of the President, Office of Management and Budget, *Special Analyses, Budget of the United States Government, 1982* (Washington, D.C.: Government Printing Office, 1981), table E-3, p. 113; *Economic Report of the President, February 1982,* table B-51, p. 303.

[a]Gross debt reduced by $10.7 billion as three government-sponsored enterprises became privately owned.

[b]M1, calendar years.

[c]Gross debt increased by $4.5 billion because of technical change in the recording of trust fund holdings of Treasury debt.

However, usually only a part of the debt is financed in this way. It is also financed by the sale of government securities to the Federal Reserve System, the U.S. central banking system, which in effect monetizes the federal government's debt by expanding the money supply. Table 6–2 summarizes the growth in the national debt, growth in the military deficit, Federal Reserve funding of the national debt, and growth in the money supply from 1954 to

1980. Monetization of the government deficit is of course only one factor affecting the growth of the money supply (which in turn is only one factor determining the incidence of inflation).[9]

Obviously, the relationship between military expenditure and inflation is not simple. The political economy of inflation includes a number of important variables as well as military spending:

1. The overall state of the economy, particularly employment and capacity utilization, in which military expenditures occur.
2. The degree to which available productive capacity is currently being utilized in sectors of the economy most affected by military demand, particularly in firms engaged in specilized military production.
3. The compensatory fiscal policy measures introduced by government, if necessary, to curb public or private civilian demand by means of tax increases or budget cuts.
4. The government's monetary policies, in particular the extent to which the budget deficit is monetized by expansion of the money supply as opposed to borrowing from capital markets or other extraordinary measures, such as bonds, that draw savings or constrain civilian demand.
5. The particular type of military expenditures, in the sense of the specialized resources required, and the rate of increase in military spending.

Military expenditure as a source of demand-pull inflation is directly and positively related to variables 1 and 2. This stimulative effect on the economy and its possible inflationary effects are basically similar to other types of government-stimulated demand at both the microeconomic level in the military sector and overall demand at the macroeconomic level.[10] On the other hand, the inflationary impact of military spending can be limited by offsetting fiscal policies, as can other types of government expenditures. Nevertheless, because military-industrial production is heavily concentrated in relatively few firms in a few sectors, general fiscal measures alone would be a crude way to deal with military-related demand-pull inflation.

Military-related monetary inflation is positively related to variable 4, a government monetary policy that monetizes the military-related deficit. In the strict monetarist perspective, such an expansion of the money supply is necessarily inflationary even without excess demand. Finally, the rate of increase in military expenditure is as relevant to its actual inflationary impact as the type of spending. Large and rapid increases in military spending strain the resources of the economy as well as the capacities of the political system.

The Political Context: Vietnam Inflation and
Policy Stress

Government policymaking is central in both the demand-pull and monetary types of military-related inflation scenarios. The assessment of the existing state of the economy and the integration of military resource allocation in the government budget and in economic policy take place within the public governmental sphere. To understand the relationship between military expenditure and inflation it is necessary to go beyond economic theory and to consider somewhat more concretely the real policymaking context.

The Vietnam Inflation

An especially interesting account of the impact of military spending on economic policy has been given by Arthur Okun, a member and later chairman of President Johnson's Council of Economic Advisors from 1964 to 1968, when the Vietnam war escalated. In principle, the potential detrimental effects of this mobilization on the U.S. economy, which was then approaching full employment, could have been compensated by higher taxes to reduce consumer spending and business investment, cutbacks in government civilian programs, or a more restrictive monetary policy to reduce private spending. In fact, sufficient and timely compensatory measures were not taken and the nation was hit by severe inflationary pressures. Okun attributes this failure to implement an effective economic policy to three principal factors: (1) the unpredictability and disruptive effects of military spending; (2) the political resistance to tax increases and other economic restraints; and (3) the shortcomings of economic analysis.[11]

The levels of defense spending required for actual combat or to meet external threat are highly unpredictable. Economic policy is based on forecasts and expectations of economic activity and government budgets, but military contingencies are a special case—"we never know how big a war we are about to fight." Constant revisions of military budget estimates require readjustments in government compensatory fiscal and monetary policies, with inevitable lags and disruptive costs. During the Korean buildup, for example, three major pieces of tax legislation had to be enacted in 1950 and 1951.

As the Vietnam war experience shows, estimates of the course of defense expenditures may also be politically biased. According to Okun's account, the January 1966 official estimates of 1967 defense spending was in fact $10 billion under the actual outlays. About $2 billion was due to an underestimate of the actual costs of planned defense programs, and about $2.5 billion was due to program decisions made after January 1966 that resulted in stepped-up Vietnam activity during the fiscal year. However, the largest share, about $5 billion in unanticipated costs, resulted from the administration's January 1966 assumption, for purposes of budgetary planning, that the war in Vietnam would end during FY 1967 and that provisions need not be made for the continuation of hostilities beyond June 30, 1967. Absurd as this decision may seem in retrospect, the administration's politically conditioned optimism about the course of the Vietnam war actually shaped budgetary planning and assumptions about economic policy.[12]

The failure to estimate the actual outlays required for military policy and programs is also an inherent source of unpredictability:

> Although large and bureaucratic, the Pentagon was light on its feet, translating new decisions promptly into increased outlays. The resulting shifts had larger and more disruptive economic effects than any surprises encountered in components of private demand during the 60's.[13]

Estimates of defense expenditure are also likely to be lower than actual outlays for institutional and bureaucratic reasons. The function of the defense expenditure estimates is to set targets, not to make forecasts. The Secretary of Defense uses the budget estimates as an administrative instrument for cost control—that is, to curb department demands for even greater expenditures—and consequently such estimates tend to err on the low side.[14]

The principal failure of economic policymaking during the Vietnam war, however, occurred at the political level. Although administration economists had underestimated the impact of the war escalation on the economy in 1965, they did recommend a general tax increase for the January 1966 budget program to avoid excess demand. However, this recommendation was not accepted and the burden of countering inflation was born by the Federal Reserve Board acting alone. In January 1967 the administration proposed a 6 percent surcharge on individual and corporate income taxes, and the Fed moved away from its policy of monetary restraint in anticipation of the proposed tax increase. However, Congress failed to act on the tax proposal because, according to Okun, of the general political unacceptability of a tax increase and Congress's unwillingness to raise taxes on the basis of mere forecasts of economic acceleration in an economy still sluggish after the monetary restraint of the previous year. Not until early 1968, when the signs of the overheated economy were unmistakable, did Congress finally enact a 10 percent surcharge on corporate and individual incomes.

This tax measure, together with a $6 billion cut in civilian expenditures in the FY 1969 budget, slowed the pace of the economic boom, although much more slowly than had been anticipated by the administration's economic advisors. This "political paralysis of the tax rates"—the reluctance of the administration to press for an early tax increase and the subsequent reluctance of the Congress to pass the surtax after it was proposed—was clearly related to the unpopularity of the Vietnam war itself.[15] The administration did not and dared not employ the kind of patriotic appeal for wartime austerity taxation that was used during the Second World War and the Korean conflict. Inflation, which averaged around 2 percent in the early 1960s, doubled to 4.1 percent in FY 1968 and 4.8 percent in FY 1969, setting off the inflationary spiral of the 1970s.

Policy Stress

Periods of sharply accelerating military expenditures are particularly subject to economic disruptions and inflationary pressures. In theory, economic policy can compensate for the economic effects of the military buildup, but in practice its capacity to intervene is subject to technical limits and political restraints, which have more often than not resulted in an inadequate or mistaken response. In Okun's opinion, deviation from economic stability in the direction of inflation and recession have been "more often and more severely" a consequence of government actions than of autonomous shifts in private demand. He cites the 1950–1951 Korean inflation, the 1953–1954 post-Korean recession, and the Vietnam inflation as examples of "fluctuations associated with inappropriate swings in the Federal budget." In each case "the defects lay in error of omission rather than in errors of commission . . . some strong force was pushing the budgetary impact in one direction; and the budget was allowed to swing in that direction rather than being neutralized by timely and adequate fiscal notion."[16]

Although in principle government can pursue a correct compensatory fiscal or monetary policy to counteract any inflationary tendency set off by military spending, the practice of government economic management of the market economy, at least in the United States, is more complicated. Aside from the technical shortcomings of measurement, the quality of economic analysis, and the uncertainties of anticipating military spending levels in wartime or the costs of major new weapons programs, political considerations have constrained the practice of the fiscal and monetary restraints necessary to control incipient inflation when military expenditure increases. Such fiscal restraints as increased taxes or reductions in government civilian programs that curb public and private civilian demand entail considerable political costs for an incumbent government. Increased taxation is seldom popular and existing government civilian programs usually have strong political constituencies.

David Ricardo, the nineteenth-century British classical economist who lived and wrote during the Napoleonic wars, advocated that wars be financed out of taxes alone to impose their economic burden on the present instead of the future: "When the pressure of the war is felt at once, without mitigation, we shall be less disposed wantonly to engage in an expensive contest, and if engaged in it, we shall be sooner disposed to get out of it unless it was a contest of some great national interest."[17] Surely Ricardo's supposition is correct; if a war or military buildup is controversial, then the reluctance to ask for tax financing of the military effort will be correspondingly greater. At a minimum, this politically conditioned reluctance in combination with the uncertainties of economic analysis and projecting military spending is likely to postpone the adoption of the needed compensatory fiscal policies considerably, as was the case during the Vietnam buildup.

Deficit financing is a politically congenial solution. It eases the political choice by displacing part of the budgetary costs and political liabilities of military spending onto future budgets and future administrations. However, it creates other problems. Insofar as the debt is financed through capital markets, private investment may be crowded out by government demand for money and related higher interest rates. On the other hand, insofar as the debt is monetized, classical monetary inflation may result, which means in effect financing the war through an inflation-tax with resultant distortions in the economy and individual hardships.

Martin Feldstein, chairman of the Council of Economic Advisors in the Reagan administration, recently considered the implications of government increases in the real deficit in a fully employed economy. Although Feldstein believes that the deficit can be increased without inflation if the interest rate on government bonds increases, the economy suffers a corresponding loss in capital intensity—that is, crowding out investment with resulting loss in real income: "An important conclusion is that such an increased deficit must raise the rate of inflation or lower the capital intensity of production or both."[18] Feldstein's conclusions are clearly also applicable to military-related deficits.

When increasing military expenditures in an underemployed economy, government has more room to maneuver to control the possibility of both demand-pull and monetary inflation. However, as the Korean buildup suggests, any initial economic slack in the overall economy may be quickly absorbed by the demand stimulation of sharply increasing military expenditures.

Cost-Push Inflation in the Military Sector

The Defense Industry

Extraordinary cost-push inflationary tendencies in the military sector itself may generate mark-up inflation, wage inflation, or general inefficiency in the use of economic resources, which Melman calls "cost maximizing/subsidy maximizing" management.[19] In mark-up inflation, management takes advantage of a favorable situation to increase profit margins. Wage inflation is a price movement set in motion by a rise in labor compensation achieved by the bargaining power of organized labor, which is then passed on by management in the form of price increases. Cost-inefficient management is said to be indigenous to the military sector because U.S. military-industrial production weakens or removes the normal incentives for cost control in the use of economic resources. (Import inflation plays no very signficant role in the U.S. military-industrial sector, although military costs are greatly influenced by fuel prices.) In practice, of course, it is often very difficult to distinguish cost-push inflation in the military sector from other types of inflation.

A great deal of the critical literature describes the special characteristics of the U.S. defense industry, particularly its organizational and managerial shortcomings.[20] Gansler, for example, uses free market theory as an analytic benchmark to identify the military-industrial features that foster the development of cost-push inflation (see table 6–3). The major factors are:

1. The high degree of concentration of military business in relatively few prime contractors and major suppliers.[21]
2. Its primary reliance on negotiated cost-plus contracting.[22]
3. Its orientation toward an essentially one-buyer market that is more quality-oriented than price-sensitive and in which procurement decisions are more bureaucratic and political than market rational.[23]

Although U.S. industry as a whole, particularly in manufacturing, deviates considerably from the market model of cost control, this process is nowhere more advanced than in the defense sector. Nevertheless, Gansler rejects the conclusions of those who regard the defense sector as an example of "the planning system" (Galbraith) or a state-managed economy (Melman). Government intervention in the industry as the principal buyer and the planning of individual weapon programs is far from the overall sectoral planning of the defense-industrial base that Gansler thinks is necessary.

One commentator has suggested that defense expenditures resemble the so-called Laffer Curve, which postulates that as government tax rates increase a zero point is reached at which tax revenues actually begin to decline.[24] The defense spending version, which Greider dubs the Maginot Curve, postulates that, given the existing structural inefficiencies and supply bottlenecks in the defense industry, the more we spend on weapons the fewer weapons we get for our money.

The Defense Logistics Agency has documented several examples of spectacular price increases in parts and supplies. The official explanations

Table 6-3
Market Imperfections in Defense Industry

Free Market Theory	Defense Market
Many small buyers	One buyer (DOD)
Many small suppliers	Very few large suppliers of a given item
Market sets prices	Monopoly or oligopoly pricing or buy into available dollars
Free movement in and out of market	Extensive barriers to entry and exit
Prices set by marginal costs	Prices proportional to total costs
Prices set by marginal utility	Any price paid for desired military performance
Prices fall with reduced demand	Prices rise with reduced demand
Supply adjusts to demand	Large excess capacity
No government involvement	Government is regulator, specifier, banker, judge of claims, and so on
Selection based on price	Selection often based on politics, sole source, or negotiation
Production for inventory	Production occurs after sale made
Demand sensitive to price	Demand threat-sensitive, or responds to availability of new technology; almost never price-sensitive
Buyer has choice of spending now or saving for later purchase	DOD must spend its annual Congressional authorization
Price fixed by market	Most business, for any risk, is for cost-plus fee

Source: Jacques Gansler, *The Defense Industry* (Cambridge, Mass.: MIT Press, 1980), table 2.1, p. 30. Reprinted with permission.

for these rises provide insight into the unique structure of the defense business that makes it particularly susceptible to cost-push inflation (see table 6-4). They illustrate the extent to which nonmarket factors determine pricing and the effect of DOD's reliance on limited or sole-source contractors. Even more impressive is the historical rise in the cost of major weapon systems. Norman Augustine, former Assistant Secretary of the Army for Research and Development, has calculated the rate of growth in the unit price of tactical aircraft, tanks, and aircraft carriers that results both from price increases in the cost of development and procurement as well as qualitative improvements.[25] Unit costs of tactical aircraft are increasing so rapidly that Augustine projects the price of one aircraft in 2036 will be the same as the Pentagon's entire 1974 budget.

This spectacular growth in unit costs has resulted in the purchase of fewer and fewer weapons in each succeeding generation. In 1945, the peak

Table 6-4
Price Increases and Official Explanations for Selected Items

	Prior Cost ($)	New Cost ($)	Defense Logistics Agency's Explanation
Static discharger	6.23 (FY 74)	7.70 (FY 75)	Previous supplier no longer certified; new source.
Relay arm	22.84 (Aug. 74)	50.51 (Oct. 74)	Original supplier bought out.
Crystal	6.53 (Jan. 72)	14.75 (Dec. 74)	Revision of specification. Item no longer commercially available.
Intersleeve connector	134.00 (FY 72)	382.15 (FY 74)	Increase in royalties.
Plug connector	2.50 (FY 73)	4.21 (FY 74)	Company absorbed. Also now only one approved distributor.
Circuit module assembly	235.46 (Apr. 73)	336.00 (Dec. 73)	Contractor claimed smaller production.
Rotary switch	132.52 (FY 73)	160.14 (Sep. 73)	Company readjusted pricing structure.
Armature	7.77 (Apr. 73)	14.73 (FY 74)	Company readjusted pricing structure.
Electron tube	135.00 (Jan. 72)	240.00 (Dec. 74)	Company became sole source.
Variable resistor	106.75 (FY 72)	158.85 (Dec. 74)	Company stopped absorbing setup costs.
Variable resistor	88.65 (May 73)	114.25 (Dec. 74)	Company no longer produces except on job-shop special basis; no satisfactory substitute available.
Loudspeaker	19.25 (FY 73)	38.00 (FY 74)	Increase due in part to cost of special metal casting. Only two firms in Midwest can do this casting, because of environmental controls.
Electron tube	3.18 (FY 73)	4.61 (Dec. 74)	Supplier recalculated cost on all items.
Wear ring	32.00 (FY 73)	161.57 (FY 74)	Loss of competition resulted in sole source.
Aerial refueling hose	1,456.00 (FY 73)	1,694.25 (FY 74)	Original source went out of business.

Source: Defense Logistics Agency Study, January 10, 1975, as reported in Jacques Gansler, *The Defense Industry* (Cambridge, Mass.: MIT Press, 1980), table 6.3, pp. 134–135.

year of World War Two production, the United States produced 50,000 tactical aircraft, 20,000 tanks, and 80,000 artillery pieces. In 1974, when defense expenditures were the same as in 1945 ($80 billion in current dollars), the United States produced only 450 tanks, 600 aircraft, and no artillery. Even adjusting for inflation explains only a fraction of this discrepancy; the United States spent only about four times as much in 1982 constant dollars for procurement, R&D, and construction in 1945 as in 1974.[26]

Cost-push inflation in the military sector affects overall inflation in two ways. First, the military sector is a significant share of the total economy (about 6 percent) and an even larger share of manufacturing (about 10 percent). If cost-push inflation in the military sector were only two times the rate of inflation in the economy as a whole, it would contribute disproportionately to overall inflation in the economy and in the key manufacturing sector. Second, the economy is an interrelated whole and, although military production is relatively concentrated in a few industries, military-oriented firms and unions (which are particularly concentrated in larger firms and in such industries as aerospace and electronics) may establish price and/or wage patterns for the rest of the economy. Furthermore, the military sector's ability to pass through costs—Melman's "cost maximizing/subsidy maximizing" management—may also negatively influence civilian management practices.[27]

An Assessment

The significance of the several types of cost-push inflation that various authors ascribe to the military sector is difficult to evaluate in more than an illustrative fashion. Nevertheless, if these theories are correct, cost-push inflation factors in the military sector should result in higher rates of inflation for goods and services purchased by the military, in particular for specialized products. Data available from the U.S. Defense Department and the Bureau of Economic Analysis (BEA) of the U.S. Department of Commerce on inflation in the military sector enables a comparison of inflation rates in the military sector with rates in other sectors of the economy.

The DOD composite inflation index rose to 230.0 between 1972 and 1982 (FY 1972 = 100), while the overall GNP deflator stood at 209.4 for the same period. The GNP price index is the ratio of GNP in current prices to GNP in constant prices. It is a weighted average of the price indexes used to deflate the components of GNP. The DOD composite price index, the ratio of DOD expenditures in current prices to the constant-price base year, is a weighted average of a DOD purchases index and increases in compensation for military and civilian personnel. Thus inflation in the military sector averaged 13.0 percent, while the increase in the GNP deflator averaged 10.9 percent for the same period—a significantly, but not dramatically higher rate of inflation in the military sector.[28]

Other sectors have different rates of inflation over this period. The cost of fuels, for example, increased over 400 percent, and the Consumer Price Index stood at 233.5 at the end of 1982, even higher than the defense deflator. Thus the defense deflator may be higher than the GNP deflator because the mix of DOD purchases of goods and services comes disproportionately from sectors with higher rates of inflation than the economy as a whole—as is the case for consumer prices.[29]

Table 6–5 shows DOD composite inflation rates by major appropriations categories from 1975 to 1982. As shown, the inflation rate for the major components of the military budget also varies considerably. (R&D and procurement categories correspond roughly to specialized military industrial production.)

Even more detailed calendar year data by sector and industry is provided in table 6–6. While the GNP deflator had risen to 206.9 (1972 = 100) by 1982, the deflator for national defense purchases had risen to 227.7 and the deflator for military equipment—military-industrial production in a narrow sense—to 233.7. The deflator for military purchases of nondurable goods had by contrast reached 488.3, mostly because of the rise in petro-

Table 6–5
Composite Inflation Rates by DOD Appropriation Category

Outlays	Fiscal Year					
	1976–1977	*1977–1978*	*1978–1979*	*1979–1980*	*1980–1981*	*1981–1982*
Military personnel	5.27	6.76	5.80	7.17	17.00	12.80
Retired pay	5.91	7.51	8.27	12.08	11.20	6.60
Operation and maintenance	8.00	7.93	7.42	16.03	11.75	5.99
Procurement	7.69	7.09	8.68	9.69	11.79	9.41
Research, development, testing and evaluation	5.97	6.82	8.03	8.91	11.39	8.68
Military construction	3.96	8.09	9.23	9.99	11.64	8.84
Family housing	6.37	7.55	8.44	9.16	11.41	8.47
DOD Composite	6.72	7.33	7.45	11.30	12.90	8.75

Source: Office of the Secretary of Defense (Comptroller), *National Defense Budget Estimates for FY 1983* (Washington, D.C.: Government Printing Office, 1982), table 5.11, p. 51.

Table 6–6
Implicit Price Deflators for National Defense Purchases
(1972 = 100)

	Line	1979	1980	1981	1982
National Defense Purchases	1	166.0	187.5	209.3	227.7
Durable Goods	2	164.3	184.0	205.8	228.4
Military equipment	3	165.6	185.7	208.6	233.7
Aircraft	4	167.0	189.2	215.9	252.9
Missiles	5	155.7	176.4	203.1	231.0
Ships	6	190.7	209.4	229.9	243.8
Vehicles	7	172.0	195.4	237.6	278.5
Electronic equipment	8	150.9	167.6	176.9	183.7
Other	9	153.4	170.0	186.7	196.8
Other durable goods	10	159.7	178.0	197.1	208.8
Nondurable Goods	11	298.1	437.8	488.4	488.3
Bulk petroleum products	12	502.4	858.6	984.6	923.7
Ammunition	13	196.6	217.0	238.8	265.8
Clothing and textiles	14	155.7	165.1	178.6	184.0
Other nondurable goods	15	181.7	202.5	215.7	225.6
Services	16	159.9	175.5	195.9	213.6
Compensation of employees	17	152.2	165.2	185.2	201.9
Military	18	147.4	161.0	184.7	205.7
Civilian	19	159.0	171.2	185.9	196.4
Other services	20	177.1	196.7	217.1	234.8
Contractual research and development	21	175.7	195.7	216.4	236.0
Travel	22	153.4	191.1	236.4	238.1
Transportation	23	186.1	224.0	237.4	243.2
Communications	24	120.4	124.1	151.8	172.4
Depot maintenance	25	178.4	188.1	215.4	246.0
Other	26	185.5	202.0	217.4	234.2
Structures	27	183.5	205.0	221.2	224.3
Military facilities	28	183.4	202.8	218.0	217.7
Other	29	183.6	209.6	226.3	235.3

Source: "National Income and Product Accounts," in *Survey of Current Business* (July 1983), table 7.15, p. 87.

leum prices. Comparison with inflation in private purchases of producers' durable equipment shows that price increases over the period are significantly higher for procurement of specialized military equipment (233.7: 182.8). However, differences are less marked in such key individual categories as aircraft (252.9:247.4), electronic equipment (183.7:161.6), and shipbuilding (243.8:238.8). Moreover, if inflation data for military equipment and producers' durable equipment from 1972 to 1979 are compared—

that is, during a slack period in military demand before the impact of the Reagan buildup—there is no significant difference (162:159.4). The big surge in inflation in purchases of military equipment may reflect demand pressure rather than cost-push factors peculiar to the military-industrial sector.[30]

In general, the evidence from NIPA data is inconclusive for cost-push inflation in the military sector which is above that for the economy as a whole (GNP deflator) or comparable production for private demand. The overall difference in inflation rates is not as great as available data on cost inflation in some individual weapons programs would indicate and it is difficult to distinguish the impact of demand pressure. Moreover, inflation data for key military-related industries shows surprisingly little difference.

The reasons for these unexpected findings are difficult to identify. Perhaps the cost-push factors attributed to the military sector are not unique to it. Specifically in the key military-related industries, the impact of the military sector may be large enough to affect price levels in the entire industry. It is also possible that data covering a longer period would reveal greater differences between price levels in military-industrial production and in comparable production for private demand. Finally, the manner in which cost indexes for military-industrial purchases are calculated by the Department of Commerce may be a reason. Price indexes measure cost increases for the same commodity over time, but military-industrial production involves unique products—particularly when generations of specialized military equipment are compared. It may be that the manner in which price increases and product improvements are defined and measured obscures important cost differences that are not reflected in published inflation rates. At the other extreme, if unit cost data are used, military inflation rates are, as noted previously, phenomenal.[31]

The Inflationary Nature of Military Spending

Some critics maintain that military expenditure is inherently inflationary because military demand removes goods and services from the economic cycle. Unlike any other economic activity, the military product leaves the economic cycle almost completely: "The incomes of the worker and the profits of the enterprises appear on the market as demand for consumer and capital goods without a corresponding increase in the production of these goods."[32] In other words, military expenditure is an exogenous stimulant to demand, which is its particular attractiveness for Keynesian demand management as a countercyclical expenditure.

There are several counterarguments to this thesis. First, military expenditure is inflationary only when resources are shifted from directly productive to nonproductive uses. Although this is true of military expenditure, it is also true of all other government purchases that are nonproductive in the sense of withdrawing goods and services from the market without any corresponding product. Second, even nonproductive military expenditure, like other government expenditures, is not necessarily inflationary if it is financed either by increased tax revenues or by borrowing from capital markets rather than by money creation.[33] Although from the point of view of economic theory military spending is not distinguishable from other government purchases, in fact it constitutes the vast bulk of federal purchases, averaging 75 percent in the 1970–1980 period. Thus its magnitude alone makes it in practice distinctive.

Moreover, other government purchases for civilian education, transportation, health services, community development, and so on represent to a significant extent public consumption which flows directly or indirectly into the living standards of the population.

Even though military expenditure can be financed in a noninflationary manner, it is in practice difficult for both technical and political reasons. In fact, wars and arms booms in U.S. history have been paid for to a considerable extent by inflationary deficit financing as government has failed, for whatever reason, to take the necessary compensatory fiscal and monetary measures. Although the formulation "inherently inflationary" is perhaps too strong, military expenditures do in practice have a strong inflationary bias, which is rooted in the political-economic characteristics of military spending.

The Impact of Military Spending on Inflation

Finally, the view that military spending is too small a percentage of total production to be a major cause of inflation (6 to 7 percent in 1982) requires explicit consideration. The magnitude of military expenditure in the general economy may be a misleading indicator of its political and economic impact. It is by far the largest element in the federal administrative budget, which in turn has been the principal instrument for Keynesian demand management of the U.S. economy since the end of World War Two. Moreover, military expenditure has been a particularly volatile and destabilizing component of U.S. public expenditures, as the Vietnam war mobilization costs indicate.

The dynamics of the impact of the federal budget on inflationary pressure are such that a relatively small deficit and excess demand in GNP terms can have disproportionate effects on economic stability. Also, the psychological impact of fluctuations in government fiscal and monetary policy, of which military expenditure is a critical determinant, can not be adequately assessed in merely quantitative terms. Furthermore, the percentage of GNP that military final demand constitutes underestimates the impact of the military sector in the light of even conservative estimates of its multiplier effect or its impact on key industrial sectors, particularly by durable goods manufacturing (see chapters 3 and 4).

Notes

1. For an effort to conceptualize military-related demand-pull and other types of inflation in market economies see *Report of the Secretary General: Study on the Relationship between Disarmament and Development* (New York: United Nations, 1981), pp. 83–87.

2. Lester Thurow, *The Zero Sum Society* (New York: Basic Books, 1980), p. 43. The Committee for Economic Development, for example, in *The National Economy and the Vietnam War* (New York, 1968) also concluded that the Vietnam military buildup produced inflationary pressures that, because of an inadequate response of government economic policy, led to a rapid rise in the rate of inflation (p. 10). See also the more detailed discussion of Vietnam-related inflation later in this chapter.

3. Jacques Gansler, *The Defense Industry* (Cambridge, Mass.: MIT Press, 1980).

4. Ibid., p. 15.

5. See chapter 2, table 2–9.

6. Gansler, *Defense Industry*, p. 15.

7. Council On Economic Priorities (CEP), *Newsletter* (July 1981), p. 7. For supporting data see David Gold and others, *Misguided Expenditure, An Analysis of the Proposed MX Missile System* (New York: 1981), table 6, pp. 158–163.

8. Caroline Atkinson, "Confounded Inflation! The Experts at Odds," *Washington Post,* August 9, 1981, p. F3f.

9. See "Military Spending Causes Higher Prices," *The Defense Monitor,* 3:1 (January 30, 1974).

10. A qualification might be required here with respect to unique features of the military-industrial sector. The planned maintenance of excess capacity to provide for surges in military demand—for example, ordnance—might make it in some instances less susceptible to sectoral demand pressures in comparison to other industries. On the other hand, the peculiar features of specialized military industrial production (such as limited competition, cost-plus contracting, orientation toward quality rather than cost-efficiency) make it more vulnerable to cost-push inflation than other industries.

11. Arthur Okun, *The Political Economy of Prosperity* (Washington, D.C.: Brookings, 1970), p. 98.

12. Ibid., pp. 73–74.

13. Ibid., p. 74.

14. Ibid.

15. Ibid., p. 72.

16. Ibid., p. 111.

17. David Ricardo, *Essay on the Funding System* (London, 1920), quoted in Gavin Kennedy, *The Economics of Defense* (London: Faber and Faber, 1975), p. 29.

18. Martin Feldstein, "Fiscal Policies, Inflation and Capital Formation," *American Economic Review,* vol. 70 (September 1980), p. 647.

19. A point repeatedly emphasized in Seymour Melman's studies of the military industrial sector and defense management. See for example, Melman's *The Permanent War Economy* (New York: Simon & Schuster, 1974).

20. More critically in Melman, ibid. and more concerned with efficient management of defense resources in Gansler, *The Defense Industry.*

21. See ibid., table 7.2, for concentration ratios in different areas of military industrial production.

22. See examples of price increases in selected parts and the official explanation given in ibid., table 6.3, p. 134.

23. For a recent thorough study of the bureaucratic-political context of weapons procurement see Gordon Adams, *The Iron Triangle* (New York: Council on Economic Priorities, 1982).

24. William Greider, *Washington Post* (March 29, 1981), p. B2.

25. Norman Augustine, "One Plane, One Tank, One Ship: Trend for the Future?" *Defense Management Journal* (April 1975), pp. 43–47. For a recent critical journalistic account of the Pentagon's technological fetishism in weapons procurement policy see James Fallows, *The National Defense* (New York: Random House, 1981).

26. In 1982 constant dollars the United States spent $538.5 billion in FY 1945 and $148.5 billion in FY 1974 (a ratio of 3.6:1); if the comparison is confined to procurement, R&D and construction expenditures the ratio is about 4:1. Calculated from historical data; see Office of the Assistant Secretary of Defense (Comptroller), *National Defense Budget Estimates for FY 1982* (Washington, D.C.: Department of Defense, 1981).

The West German Air Force plans to replace 600 F-104 Starfighters with no more than 320 MRCA (Tornado) fighters. The earlier generation Starfighter cost DM 5.0 million each in 1965; its successor was estimated to cost DM 40.3 million in 1980, an annual average increase of 15 percent over the fifteen-year period—far above the overall inflation rate. See also Gansler, *The Defense Industry,* figure 1.2, p. 16, for an update of Augustine's estimates, including data on cost increases for other types of weapon systems. Ulrich Albrecht, "Armaments and Inflation," *Current Research on Peace and Violence* (1974) no. 3, p. 162; *SIPRI Yearbook,* 1981. table 1.2, p. 9.

27. Melman, *Permanent War Economy;* and Lloyd J. Dumas, "The Impact of the Military Burden on the Domestic Economy," *Current Research on Peace and Violence,* (1980), no. 2, pp. 73–82.

28. Data from *National Defense Budget Estimates for FY 1983,* table 5–3, p. 43.

29. CPI measures average changes in the prices of goods and services typically bought by urban wage earners and clerical workers. It is based on 400 items including food, clothing, fuel, transportation, health care, utilities, and housing.

30. *Survey of Current Business* (July 1983), table 7.20, p. 89. More historical data can be found in the corresponding tables in U.S. Department of Commerce, Bureau of Economic Analysis, *The National Income and Product Accounts of the United States, 1972–76 Statistical Tables* (Washington, D.C.: Government Printing Office, 1981).

31. See also the discussion of inflation in military expenditures in chapter 2.

32. Ernest Mandel, *Marxist Economic Theory,* quoted in Albrecht, "Armaments and Inflation," p. 158; Melman, *Permanent War Economy,* makes a similar agrument.

33. This view is expressed in *Study on the Relationship Between Disarmament and Development,* pp. 83ff.

7 Impact on Balance of Payments and International Competitiveness

Military- and defense-related transactions have a major impact on the U.S. balance of payments. These effects consist of four major components:

1. Direct defense purchases from foreign sources.
2. Import content of domestic defense purchases.
3. Foreign economic and military assistance expenditures.
4. Export loss or import gain resulting from the impact of military spending on the domestic economy.

Each component is described in this chapter and estimates for each are given in table 7-1.

Direct purchases from foreign sources include the foreign exchange costs of maintaining U.S. military bases and personnel throughout the

Table 7-1
Impact of Military Related Transactions on U.S. Balance of Payments
($ billions)

	1960–1967		1970	1972	1974	1976	1977	1980
	Total	Annual Average						
Direct defense purchases	24.9	3.10	4.80	4.70	5.00	4.80	5.70	10.5
Foreign economic assistance[a]	7.0	0.88	0.72	1.10	1.40	1.90	1.70	4.3[b]
Foreign military assistance[a]	1.3	0.16	0.00	0.05	0.04	0.03	0.03	0.05
Import content of domestic defense purchases	Depends on alternative spending scenario; except for fuel purchases no particularly high import component							
Impact on U.S. foreign competitiveness	Large but unknown							

Source: Vladimir Pregelj, "The Impact of Foreign Assistance and Defense Transactions on the U.S. Balance of Payments: Summary of Statistical Data, 1960–77," *Congressional Research Service Report* 76–164E (Washington, D.C.: October 1978) and author's estimates.

[a]Net.

[b]Assumes 40% feedback ratio.

135

world. The Commerce Department publishes an estimate of "direct defense expenditures" as part of its reporting on U.S. international transactions. Direct defense expenditures were 10.5 billion in 1980 or 4.5 percent of all merchandise imports.[1] This estimate includes the foreign exchange losses attributable to the personal consumption expenditures of DOD personnel and their dependents stationed outside the United States.

The Defense Department has made strenuous efforts to reduce such outflows, among other costs. Since 1962, there has been a policy of a 50 percent preference for U.S. materials and supplies for use abroad—that is, a U.S. item would be favored over a foreign item even if it exceeded it in cost up to 50 percent; in practice, U.S. goods receive even greater preference. A similar 50 percent preference for U.S. goods on a delivery basis exclusive of duty was applied to goods for domestic use.[2] On the other hand, the total for direct defense purchases overstates the actual foreign exchange loss due to such defense expenditures because direct foreign purchases have a feedback effect. That is, they stimulate U.S. exports, and the curtailment of direct defense expenditures would thus be partially offset by a reduction in U.S. exports. A 40 percent feedback ratio has been suggested, based on studies of worldwide U.S. foreign exchange expenditures abroad.[3] Assessing the net effect of DOD expenditures abroad is further complicated by the fact that the United States has concluded a formal offset agreement with the Federal Republic of Germany, which has the largest single concentration of U.S. forces stationed abroad and accounts for 30 percent of such expenditures.

The import content of domestic defense purchases is another significant outflow of foreign exchange attributable to military expenditures. The foreign exchange loss can be estimated by resolving domestic defense purchases into final demand for commodities in the U.S. input-output tables.[4] This step allows the approximation of the direct and indirect import content of domestic production for military final demand. Ideally, from an opportunity cost perspective, the import content of domestic defense production would be compared with that of alternative civilian expenditures or with the average import conten f domestic U.S. goods and services. Domestic defense expenditures may have an above average import content because of heavy petroleum purchases—about 8 percent of U.S. consumption.

Foreign economic and military assistance expenditures represent another foreign exchange loss. Although not a direct U.S. military expenditure, such spending is closely related to U.S. national security concerns. In 1980 total net U.S. government foreign grants and credits amounted to $10.8 billion of which $3.6 billion went for military assistance and $7.2 billion for economic assistance. Foreign exchange loss due to military assistance is quite low because almost all funds go for U.S. military purchases. Assuming a 40 percent feedback effect for economic assistance, the actual foreign exchange loss for these programs would be $4.3 billion in 1980.[5]

Finally, export loss or import gain resulting from the negative impact of military expenditures on the domestic U.S. economy is potentially the largest factor, but also the most difficult to define and estimate. Critics regard the declining position of the U.S. economy in the world market as being largely a result of the deleterious effects of the arms economy on U.S. industry. After World War Two, the United States developed strong world positions in such high-technology industries as computers, commercial aircraft, nuclear power, and electronic components. These industries greatly benefited from the military's forced development of defense-releated products; many European leaders voiced fears about the development of a "technology gap." However, as Melman concludes:

> This fear did not endure very long, as European and Japanese industrialists began to reap the benefit of their sustained concentration on civilian research. . . .
>
> In American industry competent technology and industrial efficiency have become casualties of the war economy. This is revealed by the epidemic deterioration of research and production capability in major industries, by the progressive inability of many firms to hold even the domestic market against foreign competition, and by the consequent formation of capital and labor surpluses.[6]

Structural Impact on International Competitiveness

Melman may overemphasize the negative impact of the arms economy in explaining the deteriorating U.S. position in the world market; nevertheless, the arguments in this book support the thesis that military expenditure has had a significant overall negative affect on the U.S. position. This macrothesis is difficult to evaluate because, in contrast to the other components of military-related foreign exchange loss, it fails to identify specific outflows. Indeed, it postulates an alternative, predominantly civilian-oriented development of the U.S. economy since the end of World War Two. Moreover, any such assessment must be based on an estimate of net effects because in some high-technology industries, such as aircraft, electronics and communications equipment, civilian exports have undoubtedly gained from military-related R&D.

An Export-Led Growth Model

Export-led growth models have been used to explain the negative relationship of military expenditure to export growth and international competitiveness.[7] In this perspective, firms in a country with a favorable export position play a central role in the dynamics of economic expansion. As summarized by Rothschild:

> The limits of the home market will lose their force and lapses in domestic demand can be repaired through easy access to foreign markets. This will have a beneficial effect on employers' expectations and will stimulate output and investment. The acceleration of investment will increase productivity, partly because embodied technical progress can be faster absorbed, partly because with the faster expansion of (firms') capacities, economies of scale can be achieved. Productivity will be fostered by the competitive pressure emanating from international competitors and by the quicker expansion of the more productive (export-oriented) branches and enterprises.[8]

Countries with a "good export start" can be expected to experience higher rates of growth in output and productivity, further improving their competitive position and facilitating new investment as success feeds on success. The continuous expansion of exports also prevents crises in which governments would otherwise have to curtail economic growth to cope with balance of payment problems.[9] The post-World War Two growth economies of Japan and West Germany are especially relevant examples of such export-led growth models.

Export-oriented growth in the OECD countries in the postwar period is concentrated in technologically advanced goods characterized by a high degree of technical know-how and product differentiation. The negative impact of military expenditure in terms of this growth model is a result of the fact that military demand is particularly concentrated in those industries which are also the focus of export-led growth. Thus, although the unweighted average for export expansion in fourteen advanced industrial capitalist countries in Rothschild's sample rose from the base years 1956 and 1957 to 339 for total exports in 1969 and 1970, the index of chemical exports rose during the same period to 527 and that of exports of machinery and transportation equipment to 596.[11] Rothschild advances the thesis that, in addition to other factors usually mentioned as conditions of export-led growth, military expenditures can also play a significant negative role:

> High (or quickly rising) military expenditures with its large demands on the engineering and transport sector reduces the availability of machinery and transport equipment for export. The most dynamic export sector is thus handicapped and this creates a tendency for slower export growth which in turn tends to dampen GNP-growth.[12]

Rothschild's analysis does not attempt to distinguish between the impact of the level of military expenditures and the impact of rising military expenditures. The latter situation seems to have a clearly negative effect because of supply bottlenecks and inflationary pressures that can be expected when the affected industries are already experiencing a high rate of capacity utilization. Extended delivery times or higher prices may both decrease exports and increase imports as domestic demand turns to foreign suppliers.

The Vietnam military buildup was a classic case of this scenario. Dudly and Passell estimated the negative impact of the Vietnam increment in military spending at $1.38 billion in 1967.[13] Although the negative impact seems clear, estimates are of course extremely speculative.[14] In addition, even during periods of peace, the episodic rhythm of major weapons programs makes military procurement itself much more variable than overall military spending.

Rothschild's analysis of the conflict between military-industrial demand and export-oriented growth also rests on a structural analysis. In this broader sense, it merges with the analyses of Melman and others who suggest a structural distortion of the U.S. economy resulting from the heavy military orientation of its most advanced and export-oriented sectors. Rothschild's explanation of the possible relationship between the U.S. arms economy and the deterioration of the U.S. competitive position in world markets is much more structurally elaborate than Melman's largely descriptive account. A more detailed investigation would be required to substantiate Rothschild's thesis and to appraise the extent to which the arms economy has been a significant drag on U.S. export growth.

Foreign Military Sales

Military- and defense-related transactions also have favorable impacts on the U.S. balance of payments if foreign military sales are included in the assessment. Such sales are not a direct result of U.S. military spending but rather a byproduct. They are primarily an instrument of U.S. foreign policy but have also become a major foreign exchange earner since the early 1970s.

Table 7-2 shows total U.S. arms transfers under the foreign military sales and military assistance programs for the 1970–1980 period. Although the total dollar value of U.S. military transfers has not changed dramatically (and has actually declined as a percentage of total U.S. exports, which expanded rapidly over the reference period), almost all U.S. military transfers are now sales as opposed to grants. The turnabout apparently reflects a deliberate decision to promote foreign military sales in response to U.S. international trade and payments difficulties, resulting from the first U.S. foreign trade deficit in seventy-eight years in October 1971. This policy

Table 7–2
U.S. Arms Sales 1970–1980
($ millions)

	1971	1972	1973	1974	1975	1976	1977	1978	1979	1980
Foreign military sales deliveries	1,346	1,450	1,510	3,159	3,502	5,798	7,022	7,408	7,506	7,698
Commercial exports	428	481	362	502	547	1,402	1,523	1,676	1,527	1,770
Total	1,774	1,931	1,872	3,661	3,049	7,200	8,545	9,084	9,033	9,468[a]

Source: U.S. Department of Defense, Security Assistance Agency, *Foreign Military Sales and Military Assistance Facts*, December 1980, pp. 7–8, 25–26.
[a]Estimate

was reinforced by the doubling of oil prices in 1973/74 and the resulting balance of payments crisis.[15]

The value of foreign military sales does not accurately reflect the impact on balance of payments of these exports. Payment is usually not in cash; rather, the purchases are financed over several years, often with a significant grant or consessionary component. Moreover, foreign military sales are frequently tied, formally or informally, to offset agreements for the purchase or production of major parts in foreign countries. Therefore, the nominal value of the sale overstates the balance of payments gain which the sales entail.

For example, Canada negotiated an elaborate coproduction agreement in connection with its purchase of 138 F-18s from McDonnell Douglas for $2.37 billion. This sale by no means represents an unqualified boon to the U.S. balance of trade and balance of payments. In fact, the agreement includes an estimated $2.9 billion in offsets such as the production of parts for the F-18 in Canada, which will be assembled in the United States; transfer of such proprietary technologies as the manufacture of advanced composite materials, fiber optics, and computer-aided design; provision of a $60 million Canadian plant for the manufacture of compressor blades and vanes for jet engines and a $3 million advanced controlled machinery center; a promise to give "stretch work" on the DC-10 commercial jet to Canadian firms; promotion of Canadian tourism; and the development of an export marketing program for Canadian goods.[16]

Although the offsets negotiated in the sale of the F-18 to Canada are unprecedented, many foreign military sales include similar agreements. For example, when General Dynamics sold 346 F-16s to Denmark, Norway, Belgium, and The Netherlands in 1975, it agreed to purchase parts from its European purchasers. According to a complicated formula, such parts purchases would offset at least 58 percent of the purchase price. According to a Treasury Department study, U.S. firms have signed such coproduction agreements totaling $13.9 billion over the last five years, but the associated offsets negotiated are estimated at $8.6 billion.[17]

The Price of Hegemony

Foreign military expenditures may also benefit the U.S. economy in another way. That is, the United States has been the policeman of the capitalist world, and although this role has certainly entailed costs, there have also been corresponding economic benefits. For example, profits derived from U.S. foreign investment might be considered in any cost-benefit analysis of U.S. military expenditures abroad.[18] However, the overall effects on the U.S. economy of this special role are ambiguous. A recurrent theme in the literature is that Western economic competitors, particularly Japan and West Germany, have reaped the benefits of U.S. defense of the world capitalist economies without sharing correspondingly in the costs.[19] Indeed, U.S. policymakers in the Reagan administration now view this unequal burden-sharing as a principal concern.[19] On the other hand, the problem of the U.S. military share will become even larger as a result of the budgetary shifts set in motion by the Reagan administration.

Confining the analysis to estimated direct net outflows as a result of U.S. military-related expenditures (table 7–1) and gross inflows from U.S. foreign military sales (table 7–2), the arms economy shows a foreign exchange loss of about $5 billion in 1980, after having shown a surplus of about $1 billion as late as 1977. If collateral offset agreements were considered, the balance of payments "deficit" of the arms economy would increase by several billion more. Nevertheless, in the context of a total international trade volume of over $600 billion in 1980, this is a significant but not a dramatic source of U.S. balance of payment problems. The broader negative impact of overall military spending on the competitiveness of the economy is probably much more important.

Notes

1. "Military Transactions in U.S. International Accounts," 1976–1982," *Survey of Current Business* (May 1983), table 2, p. 21.

2. Office of the Secretary of Defense (Comptroller), *The Economics of Defense Spending* (Washington, D.C.: Department of Defense, 1972), p. 69.

3. Douglas R. Bohi, "War in Vietnam and the United States Balance of Payments," *Review of Economics and Statistics,* vol. 51 (1969), p. 473. Bohi cites an unpublished 1967 AID study, "Effects of Untied Aid on U.S. Commercial Exports," (July 1967). Rolf Piekarz and Lois Stekler suggest a somewhat higher figure of 60 percent for developing countries. See "Induced Changes in Trade and Payments," *Review of Economics and Statistics* (November 1967).

4. This method is suggested by Leonard Dudley and Peter Passell, "The War in Vietnam and the United States Balance of Payments," *Review of Economics and Statistics,* vol. 50 (1968), pp. 438–439.

5. *Statistical Abstract of the United States* (Washington, D.C.: GPO, 1982) table 1476, p. 827.

6. Seymour Melman, *The Permanent War Economy* (New York: Simon & Schuster, 1974), pp. 88–89, 103–104.

7. Kurt W. Rothschild, "Military Expenditure, Exports and Growth," *Kyklos* (1973), pp. 804–814.

8. Ibid., p. 805.

9. Ibid., p. 806.

10. Ibid.

11. Ibid. Rothschild regards chemical exports as also being particularly important to the growth model. But, in this case, the impact of military production is not in fact great.

12. Ibid., p. 808. For the fourteen countries, Rothshild's rank-order correlation coefficients between growth of total exports and growth of real per capita GNP (+0.57) and between growth of machinery and transportation exports and growth of total exports (+0.57) are significant at the 5 percent level. The rank-order correlation coefficient of military expenditure is negative (1967–1970, –0.45) but significant only at the 10 percent level.

13. "War in Vietnam."

14. See Bohi, "War in Vietnam," pp. 471–474, for a critique of Dudley and Passell's estimates.

15. See Michael Klarc, "The Political Economy of Arms Sales," *Bulletin of Atomic Scientists* (November 1976), pp. 11–18.

16. Michael Gordon, "Pentagon Contractors Divided Over Foreign Arms Co-Production Deals," *National Journal,* 14:8 (February 20, 1982), pp. 332–333.

17. Ibid., pp. 331, 332.

18. See, for example, Harry Magdoff, "Militarism and Imperialism," *American Economic Review* (May 1970), pp. 237–242.

19. See Bruce Russett's discussion of burden-sharing in *What Price Vigilance?* (New Haven, Conn · Yale University Press, 1970), chapter 4, as well as the current U.S. policy discussion on burden-sharing within NATO.

8

The Reagan
Military Buildup and
Reaganomics

The Reagan administration began to put its mark on the country with the presentation of its economic program to the Congress and the public only four weeks after taking office on January 20, 1981. It then made detailed revisions to the FY 1982 budget, originally submitted by the outgoing Carter administration. The revised budget proposals and related policy statements represent the first practical definition of Reagan's policy goals, economic assumptions, and budgetary priorities.

The Reagan Economic Program

The new administration's economic program confronted the problems of sluggish growth, unemployment, inflation, declining productivity, and loss of international competitiveness with a number of policy goals that constituted a sharp break with the recent past: (1) a substantial reduction in the growth of federal expenditures; (2) reduced taxes; (3) reduction of the government regulatory burden; and (4) a monetary policy aiming at steady growth of the money supply at lower levels.[1]

Federal Expenditures

The Reagan program aimed at achieving a sharp reduction in the growth of federal expenditures from the high of 23 percent of GNP in 1981 to 19 percent of GNP by FY 1986. Its revisions called for an immediate cut of $43.9 billion in FY 1982 outlays, or a 5.9 percent decrease in the outgoing Carter administration budget. Although startling in itself as a reversal of past trends, this overall figure contained even more drastic internal shifts in budget priorities.

The 1982 Reagan budget called for further increases in defense expenditures over and above the large increases already planned by the Carter administration, with the goal of increasing defense expenditures by an average of 9 percent in real terms each year until 1986. At the same time the administration designated certain social safety net programs—including social security benefits for the elderly; basic unemployment insurance benefits; cash benefits for dependent families, elderly, and the disabled; and veterans benefits—as being exempt from major cuts. Together, military spending and safety net programs, plus high interest payments on the federal debt, constituted approximately 70 percent of 1981 federal outlays. As a result, the planned budget cuts and increases in military spending required eliminating or sharply curtailing economic and social programs accounting for only about 30 percent of federal outlays.

Reduced Taxes

The administration's economic program called for sharply reduced personal income and business taxes. Personal income tax cuts were proposed in the form of a 30 percent across-the-board reduction in marginal tax rates phased in over three years, reflecting the administration's view that high marginal tax rates are a significant disincentive to work, savings, and investment. The administration also proposed new accelerated depreciation schedules for business investment (for example, five years for capital equipment) in terms of which the cost of new investments can be written off against earnings in determining tax liability. The rationale was to provide a strong tax incentive for new investment by business firms. The administration estimated that these changes would result in a revenue loss of $53.9 billion in 1982 rising to $221.7 billion in 1986.

Although the Reagan administration budget revisions reduced federal expenditures considerably from the levels estimated in the January 1981 budget of the Carter administration, tax reductions reduced anticipated revenues even more. The net effect was that the planned budget deficit for FY 1982 was almost twice as large in the Reagan budget revisions as in the original Carter administration budget.

The Government Regulatory Burden

In the administration's view, excessive regulation is a significant cause of current economic woes, adding $100 billion a year to the cost of goods and services produced. More important, excessive regulation is deemed to have a negative effect on economic growth, "discouraging innovative research and development, reducing investment in new plant and equipment, raising unemployment by increasing labor costs, and reducing competition."[2]

Monetary Policy

The administration's goal was to gradually reduce the rate of growth of the money supply to about one-half the 1980 levels by 1986. Under the influence of monetarist economic theories, the administration regards excessive increases in the money supply as a major cause of inflation. Moreover, it feels that past attempts to manipulate money supply growth for short-term policy objectives through management of interest rates resulted in business uncertainty, which in turn hampered long-term investment decisions and economic growth. The monetary policy goals of the administration were to be flanked by a reduction and subsequent elimination of federal deficit spending (which, of course, proved to be wildly illusory).

These "four complimentary policies" are in the administration's view, "an integrated and comprehensive program." Their aim is to "revive the incentive to work and save" and to "restore the willingness to invest in the private capital required to achieve a steadily rising standard of living."[3]

Although critics may doubt the wisdom of the administration's economic program, particularly the validity of many of its economic assumptions, it is ideologically consistent: "The most important cause of our economic problems has been the government itself."[4] In general, the administration's economic program was at best a high-risk wager based on largely untested premises.

The new administration was remarkably successful in getting its economic program adopted. Reagan's revisions of the 1981 and 1982 Carter administration budgets won stunning victories in the Congress, which endorsed the new national defense budget authority and spending levels proposed by the administration as well as most of the proposed drastic cuts in domestic programs. Congress also enacted—and in some cases even surpassed—the tax cuts proposed by the administration. The independent Federal Reserve Board acted to counter inflation by cutting back money-supply growth. Reagan officials adopted controversial, "pro-growth" regulatory policies at the Interior Department and other executive agencies.

The Reagan Record

The Reagan administration's record in achieving its economic goals has been mixed. The first (1982) Reagan budget estimated that his program for economic recovery would produce a slight budget surplus by FY 1984 and increasing thereafter. However, these projections were based on optimistic "supply-side" assumptions about the favorable impact of tax cuts on labor supply and on savings and investment. The economy plunged into a deep recession in 1981–1982 as the expansionary fiscal policy came into conflict with the Federal Reserve Board's restrictive monetary policy. After mid-1982 the Federal Reserve changed course in monetary policy and pushed down interest rates, leading to a surprisingly strong recovery throughout 1983 and into 1984. Inflation, which had fallen sharply during the recession, remained low during the first 18 months of the recovery—despite continuing large government deficits. But unemployment remained stubbornly high, averaging 9.5 percent during 1983. Although U.S. interest rates remained relatively high—especially long-term interest rates—they have not yet had a dampening effect on the recovery or risen as much as the administration's critics expected. Still, the resulting overvalued U.S. dollar further weakened the international competitiveness of U.S. industry.[5]

The administration has been successful in reducing taxation but not government spending. While federal tax revenues declined from 20.1 percent of GNP in 1980 to 18.8 percent in 1983—even surpassing the goal of 19 percent by FY 1984—federal spending rose from 22.9 percent to 25 percent of GNP. The FY 1985 budget projects that spending will be 22.2 percent of GNP in 1989—far above the original goal. Even this figure is probably optimistic.[6]

The administration has, of course, failed spectacularly in its goal of balancing the budget, incurring the largest budget deficits in the postwar era. It now forecasts 1984–89 deficits totaling $812 billion. According to the more pessimistic projections of the Congressional Budget Office (it expects no significant drop in interest rates) the total will be $1.1 trillion.[7]

Although unsuccessful in controlling overall spending or balancing the budget, the Reagan administration has been able to reverse the historic trend toward increased domestic spending and dramatically increase military spending. Constant dollar domestic spending (excluding interest payments) was lower in FY 1984 than in 1981, while DOD spending increased by 38 percent, with even greater increases programmed.[8]

Military Buildup vs. Economic Goals

The Reagan military budget for FY 1982 proposed an average real growth of 9.2 percent in budget authority and 8.4 percent in outlays over the five-year (1982–1986) defense budget. (See table 8–1.) The contrast with the Carter administration is one of degree: It too had proposed smaller increases—5.5 percent and 5.0 percent respectively—over the same period. Actual real growth in budget authority closely reflects the original Reagan program until FY 1984, when critics were successful in forcing some cuts. The FY 1985 DOD budget request attempts to win back lost ground.

Table 8-1
Reagan Defense Budget, 1981–1986
($ billions)

	FY 1981	1982	1983	1984	1985	1986	Average Real Growth
Budget Authority							
Projected							
March 1981	178.0	222.2	254.8	289.2	326.5	367.5	
Real growth (%)	12.4	14.6	7.3	7.0	7.0	7.0	9.2
Actual & Projected							
January 1984	178.4	213.8	239.5	(258.2)	(305.6)	(349.6)	
Real growth (%)	12.5	12.1	7.5	(3.7)	(13.0)	(9.2)	(9.7)
Outlays							
Projected							
March 1981	158.6	184.8	221.1	249.8	297.3	336.0	
Real growth (%)	7.0	6.2	11.3	6.1	12.5	7.4	8.4
Actual & Projected							
January 1984	156.1	182.9	205.0	(231.0)	(264.4)	(301.8)	
Real growth (%)	4.7	7.8	7.1	(8.8)	(9.3)	(8.4)	(7.7)

Source: Executive Office of the President, Office of Management and Budget, *Budget of the United States Government, FY 1985* (Washington, D.C.: GPO, 1984); *America's New Beginning: A Program for Economic Recovery* (Washington, D.C.: GPO, 1981); Congressional Budget Office, *An Analysis of President Reagan's Budget Revisions for FY 1982*, Staff Working Paper (March 1981). January 1984 real growth percentages from DOD press release as reported in *National Journal*, 16:5 (February 4, 1984), p. 206. All data are for DOD military spending.

Reagan administration increases in military spending are concentrated in the area of procurement—largely for purchases of major weapon systems. The FY 1985 budget requests $107.6 billion for procurement or 305 percent above the 1980 level.[9] Because of the long lead time for major procurement purchases, actual outlays will rise more slowly.[10] Current dollar spending is less than originally projected due to lower inflation.

The Reagan administration's massive military buildup proved to be incompatible with its economic program. The administration's effort to reduce the growth of federal spending while dramatically increasing defense spending ran up against the limits of fiscal possibility—particularly when politically sensitive safety net social programs were exempted from major cutbacks. While federal domestic spending declined from 15 percent to 14 percent of GNP between 1980 and 1984, defense and other national interest expenditures (including NASA, international affairs and other related programs) increased from 5.8 percent to 7.4 percent.[11]

The costs of the military buildup are also a principal cause of the Reagan administration's failure to control federal deficits, which are considerably larger than it originally estimated. The administration's tax reductions, which far exceeded the initial cuts in domestic spending, mean that increased military spending is in fact being financed by increased borrowing. The rising cost of interest payments on the federal debt ($53.4 billion in 1980 and $96.5 billion in 1983) has more than offset any savings in domestic programs.[12]

The administration's heavy reliance on monetary policy might have been more successful, and might have required less-prohibitive interest rates, without the fiscal impact of the large military increases or deep cuts in federal tax revenues; but without one or the other it proved to be disastrous. Interest rates soared and by Fall 1982 the United States experienced unemployment rates unprecedented in the postwar period. Economic policy in the current recovery remains hamstrung by the continuing deadlock between the administration and Congress on fiscal and tax policy.

Military spending not only played havoc with administration economic policy but is also incompatible with its long-term goal of restoring the health and competitiveness of the U.S. economy. The increases in military spending are concentrated in procurement and R&D—that is, military-industrial demand. Thus, at a time when major U.S. industries such as auto, steel, and consumer electronics are foundering, and even U.S. preeminence in computers, civil aviation, and microprocessors is facing stiffening foreign competition, the economic effect of the Reagan program is to shift capital investment, skilled labor, and R&D resources from the civilian to the specialized military sector. The United States shoulders an ever-increasing military burden larger than its major allies and economic competitors, who have failed to follow the U.S. administration's policy of shifting national resources toward military priorities.

Finally, the military priorities of the Reagan administration mean the dramatic expansion of a sector of the economy that is essentially statist in terms of federal government employment and federal government purchases of goods and services. Such a big government role is entirely at odds with the professed market economic ideals of the Reagan administration.

Reagan Buildup vs. the Korean and Vietnam Buildups

Korea

The Korean crisis and resulting rearmament took place in two stages: first, the initial outbreak of hostilities in June 1950 and the U.S. decision to intervene in support of South Korea; and second, the entry of China, with Soviet backing, into the war in November 1950, in support of North Korea. Although the first stage was regarded as a police action by the Truman administration, the entry of China into the conflict led to the U.S. declaration of a national emergency and a sharp upward revision of military requirements in the direction of full-scale mobilization. Military spending increased from 4.7 percent of GNP in 1950 to 13.8 percent in 1953 (see table 8–2).

The U.S. economy in June 1950 was recovering from the first postwar recession; industrial production increased by more than 10 percent between February and June, surpassing the postwar record level established in 1948. In its year-end report in January of 1951 the Council of Economic Advisors saw the Korean war as falling upon an economy "with few slack resources or signs that the boom was leveling off."[13]

The immediate impact of the U.S. entry into the Korean conflict was a surge in consumer demand induced by panic buying and hoarding, which resulted in a rapid jump in price levels. This response reflected consumers' anticipation of shortages like those in World War Two rather than the effect of increased military demand. Business investment reacted sharply to increased consumer demand and the prospects of expanded military purchases, and the recovery became an inflationary boom in the latter half of 1950. Wholesale prices rose 15.4 percent during 1950 (10.4 percent between June and December) and consumer prices increased by 6 percent. Although the civilian economy was approaching capacity limitations at the time of the outbreak of the Korean conflict, the country still had considerable unused military production capacity left over from the war that was reactivated to meet the needs of the Korean buildup.

The administration was committed to financing rearmament and Korean operations on a pay-as-you-go basis. Several tax increases were enacted, substantially raising government revenues. As a result, the FY 1951 budget showed a substantial surplus in the first year of the war, which largely offset deficits in the next two years of the buildup, FY 1952 and FY 1953. The administration was explicit in its call for sacrifices in civilian consumption to support the military effort: "the real economic cost of this defense effort is that we must work harder, reduce consumption, and forego improvements in farm, business and household equipment."[14]

In addition to tax and fiscal policy the administration also was granted broad powers of control over the economy in the Defense Production Act of 1950, including powers to allocate materials and limit their use, to limit credit for consumers and housing construction, as well as to control wages and prices. These controls were selectively used to support military production and economic stabilization; wages and prices were frozen in January 1951.

The Korean buildup was, of course, more than a response to the exigencies of the Korean war. It was the beginning of a broader rearmament program, and military spending remained at the new higher plateau even after the Korean hostilities ended.

Vietnam

The Vietnam war military buildup from 1965 to 1968 took place in an economy already experiencing rapid economic expansion and high rates of capacity utilization since the business expansion starting in 1962, with rates of real growth in GNP of 5.8 percent, 4.0 percent, 5.3 percent, and 5.9 percent in 1962, 1963, 1964, and 1965 respectively. This expansive phase was also the era of the "new economics" of Keynesianism, embraced by the Kennedy administration. Although the Kennedy administration's economic strategy is best known for its policy of tax cuts and resulting planned deficits to stimulate business expansion, in terms of fiscal policy the administration vigorously expanded government spending primarily by means of increased military and space expenditures. Government defense purchases of goods and services, after having remained constant and declined in real terms during the second Eisenhower administration, rose from $44.5 billion in 1960 to a high of $51.1 billion in 1962. Space program expenditures rose even more dramatically from $0.4 billion in 1960 to more than $5 billion by 1965.[15] Including related space expenditures, the Kennedy economic strategy represents the purest and most successful example of military Keynesianism in the history of U.S. national economic policy.

An intensive military buildup for Vietnam began in 1966. Economists then generally felt (and in retrospect unanimously agreed) that a tax increase was necessary to finance the arms program. In 1966 defense purchases increased by $10 billion in a fully employed economy. The Johnson administration and Congress put off increasing taxes until 1968, a delay

that is generally considered to be the cause of the subsequent rapid inflation. Clearly the administration was reluctant to resort to increased taxes to
finance the war for fear of losing public support for its policy of military
escalation (see chapter 6).

The Johnson administration pursued a declared policy of both guns
and butter and continued to push for its domestic reform program despite
the financial pressure exerted by the war. In his 1966 economic report, President Johnson posed the rhetorical question: "Can we move ahead with the
Great Society Programs and at the same time meet our defense needs?"
And his answer was a confident "yes." Thus, although military expenditure
increased over the 1965–1968 period from $47.5 to $78.8 billion, total nondefense budget expenditures increased from $71.1 to $101.1 billion over the
same period for domestic social programs. Only the budget for FY 1969
reflected a clear tradeoff between increased military expenditure and
domestic program funding levels under the fiscal stringency made necessary
by the war.[16]

In the FY 1967 budget (presented in January 1966) the Johnson administration seems to have made a deliberate decision to underestimate the cost
of the war and postpone any tax increase proposal to safeguard the enact-
ment of its Great Society budget proposals. The administration's disingenu-
ous assumption in the January 1966 budget that the war would end by June
30, 1967, is described in chapter 6. The consistent underestimation of the
costs of the war was also rooted in the politically calculated optimism of the
administration about the course of the war itself.[17]

The result of this pattern of economic policy, or nonpolicy, was a further stimulation of an already overheated economy and increasingly large
government deficits of $8.7 billion in FY 1967 and $25.2 billion in FY 1968.
As one critic said: "It would be difficult to find a more perfect example of
irresponsible government action that would inevitably have serious inflationary consequences."[18] Inflation (GNP deflator) rose from under 2 percent, the 1960–1965 level, to 3.3 percent in 1966, fell to 2.9 percent in 1967
during a brief economic slowdown resulting from tighter monetary policy
by the Federal Reserve Board, and rose again to 4.5 percent and 5.0 percent
in 1968 and 1969 respectively.[19]

Korea vs. Vietnam

During the Vietnam buildup, national defense outlays increased from $69.3
billion in 1965 to a high of $101.7 billion in 1968 in 1972 dollars, or from 7.2
percent to 9.5 percent of GNP. The Korean buildup by contrast was from
$29.7 billion in 1950 to a high of $96.6 billion in 1953 or from 4.7 percent to
13.8 percent of GNP (see table 8–2). Although military expenditure was

Table 8-2
Three U.S. Military Buildups: Korea, Vietnam, and Reagan

	Change in National Defense Budget Share (%)	Change in Military Burden (% GNP)	Increase in Defense Budget Outlays ($ billions; 1972 dollars)
Korea (1950–1953)	29.1–65.6	4.7–13.8	29.7– 96.6
Vietnam (1965–1968)	40.1–44	7.2– 9.5	69.3–101.7
Reagan (1981–1987)	23.2–32.6	5.2– 7.4	71.3–118.9

Source: Office of the Assistant Secretary of Defense (Comptroller), *National Defense Budget Estimates for FY 1983*, tables 7–8 and 7–2. Reagan projections from Executive Office of the President, Office of Management and Budget, *Budget of the United States Government, Fiscal Year 1985*, pp. 2–11, 9–61. Defense spending is equivalent to national defense function budget outlays.

higher in constant dollars in 1968 than in 1953, both the military burden as a percentage of GNP and the magnitude of the military expansion were considerably lower for Vietnam than for Korea for two reasons: higher GNP levels and the historically unprecedented high plateau of military expenditures since the conclusion of the Korean hostilities.

Although the Vietnam buildup was, both absolutely and in terms of the share of national resources it consumed, smaller than the Korean buildup and hence potentially more manageable, it had a significantly greater disruptive economic impact. For one reason, the economy was already operating at a high rate of capacity utilization; however, the major cause was the failures of economic policy during the Johnson administration. This failure was not so much a failure of economic analysis as it was a failure of political resolve to confront the economic implications of the war with appropriate policies to minimize its disruptive effects. The Johnson administration was both reluctant to sacrifice its domestic social welfare program to the growing budgetary claims of the war and reluctant to propose tax increases to the Congress and the public to finance an increasingly unpopular war.

The new Nixon administration tried in vain to cope with the continuing inflation by inducing an economic recession in 1969 and 1970 through restrictive fiscal and monetary policies and then by the imposition of wage and price controls in mid-1971. In contrast to the Korean buildup, in which an initial spurt of inflation was subsequently successfully controlled by resolute economic policies, the Vietnam inflation began at a crawl and then became an inflationary spiral deeply rooted in the economy as a part of a new pattern of stagflation.

The postwar deescalation in Vietnam, like that in Korea, was as problematical for the economy as the initial escalation. The deflationary economic policy program of the incoming Nixon administration plunged the country into a short but sharp recession with negative growth in 1969 and 1970. In a similar circumstance the peaking out of the Korean escalation had led to an economic recession in 1954.

Economic and Social Consequences of the Reagan Military Buildup

In terms of resource allocation within the federal budget, the Reagan buildup entails a massive tradeoff in favor of the military (see table 8-2). About 10 percent of the budget will have been shifted from domestic to military programs in the 1980-1987 fiscal period. If relatively uncontrollable budget items like trust fund expenditures and interest on the federal debt are excluded, then the magnitude of the shift is in excess of 20 percent. Moreover, the share of all national resources allocated to the military effort (military burden) will increase markedly. The FY 1985 budget projects that the defense share of GNP will rise to 6.9 percent in 1985 and to about 8 percent in 1989—which underestimates the actual military burden because it uses a narrow measure of military spending.[20]

The percentage of budget resources shifted to the military is larger than during Vietnam but smaller than the Korean buildup. Although the military burden was greater during Vietnam, the Reagan buildup of 2 percent of GNP is already as large and is expected to total 3 percent by the end of the decade. The Korean buildup was of course much larger. Barring major cuts, Reagan administration military spending in 1972 constant dollars will surpass peak Korean and Vietnam expenditure levels in 1985.

The effect of the Reagan military buildup is, of course, not confined merely to a diversion of resources from civilian to military uses but also has a dynamic impact on economic growth, employment, inflation, and the international competitiveness of the U.S. economy. The short-term negative implications for growth come from the disruptive effects of the military expansion on the administration's own economic strategy. The deficit financing of an enormous military buildup with reliance on monetary policies to control the resulting inflationary pressures led to record high interest rates, sluggish growth, and then deep economic recession. For the first time military Keynesianism failed, at least initially, to stimulate business expansion as it did during the Korean, Kennedy, and Vietnam buildups.

The surprisingly strong 1983-84 recovery followed the Federal Reserve Board's reversal of monetary policy and lower interest rates, although real interest rates remained historically high. Mainstream economists had generally expected that the deficits—$200 billion in 1983—would crowd out private borrowers and cut short any recovery. Several fortuitous circumstances have been cited to explain why the deficits failed to have a greater impact on interest rates and the recovery. First, new tax depreciation rules lowered federal revenues and increased the deficit but also provided corporations with additional cash flow; public borrowing replaced private borrowing without increasing total borrowing requirements. Second, state and local governments are generating large surpluses—around $65 billion in 1984—significantly offsetting federal borrowing requirements. Third, high U.S. interest rates have attracted large amounts of foreign capital—an estimated $44 billion in 1983 and a projected $75 billion in 1984.[21]

The longer-term implications of the administration's economic and military programs are for a restructuring of the U.S. economy in terms of the requirements of the military buildup and increased military competition with the Soviet Union. The military procurement share of the manufacturing base (GNP excluding services) is expected to rise from an estimated 5.4 percent to 10 percent.[22] In contrast to Korea and Vietnam, procurement rather than increases in military personnel will account for almost all the proposed expenditure increases. Unlike the wartime military procurement patterns of Korea and Vietnam, the current buildup is concentrated in the aerospace, electronics, and communications industries, which will do little to help such ailing sectors as steel, rubber, and autos.

This rapid growth of the military-industrial manufacturing base will absorb a very large share of increments in investment, skilled labor, and R&D during the next several years. According to Charles Schultze, former Chairman of the Council of Economic Advisors, "some 30% of the increase in 'goods-producing' GNP over the next four years will go to the military."[23] A recent Defense Department study estimates that direct and indirect defense sector employment will grow at an annual rate of 7 percent of resources in the 1982–87 period, while non-defense, non-agricultural employment will expand at a rate of only 1.5 percent.[24] This loss to the military sector can only exacerbate the structural problems of the U.S. economy and impede the restoration of an internationally competitive civilian industrial base.

Despite the 1981–1982 recession and stagnation tendencies in the economy since 1979, there may in fact be little economic slack in the form of excess industrial capacity and labor resources on which the military buildup can draw. According to Lester Thurow, for example, the stagflation pattern in the U.S. economy has actually been a mixture of boom and depression. The economy in some states such as Texas, California, Florida, and Massachusetts, where such industries as semiconductors and computers are concentrated, has been booming, while the Midwest, which relies on the steel and auto industries, has been experiencing a deep recession:

The idle capacity of both workers and equipment is concentrated in a few regions and industries, but the industries and regions where idle capacity exists are not those where military equipment is purchased. As a result, the defense buildup is likely to exacerbate both the shortage of resources in the high technology and defense industrial sectors, and the regional imbalances in the national economy.[25]

These imbalances imply a high inflationary potential as the recovery progresses.

The employment effects of the Reagan buildup are above all a result of its exacerbation of short-term stop-and-go stagnation tendencies and long-run growth loss attributable to the military use of resources. Moreover, the switch from civilian programs, and, in particular, social welfare programs to the purchase of sophisticated high-technology military equipment will result in an immediate loss of employment because social spending results in a higher level of employment than the equivalent in military hardware spending. Assuming that the domestic programs foregone would create about 35,000 more jobs per $1 billion consumed by the military buildup (see table 5-4), the projected 1980–1985 buildup ($30 billion in 1972 constant dollars) will have cost the nation about 1 million jobs in direct employment effects.

The regional distribution of employment will also change because military procurement expenditures favor the Sun Belt as opposed to the Frost Belt. Northern senators and representatives have expressed their concerns about such geographic reallocation of employment as a result of the Reagan administration's military priorities.

The possible inflationary effects of the Reagan buildup have received considerable attention, particularly the prospects for sectoral bottlenecks and inflationary tendencies in the military-industrial sector. Special cost-push factors in the military sector as well as excess demand cause such inflation. At present the military buildup that began in the latter part of the Carter administration has significantly strained capacities in the military-industrial sector, primarily at the level of subcontractors and suppliers of materials, components, and subsystems. As Robert Furman, Chairman of the 1980 Defense Science Board Task Force on Industrial Responsiveness, told Congress:

"lead times for essential components have been increasing rapidly. Thus, for example, between 1976 and 1980 the lead time from order to delivery of aluminum forgings increased from 20 to 120 weeks; for aircraft landing gears from 52 to 120 weeks (1977–80); and for integrated circuits from 25 to 62 weeks (1978–80)."[26]

Defense industry spokesmen are also concerned about shortages of skilled manpower. Even before the current Reagan buildup, Furman projected a shortage of 250,000 machinists by 1985. Labor shortages in defense production can no longer be met by such quick fixes as drawing on a reserve labor pool or transferring skilled workers from civilian industries because of the increasingly divergent character of specialized military industrial production.[27]

The 1981–1982 recession reduced demand for civilian aircraft and electronics as well as for other components of civilian demand that compete with military production for materials, industrial capacity, and skilled labor. On the other hand, the greatly accelerated procurement program of the Reagan administration is now exerting strong additional pressure (see table 6-6). In contrast to Korea and Vietnam, the general inflationary demand-pull effects of the military buildup were initially limited because of the overall depressed state of the economy. The strong inflationary potential of increased government demand thus remained largely confined to the military-industrial sector itself. Without compensatory fiscal policies, the current military buildup financed by deficit financing can be expected to produce strong inflationary pressures as the economic recovery continues.[28] Alternatively, a new phase of high interest rates and restrictive monetary policy may offset the inflationary potential at the cost of renewed economic stagnation. There appears to be no way the administration can resolve this dilemma without abandoning basic features of its economic policy or military buildup.

The Reagan buildup and related deficits have contributed to higher interest rates and the resulting overvaluation of the dollar, which has further undermined U.S. international competitiveness. This factor—and the rapid pace of the U.S. recovery—resulted in a $60 billion merchandise trade deficit in 1983.[29] In the long run the allocation of increased resources to military production can be expected to have further negative effects through the unproductive absorption of R&D and investment resources, among other factors. As a structural policy for the restoration of U.S. international competitiveness, the military buildup represents the worst possible medicine. For example, the Defense Departments Very High Speed Integrated Circuit (VHSIC) program and the new Strategic Computing program are designed to orient the U.S. semiconductor industry and computer technology toward the specialized requirements of military high-tech weaponry. DOD received more than half of the $201.8 million allocated to basic computer research in the 1984 budget. The corresponding Japanese government-sponsored programs for supercomputers and artificial intelligence have a purely civilian orientation.[30]

Some voices within the administration regard an accelerating arms race as a form of economic competition with the USSR, which the larger and more productive economy of the United States can expect to win. However, the greater size and higher productivity of the U.S. economy are not in themselves sufficient indicators of endurance in such an economic race. Not only does the character of the Soviet political system give it a greater capacity to extract sacrifices from its population, short of an all-out wartime mobilization of U.S. resources, but, even more important, the U.S. market economy must hold its own domestically and in foreign markets with world market competition. In this case, the U.S. economy may be more vulnerable to the negative economic consequences of the arms race, despite the relatively greater military burden borne by the Soviet economy.

Notes

1. Executive Office of the President, Office of Management and Budget, *America's New Beginning: A Program for Economic Recovery* (Washington, D.C.: Government Printing Office, 1981).

2. Ibid., p. 18.

3. Ibid., pp. 1–2.

4. Ibid., p. 4.

5. See *Economic Report of the President, February 1984* (Washington, D.C.: Government Printing Office, 1984).

6. Executive Office of the President, Office of Management and Budget, *Budget of the United States Government, 1985* (Washington, D.C.: Government Printing Office, 1984), table 24, p. 9–60.

7. Ibid.. The Congressional Budget Office estimates are cited in *National Journal,* 16:9 (March 3, 1984), p. 419.

8. *Budget of the United States Government, 1985,* pp. 3–3, 3–8.

9. Ibid., table 6, p. 9–10.

10. By January 1984 unfilled orders for defense products reached $112.8 billion. *Business Conditions Digest* (March 1984), p. 91.

11. *Budget of the U.S. Government, 1985,* pp. 3–2ff.

12. *Economic Indicators* (March 1984), p. 34.

13. *Economic Report of the President, January 1951* (Washington, D.C.: Government Printing Office, 1951), p. 34.

14. Ibid., p. 17.

15. *Economic Report of the President, February 1982* (Washington, D.C.: Government Printing Office, 1982), tables B–1, B–2.

16. Office of the Assistant Secretary of Defense (Comptroller) *National Defense Budget Estimates for Fiscal Year 1983* (Washington, D.C.: Department of Defense, March 1982), table 7–1, p. 77.

17. See chapter 6.

18. Wallace Peterson, *Income, Employment and Growth, 4th ed. (New York: Norton, 1979,* p. 447, note 31.

19. *Economic Report of the President, February 1982,* table B–3.

20. *Budget of the United States Government. 1985,* pp. 3–2ff. . . .

21. See, for example, the estimates cited in *Business Week* (January 30, 1984), p. 12. Estimated capital inflow data from *Economic Report of the President, February 1984,* pp. 36, 56.

22. Testimony of Gary Wenglowski, Goldman Sachs Economics, before Joint Economic Committee, U.S. Congress. Joint Economic Committee, *The Defense Buildup and the Economy.* 97th Cong., 2d. sess., 1982. Committee Print, pp. 15–16.

23. Ibid., p. 20.

24. Findings of a Data Resources Inc. study reported in *National Journal,* 14: 51 (December 12, 1982), p. 2177.

25. *The Defense Buildup and the Economy,* pp. 19–20.

26. Quoted in U.S. Congress. House Committee on the Armed Services, *The Ailing Defense Industrial Base,* Report of the Defense Industrial Base Panel, 96th Cong., 2d. sess., 1980. Committee Print, p. 13. See also table 6–4 in chapter 6, this book.

27. Ibid., p. 15.

28. See, for example, the discussion by Jacques Gansler in "Can the Defense Industry Respond to the Reagan Initiative?" *International Security,* 6:4 (Spring 1982).

29. *Economic Indicators* (March 1984), p. 36.

30. Secretary of Defense, *Annual Report to the Congress, 1985* (Washington, D.C.: Government Printing Office, 1984, p. 260 ff.; *National Journal,* 15:14 (April 2, 1983), p. 691 cites National Science Foundation data on computer research in the 1984 budget.

9

The Economic and Social Consequences of Disarmament

The domestic economic and social consequences of disarmament, like those of the arms race, depend on the particular scenario envisaged: the overall size of the planned reductions in military spending, the types of expenditures affected by the disarmament measures, and the timing of the reductions. Size is obviously the most important factor. Efforts to specify the impact of military cutbacks generally rely on some postulated overall percentage reduction. The actual components of the reduction in military spending will determine the human and material resources released. For example, disarmament scenarios concentrated in the area of military personnel or operations and maintenance costs have an impact quite different from cuts concentrated in military procurement (that is, purchases of specialized military equipment). Timing—whether rapid and dramatic or gradual—is a major factor. Sudden drops in military spending, like rapid increases, are particularly disruptive.

Unfortunately, there is too little experience with disarmament. The few successes in disarmament negotiations, either bilaterally or within the framework of the United Nations, have been arms control or arms limitation agreements rather than disarmament in a strict sense. However important such agreements have been, they do not necessarily entail either overall reductions in U.S. military expenditure or the actual release of any significant resources.[1] For example, the multilateral agreements that restrict the military use of Antarctica, outer space, and the seabed prevent the introduction of armaments into certain areas where they did not yet exist. Other international agreements, such as the Partial Test Ban Treaty, the Nonproliferation Treaty, and the Convention on the Prohibition of Bacteriological Weapons, may have released some resources, but this was clearly not their primary significance.

Even such major bilateral agreements as SALT I and the unratified SALT II treaties merely placed largely quantitative limits on the future deployment of certain weapons, and the limits were in almost every case higher than existing force levels. Thus in the SALT I treaty the United States and the Soviet Union agreed to limit their deployment of antiballistic missiles to 100 each—a number that neither side had yet attained. Any disarmament resulting from these agreements is merely prospective—that is, military expenditures may be lower in the future than they would be without such agreements.

Such prospective savings resulting from arms control agreements are speculative and may merely displace U.S. military effort into other areas where the treaty restrictions do not apply. For example, monies earmarked for the ABM program were reallocated to the Trident and B-1 programs. The expected savings from SALT II were likewise largely prospective, and therefore uncertain, representing at best "cost avoidance" rather than "cost reductions."[2]

Reductions in military budgets by a certain specified percentage are another disarmament approach. Many proposals of this sort have been made at the United Nations, and the standardization of military budgets and the problems of cross-national comparison of military expenditures have been studied extensively.[3] In the United States, across-the-board percentage cuts in military spending have frequently been proposed by critics of U.S. military spending, and such scenarios have been prominent in studies of the domestic impact of disarmament (see Bezdek and Dresch, for example). In general, the economic and social consequences of disarmament can only be meaningfully discussed in terms of relatively specific scenarios.

The Conversion Problem

Disarmament is a social and economic process as well as a political one. It would require formidable adjustments in the arms economy and national security state engendered by the post-World War Two arms race. In this section the principal dimensions of the conversion problem are sketched, and in the following section U.S. experience with conversion and conversion planning is surveyed.

Two dimensions to the conversion problem must be distinguished for both analytic and policy purposes. Microlevel conversion is the adjustment process as it affects individuals, enterprises, and localities as well as the military services and military departments of government whose activities must be either reoriented toward civilian endeavors or phased out. Indeed, disarmament literature is largely dominated by this aspect of the conversion problem. By contrast, macrolevel conversion pertains to adjustment processes at the level of the overall economy in which a significant share of societal resources is reallocated to alternative civilian uses with minimal disruption. In this case, policy measures are focused on broader economic and societal parameters.

Macrolevel Adjustments

The major macrolevel compensatory policy options for government in response to reductions in military spending include:

1. Reductions in either individual or business taxes.
2. Expansion of government civilian programs in such areas as education or social welfare, or economic infrastructure.
3. Changes in monetary policy or government loan programs designed to spur private consumption and investment.

These dimensions of possible government compensatory policies to maintain aggregate demand and reorder national priorities are quite general of course. A wide variety of individual programs are conceivable. In practice, the mix of effective government policies would be determined by political priorities and the state of the economy at the time disarmament measures were being implemented.[4] The compensatory macroeconomic policies initiated in conjunction with disarmament must also reflect the actual industrial and labor resources that become available.

Microlevel Adjustments

Although marginal reductions in military spending can probably be dealt with at the level of macroeconomic policy alone—that is, by relying on normal market forces to achieve a satisfactory reallocation of resources—any significant reductions in levels of military spending will also require specific measures to deal with the impact of the disarmament on individual firms, localities, and groups of workers. The dimensions of the conversion problem at this level are implicit in the descriptions of the resources allocated to the military effort in chapters 3 and 5. Disarmament will have specific effects on the aerospace, electronics, and shipbuilding industries; in certain localities where such firms are located; in certain occupational groups, such as aeronautical engineers, physicists, and machinists; and up to 2 million military personnel and 1 million civilian employees of the Department of Defense.

Cuts in military-industrial production will have different effects on those firms and workers engaged in specialized military production (such as aircraft, missiles, tanks, armored vehicles, ships, and their specialized suppliers of major components) than on those producing nonspecialized military goods and services. The U.S. military consumes vast amounts of materials, fuel, office machines, and vehicles that are similar or the same as civilian products.

Specialized military production represents a special conversion problem. Two factors must be considered: the degree of dependence on the military market that makes certain firms economically vulnerable to disarmament measures and the specialization of plant and equipment, employee skills, and management style in military products and the military market, which is a significant barrier to their conversion to other products and markets.

The procurement item in the Defense Appropriation Act is a rough index to specialized military production, largely hardware purchases. In FY 1982, such procurement was $41.3 billion or approximately 24 percent of DOD outlays—a significant but, in a $3,000 billion economy, not an intimidating sum.

The disruptive impact of disarmament on individual firms, localities, and affected workers can be mitigated to the extent that alternative civilian work can be found for the material and skilled human resources previously engaged in specialized military-industrial production.[6] However, most engineers and scientists in military-related work become extremely specialized. They often move from civilian to military-oriented work, but movement in the opposite direction is unusual—both because of the specialized nature of the work and the loss of pay and qualifications that such a switch would entail. Military-related R&D stresses performance characteristics and cost considerations play a subordinate role.

Cost-plus contracting effectively eliminates much pressure for cost-consciousness in the design and development of weapon systems. In contrast, civilian R&D heavily emphasizes cost reduction and continually trades off qualitative features against the projected cost of the final product. Thus engineers and scientists transferring from a military-related environment will require extensive training and reorientation. According to Dumas, the difficulties in such transfers are suggested by the tendency for those laid off as a result of termination of defense contract either to move to another geographic area in which new defense contracts have been acquired by other firms, seek jobs outside of the area of their previous professional training, or simply remain unemployed in the expectation that their former employer will receive a new defense contract. At the same time, there have been critical shortages of engineers in other areas such as power plant design.[7]

Similarly, specialized military-oriented firms or their subdivisions develop capabilities quite different from those required for successful entry into civilian markets (see table 6–3). For example, the Lockheed Corporation rose above a number of failures and embarrassments to the position of the largest U.S. defense contractor between 1971 and 1975. According to Dumas: "Clearly, one cannot expect managers accustomed to operating in a situation in which there is no risk, high costs are not merely tolerated but become the path to success, and only one rich customer need be serviced, to operate successfully in a risky, cost-sensitive, multi-customer civilian markets without substantial retraining and reorientation.''[8]

Weinbaum points out that, in addition to their lack of commercial marketing experience and lack of experience in high-volume low-cost mass production, defense firms also have a relatively low capitalization—that is, the ratio of stockholders' investment to sales volume is relatively low. In the defense sector the government provides the major portion of the required capital assets.[9]

Office and production workers—whether in defense-oriented firms, the armed services, or DOD civilian employees—either hold relatively non-skilled positions or do not have the degree of specialization of their scientist or engineer counterparts. Although their skills are transferable, their sheer numbers may not be absorbed by the civilian economy and certainly compensation may be lower.[10] Similarly, the professional cadres of the armed forces—particularly those in combat branches—would suffer loss of their occupational qualifications.

Even if skills can be converted to civilian employment, status and pay levels may suffer. In both public and private employment in the United States, pay and status depend on both skill and seniority. Conversion programs might well incorporate measures to protect seniority, pay, and other benefits for those displaced as a result of disarmament. Such disruption would be minimized where conversion takes place at the level of the employing firm.[11]

A California study[12] of the potential transfer of industrial skills from defense to nondefense industries concluded that workers could transfer with little or no additional training, depending on demand in counterpart occupations, comparability of wages, union regulations, and company hiring practices. The median wage rate for counterpart occupations is found to be about 5 percent lower than in defense occupations. According to the study, even apparently specialized defense production jobs can be broken down into their component segments and related to nonmilitary counterparts.

Finally, disarmament will affect plant investment. Although some defense-industrial equipment and facilities can be easily converted to civilian uses, a large share will require major overhaul and considerable investment, even if an appropriate civilian market can be found.

In summary, the specialized military-industrial sector would experience considerable difficulties in undergoing conversion to production of civilian products. The development of compensatory programs at the macrolevel to maintain aggregate demand in the economy as a whole must be coordinated with the conversion problems of industries engaged in specialized military-industrial production. For example, uncoordinated compensatory measures that focused on a major expansion in the education and health sectors would not draw upon the same or similar specialized resources and might merely create shortages elsewhere.

In general, the United States, in comparison to many West European nations, lacks the experience with industrial and active labor market policies that would minimize the social and human costs of conversion. However, at the macroeconomic or macroconversion level, the United States does have considerable experience in economic policymaking that could help shape successful disarmament measures.

At both levels, the difficulties of conversion will depend on the extent to which the government and the affected industries, firms and localities have made advanced preparations. This process would include more information about the structure of military-industrial production and possible effects of arms reduction at the microlevel, as well as contingency planning that develops policy options and priorities.

The importance of advanced planning was suggested by a study done under the auspices of the United States Arms Control and Disarmament Agency, which focused on the timing of the impact of government expenditures on the economy—particularly compensatory expenditures upon the implementation of disarmament measures. It distinguished between the "inside lag," the time elapsing between the initiation of policy action within government and the actual obligation of funds, and "outside lag," the time between the obligating of government funds and actual expenditure or employment effects. The inside lag in the executive and legislative policy-making process was the major source of lengthy delays (up to two and a half years) in the development of typical offset programs (such as highway construction, space and ocean exploration, and urban mass transit). The outside lag depended on such factors as the degree of excess capacity and the affected economic sectors, and the size and complexity of the projects commissioned.[13]

Conversion contingency planning at the macro- and microlevels is obviously necessary to minimize the disruptive effects of a major shift in economic and social priorities from the arms race to disarmament. As military escalation in U.S. history indicates, sudden shifts in the level of military demand are highly disruptive; indeed, they tax the adjustment capacities of the political and economic system as much or more than the absolute level of such expenditures (within certain limits). When disarmament sharply reduces military expenditures, the problem would be similar but the direction of change would be different. Just as the United States maintains contingency mobilization planning for increasing current levels of military effort in a crisis, demobilization or conversion planning is also required.

U.S. Experience with Postwar Conversion

The United States has had some experience with military to civilian conversion after World War Two, Korea, and Vietnam. In addition, there is a continuing problem of conversion at the microlevel as the result of shifts and cancelations in military programs.

World War Two

The most important U.S. experience with disarmament and conversion followed World War Two. At its peak in 1945, the U.S. military employed slightly over 12 million active-duty military personnel and 2.6 million civilians—about 15 million—in the war effort. After the conclusion of hostilities the U.S. forces were rapidly, sometimes chaotically, demobilized. Two years later, there were 1.6 million active-duty military personnel and 860,000 civilian employees, as total defense manpower decreased by about 12.6 million with 10 million of this decrease occurring between 1945 and 1946. Military manpower levels remained at approximately that level until the beginning of the Korean rearmament in 1950.

At peak military production levels reached in 1943, approximately 13.4 million people were employed in defense-related industries—29 percent of private sector employment. More than half of U.S. industrial production was devoted to military needs. At the end of hostilities in 1945, approximately 11 million people were engaged in defense-related employment when war-related defense purchases were very rapidly terminated. Within one year this figure had dropped to about a million persons. National defense expenditures dropped from a war time peak of 38.7 percent of GNP in 1944 to 37.7 percent in 1945, 20.6 percent in 1946, and 5.2 percent in 1947, reaching a postwar low of 3.2 percent in 1948. Military expenditure declined more slowly than did employment and production because of expenditures related to demobilization and the termination of outstanding defense contracts.[14]

Wartime mobilization dramatically transformed the U.S. economy. Rearmament had overcome economic stagnation and mass unemployment in the United States. GNP more than doubled between 1940 and 1945 and unemployment fell from 8.8 million to 855,000; at the same time, the labor force expanded from 56 to 66 million.[15] Only about 2.75 million of this increase was the result of normal growth of the working age population. Of the remaining additions, about 3 million were women. Another 3 million young people who would have normally been in school joined the labor force under wartime conditions; and an estimated 500,000 older people left or postponed retirement.[16]

This great wartime expansion of the U.S. economy was subject to military priorities that distorted the economy in important ways that affected conversion to civilian production. Growth was particularly concentrated in the industrial sector; it accounted for 38 percent of national income in 1944 as compared to 29 percent in 1939. During the 1940–1944 period, the volume of U.S. industrial output increased by over 15 percent a year, and the total output of manufactured goods increased 300 percent; government-financed expansion of industrial buildings and machinery to meet military requirements amounted to $16.1 billion. Federal Reserve indexes of manufacturing output showed the largest increases (1939 = 100) in directly combat-related production between 1940 and 1944: aircraft (2,805) explosives and munitions (2,033), shipbuilding (1,710); a number of military-related industries were rapidly expanded to meet wartime demand: locomotives (770), aluminum (561), rubber products (206), industrial chemicals (337), and steel (202). (Numbers in parentheses are wartime peaks.) Although these industries supplied intermediate inputs for the war industries, insofar as their expanded wartime production was in excess of expected postwar civilian demand, they also constituted part of the postwar reconversion problem.[17]

Public and private planning for postwar reconversion began quite early during the war years and was in place when all hostilities ceased with the sudden surrender of Japan in August 1945. As early as November 12, 1940, the National Resources Planning Board (NRPB) was instructed by President Roosevelt to "collect, analyze and collate all the constructed plans for significant public and private action in the post defense period."[18] Public, congressional, military, and executive concerns about the problems of postwar readjustment began to take the form of a policy discussion in the latter half of 1943 and by 1944 policy decisions had been made and the necessary legislation passed. In addition to the Servicemen's Readjustment Act of 1944 (GI Bill), the most important industrial reconversion legislation was the War Mobilization and Reconversion Act of 1944. Among other provisions, it established the Office of War Mobilization and Reconversion to replace the Office of War Mobilization and gave its director broad powers to deal with reconversion problems.[19] Reconversion planning was a self-evident necessity because of the size of the impending reconversion process in the postwar era and to allay widespread fears of a return to prewar depression conditions.[20]

Generally the post-World War Two reconversion process, with notable exceptions (especially in the aircraft industry), was remarkably successful. Industrial production fell sharply in 1945 and 1946 and thereafter recovered slowly, but there was no return to prewar condition. By 1947, after a slight downturn in 1946, GNP had again reached and surpassed its wartime heights. Unemployment rose from a wartime low of 1.2 percent to 3.9 percent after demobilization and remained at about this level until the 1949–1950 recession. Between 1945 and 1947 the level of unemployment was abated by the withdrawal of women from the workforce; their labor force participation fell from the wartime peak 36.5 percent in 1944 to 31 percent in 1947. Similarly, the male labor force participation rate fell from 87 percent in 1944 to 82.6 percent in 1946, rising again to 84 percent in 1947.[21] At the same time, consumer prices rose sharply, increasing by 34 percent between 1945 and 1948.[22]

Two kinds of postwar reconversion programs can be distinguished: those aimed primarily at the reintegration of the military and military-industrial labor force and those primarily aimed at industry and industrial reconversion to the needs of the civilian economy. Returning veterans were the primary beneficiaries of specific government programs for reintegration into the peacetime economy. First, demobilized military personnel were counseled on their employment rights as veterans and on civilian jobs related to their skills and training at military separation centers. These trained counselers were usually representatives of the U.S. Employment Service, who identified civilian jobs corresponding to the soldiers' military specialty, offered educational and vocational guidance, and provided information on state and federal veterans' rights. However, returning service personnel probably received little individual attention. According to Ballard, a typical separation center had two lines for enlisted men and one for officers and, operating 24 hours a day, processed about 3,000 persons a day.[23]

Veterans were also guaranteed by law the right to return to their former employment with protection of seniority. However, about 4 million veterans (about 40 percent) had not held a job before their military service and thus could not benefit from this provision. In addition, veterans received preferential consideration for federal civil service jobs as well as for government employment in some states.[24]

Under the GI Bill, veterans were entitled to a readjustment allowance of $20 a week for periods of unemployment after separation from the service up to 52 weeks. This relatively generous provision amounted to about 50 percent of average gross earnings of production workers in industry. They received, in addition, a one-time lump sum separation payment of $300, as well as guaranteed loans of up to $2,000 for a home, farm, or business and educational benefits.[25]

There were no special readjustment programs for workers displaced from private industry as wartime contracts were canceled and returning veterans claimed their job rights. These workers were eligible for unemployment insurance and U.S. Employment Service programs. Military-industrial production peaked in 1943, and such employment had already declined about 25 percent by 1945. For example, employment in the aircraft industry reached a wartime peak of 2.1 million in December 1943 and declined to 1.2 million by July 1945, one month before the Japanese surrender. An estimated 6 million workers were employed in the production of combat munitions and war equipment at the end of the war, a narrower definition of military-related employment.[26] The number of women in nonfarm employment declined by 2.2 million between August 1945 and February 1946. In addition an estimated 3 million younger and older workers withdrew from the labor force.

Because of the intensive wartime production schedules (in war industries the average utilization of plant was 90 hours a week), the average work week in manufacturing had been 45.2 hours in 1944; it declined to about 40 hours a week in the immediate postwar period, which offset in part the disemployment effects of the decline in military demand. The employment situation was further helped by the fact that many veterans did not immediately seek jobs (an estimated 1.7 million) and over 800,000 enrolled in colleges in 1946 with the help of education benefits in the GI Bill. Nonagricultural employment in the labor force actually increased between 1945 and 1947 by 5 million persons. This recovery of civilian employment was, in addition to these labor market policy measures and developments, the principal reason for the success of the post-World War II disarmament and reconversion process.[27]

Industrial reconversion at the microlevel largely focused on prompt termination and settlement of military contracts to facilitate rapid reconversion to civilian production: "The government must pay its debts, and pay them quickly and fully, so that business will have its working capital freed for payrolls and purchase of materials."[28] An Office of Contract Settlement was established within the Office of War Mobilization and Reconversion to administer this process. As early as Fall 1943, extensive preparation in the field level were already taking place to acquaint businessmen with government termination procedures. Many pretermination agreements had already been negotiated before the war ended and thousands of termination telegrams had been prepared in advance. According to Ballard, 33,700 telegrams terminating contracts were sent out during the night of August 14, 1945, immediately following the Japanese surrender. Within one month, 95 percent of all contracts had been canceled and 80 percent had been settled by the end of 1945. Similar prompt methods were applied for the disposal of wartime inventory to clear factories for civilian production.[29]

Industry also began to make its reconversion plans early. A great many plants required no changeover because they had not been engaged in specialized military production, although the demand for their products may have been affected by the termination of government orders. Steel plants, for example, basically continued to make steel with some adjustments in level and composition of output. Civilian production had actually increased during the war constituting about half of the total industrial output at the war's end. Plants that had been converted to wartime production had carefully stored machine tools that could be returned to civilian use relatively quickly. Charles Wilson of General Motors predicted that auto production could be resumed within sixty days after the end of the war and could achieve volume output within six months.[30]

Rapid contract settlement freed capital for reconversion to civilian production. Moreover, corporations had earned and retained record profits from wartime production that financed reconversion plans and buffered downturns during the transition period. Savings and retained profits during the wartime period resulted in historically low interest rates, which further eased access to needed capital. Accumulation of corporate reserves had been greatly facilitated by a liberal five-year tax depreciation writeoff of new investment in plant and equipment.

Furthermore, consumer demand and high levels of consumer savings seemed to augur for very favorable business prospects. Personal holdings of liquid assets had risen from $48 billion at the end of 1940 to $146 billion by the end of 1945. The Revenue Act of 1945 provided for a $6 billion tax cut for both businesses and corporations in the transition period. Unemployment compensation, veterans benefits, mustering out payments, and other benefits provided an additional compensating stimulus. Private construction activity, in particular housing, increased fivefold in 1945 and 1946 as wartime restrictions were loosened. State and local governments commissioned many long-delayed public works projects, and relief to wartorn areas provided additional demand stimulus for the U.S. economy.[31]

Excess demand quickly outstripped available civilian production capacities and supplies, a situation exacerbated by a wave of postwar strikes. By the end of 1946, federal spending moved toward fiscal restraint in response to the inflated inflationary pressures; for example, a sixty-day moratorium on all new federal public works projects was ordered. Other public works programs developed to maintain employment were indefinitely delayed; for example, a $500 million matching grant program for state highway construction and a $1 billion flood control project were postponed.[32]

The spurt of postwar inflation which quickly developed was the result in part of the rapid loosening of wartime wage and price controls under pressure from the Republican Congress elected in 1946. Overall, federal fiscal policy reduced the deficit to $15.8 billion in 1946 and moved to a large surplus of $3.8 billion in 1947 and a highly deflationary surplus of $12

billion in 1948. The reduced deficit in 1946, the first year of postwar reconversion, was the combined result of the dramatic reduction in government
wartime outlays as total spending fell from $92.6 to $55.2 billion and the $6
billion reduction in tax revenues. By contrast, government borrowing had
amounted to $47.5 billion in the last year of the war. Military-related expen-
ditures were still relatively high because of generous benefit programs for
veterans and the momentum of wartime expenditures.[33]

The effects of conversion were not uniformly favorable for all industries Those engaged in specialized military production that had no ready
alternative civilian market faced a deep crisis—particularly the aircraft,
shipbuilding, and munitions industries. In some industries, particularly
aluminum and magnesium production, the rapid expansion of capacity during the war already exceeded wartime demand by 1944, and they inevitably
faced large excesses in postwar production capacity. Still, for most industries, the postwar period meant reconversion—reverting to production for
established civilian markets, as in the auto industry.

The relatively successful transition from a war economy to peacetime
prosperity following World War Two does not provide a clear pattern for
dealing with the economic effects of disarmament today for several reasons:

1. The most successful postwar industries simply reconverted to civilian
    production.
2. Pent-up demand, especially for consumer durables, and accumulated
    savings provided a favorable economic context for conversion or rede-
    ployment of resources (such accumulation is the aftermath of a war
    economy and would not be true of conversion from the present arms
    economy).
3. The conversion policies were not successful on a microlevel for special-
    ized military-industrial production, which is the core of the arms
    economy. Rather, an unusually favorable macroeconomic situation
    provided a context for the redeployment of resources.
4. Although the postwar demobilization of military personnel, special
    transitional counseling, and payments are applicable to any future
    demobilization under disarmament, structural elements that eased the
    transition—in particular, the right to return to former civilian
    jobs—were specific to the postwar situation of reconversion.
5. The manipulation of the size and composition of the labor force that
    greatly eased the demobilization and successful reintegration of
    military personnel was the result of the "exceptional" war economy.
    To a certain extent, educational benefits for former military personnel
    would be a feasible solution under disarmament, but probably not an
    overt policy of removing women and older workers from the labor
    market.

6. Tax reductions and alternative public expenditure programs played a surprisingly small role in the postwar disarmament readjustment process, although both were conceived as deliberate policy instruments. Retained business profits, private savings, and pent-up consumer demand seem to have been the determining factors following World War Two. But a transition from the present arms economy to disarmament would require greater reliance on such government policy measures.

7. Advanced planning was a very important part of the successful reconversion of the wartime economy, both at the governmental level and at the enterprise level, as it would be today. However, an essential condition of the readiness of government and firms to engage in such planning was a clear awareness that the war economy was a temporary situation. In contrast, today's arms economy is largely perceived as being of indefinite duration, and there is no corresponding incentive to plan for its end.

Korea

The post-Korean adjustment was not as dramatic and wrenching as the conversion following World War Two (see table 9-1). First of all, the Korean buildup represented only a limited mobilization of U.S. economic resources. Between 1950 and the peak year of the Korean buildup in 1953, national defense expenditures roughly quadrupled from $12.9 billion to $48.5 billion. This increase represented a rise in the defense burden from 4.9 percent of GNP to 13.4 percent of GNP in 1953.[34]

More important, in contrast to the post-World War Two demobilization and reconversion, there was only a limited reduction in U.S. military expenditure and the military burden after the Korean armistice. The Korean buildup was only in part a response to the immediate military requirements of the Korean War. It also served to mobilize U.S. resources for a worldwide confrontation with the Soviet Union in the spirit of NSC-68 (see chapter 1). After Korea, defense spending in current dollars decreased by only about 20 percent from $49.9 billion in 1953 to $39.8 billion in 1955. National defense purchases in the national income accounts dropped from $48.5 to $38.9 billion. In terms of the military burden on GNP, the decline was from 13.4 percent of GNP in 1953 to 9.4 percent in 1956, the immediate post-Korean low. These cuts represented a scaling down to cold war levels of military spending that have subsequently prevailed as "normal."[35]

Active-duty military personnel declined by about 800,000 from 3.6 million in 1953 to 2.8 million in 1956; DOD civilian personnel declined by about 300,000 in the same period. Defense-related industry employment declined from an estimated 4.1 million to 2.5 million. Thus the estimated

Table 9-1
Three U.S. Postwar Conversion Experiences: World War Two, Korea, and Vietnam

	Military Spending Decrease ($billions; 1972 dollars)	DOD Military and Civilian Employees (millions)	Defense Industry Employment (millions)	Total Military-Related Employment (millions)	Postwar Economic Indicators			
						Unemployment (percent)	Inflation (percent)	Growth (percent)
World War Two (1945–1947)	255.5–30.4	14.8–2.4	11.0–0.8	25.8–3.2	1945	1.9	2.4	−1.5
					1946	3.9	15.7	−14.7
					1947	3.9	12.9	−1.7
					1948	3.8	6.9	4.1
Korea (1953–1955)	96.6–77.0	5.4–4.5	4.2–2.5	9.5–7.0	1953	2.9	1.6	3.8
					1954	5.5	1.2	−1.2
					1955	4.4	2.2	6.7
					1956	4.1	3.2	2.1
Vietnam (1968–1972)	101.7–76.6	5.0–3.5	3.2–2.0	8.1–5.5	1968	3.6	4.4	4.6
					1969	3.5	5.1	2.8
					1970	4.9	5.4	−0.2
					1971	5.9	5.0	3.4
					1972	5.6	4.2	5.7

Sources: Data on military spending in constant 1972 prices and on employment are for fiscal years and derived from Office of the Assistant Secretary of Defense (Comptroller), *National Defense Budget Estimates for FY 1982* (March 1982), tables 7-2 and 7-7. Data on growth, inflation, and unemployment are for calendar years and derived from *Economic Report of the President, 1982* (Washington, D.C.: Government Printing Office, 1982), tables B-2, B-3, and B-29.

total decline in direct and indirect defense employment between 1953 and 1956 was on the order of 2.7 million.[36]

The impact of the postwar adjustment on the economy led to a sharp recession and, after a brief recovery in 1955, sluggish growth in 1956 and 1957.[37] Unemployment rose from its wartime low of 2.9 percent in 1953 to 5.5 percent in 1954 and, after declining to slightly more than 4 percent in the immediate postwar years, increased again in the 1958 recession to 6.8 percent.[38] Consumer prices increased less than 1 percent in the two immediate postwar years.

With the new commitment to a large permanent military establishment, postwar levels of military procurement purchases remained high by historical standards, and thus the adjustment in this sector, though sharp, was not as great as after World War Two. In particular, the shift from a war to a cold war military posture led to a displacement in the relative importance of various purchases of specialized military equipment. During the Korean war, military procurement was concentrated in such conventional weapons as combat vehicles, artillery, rifles, ammunition, and surface ships. However, the cold war requirements as well as the military strategy of the Eisenhower administration put more emphasis on the Air Force; aircraft purchases constituted three-fifths of total procurement by 1955.[39]

The Eisenhower administration devoted relatively little attention to the problems of conversion or reconversion. Although Korean veterans were guaranteed their former civilian jobs, preference in civil service appointments, and benefits, no new programs were introduced. Industrial workers who lost their jobs when wartime contracts were terminated had to rely on the existing unemployment insurance and employment service systems. No special conversion programs were developed to alleviate the problems of industries adjusting to the termination of wartime contracts.

At the level of government fiscal policy, there was no evident perception of the need to offset the decline in military purchases of goods and services; federal nondefense expenditures were cut back by one-third between 1954 and 1957 (averaging $5.2 billion annually below the 1953 level). Federal revenues actually increased by an average of $3.6 billion above 1953 levels during this period. As a result, there was a cumulative Federal budget surplus of $11.5 billion during this three-year period, which had a sharp deflationary effect: "three years of industrial growth were wasted." The post-Korea industrial slowdown was not a result of the arms cut itself but of "a defective adjustment to the arms cut . . . the failure to provide adequate offsets."[40]

Vietnam

In contrast to World War Two and Korea, the U.S. engagement in Vietnam did not end abruptly but wound down more slowly. The peak year of war activity was 1968; 1972 can be considered as the postwar low. DOD total obligational authority declined approximately 20 percent in constant 1983 dollars (from $238.8 billion to $187.4 billion; because of inflation there was no decline in current dollars). The military burden declined over the same period from 9.0 percent of GNP to 6.4 percent. Active-duty military manpower declined from the 1968 high of 3.8 million to 2.3 million in 1972, DOD employment, including DOD civilian personnel, declined by 1.7 million. According to DOD estimates, defense-related industry employment declined from 3.2 million to 2.0 million persons.[41] Together 3 million jobs in defense-related employment were lost in the 1968–1972 adjustment period. The wartime boom had brought the unemployment rate under 4 percent for the first time since the Korean war (3.8 percent in 1968); unemployment rose to its immediate postwar high of 5.9 percent in 1971. Inflation had been the principal preoccupation of economic policy in the last years of the war (see chapter 6) and consumer prices rose 21.3 percent between 1968 and 1972.[42]

In contrast to the Eisenhower administration's laissez-faire attitude toward the post-Korean adjustment, the Johnson administration did make some efforts to develop a postwar adjustment policy. The report of the Cabinet Coordinating Committee on Economic Planning for the End of Vietnam Hostilities was published as an appendix to the *Economic Report of the President* in January 1969.[43] The committee considered a range of possible compensatory programs, including a tax reduction; adjustments in monetary and financial policies; expansion of government expenditure programs, such as public works and long-term health, education, and environmental programs. The report generally foresaw the need for compensatory programs to offset any rapid decline in defense spending to avoid a recession like that at the end of the Korean War. Except for elimination of the temporary 10 percent income tax surcharge adopted during the war, the committee generally favored the expansion of public sector programs rather than further tax cuts. It also recommended some specific measures for the benefit of affected communities and individuals—particularly the strengthening of job placement and training—but otherwise focused on more general measures for the maintenance of aggregate demand as well as on existing labor market programs.

The committee estimated that altogether 1.3 million workers might seek new civilian jobs over the six quarters following the end of the war, or an average of 75,000 a month. In general, its report emphasized the dynamism and normal adaptive capacity of the economy and labor market, noting that, in manufacturing alone, the average number of layoffs per month was 250,000 in 1966–1967 and voluntary separations 470,000, while manufacturing workers were hired at an average monthly rate of 685,000 over the same period. Still the committee proposed the establishment of a cabinet-level coordinating committee to deal with the special problems of defense-dependent areas. According to committee data, defense employment increased by more than 5 percent of the total work force in thirty-eight localities during the Vietnam buildup from 1965–1967.

In 1969, the Nixon administration focused primarily on countering inflation and actually cut back, in real terms, civilian as well as military purchases. The result was the sharp, induced recession of 1970–1971. At the level of macroeconomic policy the administration seems to have decided to reduce military expenditure without any offsetting stimulus to aggregate demand: "The Administration chose deliberately and consciously to use the defense cutback as a vehicle for fiscal restraint in order to fight inflation and worked hard to insure that this was not offset by increased civilian expenditures."[44]

Conversion Planning

Economic Adjustment Office

Since 1961 the Economic Adjustment Office in the Department of Defense has aided communities in adapting to the curtailment of defense employment. In 1971 the President's Economic Adjustment Committee (EAC) was established to plan for the aftermath of the Vietnam War; it includes eighteen federal departments and agencies and is chaired by the Secretary of Defense; the Office of Economic Adjustment within the Department of Defense serves as its permanent staff.[45] By 1979, 260 economic adjustment projects had been completed at military bases under this program. According to a survey published by the Economic Adjustment Office, 124,500 new jobs were created in 86 communities that received major assistance, while 122,000 jobs were lost as a result of DOD realignments.[46]

Planning and preparation for reductions in military spending is, as these examples show, more than an expression of a vaguely utopian hope. Levels of military spending have fluctuated significantly in the post–World War Two period in response to the international situation and domestic changes, and this pattern can surely be expected to recur. Downturns in the cycle of the arms race and military spending regularly present the U.S. economy with difficult problems of local adjustment. Moreover, fluctuations in the composition of military spending create similar problems.

Since the end of World War Two, the United States has switched from spending for mainly conventional land and sea weapons (such as combat vehicles, artillery, surface ships, and ammunition during the Korean War) to higher outlays for aircraft in the latter 1950s, and now to increasingly dominant purchase of missiles and the space program.[47] These interindustry shifts in the composition of military demand have also been accompanied by interregional shifts. Within industries, individual firms and plants are even more subject to the vicissitudes of fluctuations in military demand.

A Proposal for Improved U.S. Conversion Planning

Legislation proposed in 1979 by then Senator George McGovern illustrates elements of a more effective U.S. conversion program (S. 1031, 96th Congress, 1st session). The bill—it was not enacted—provides for the establishment of a Defense Economic Adjustment Council within the Executive Office of the President. Its members would be department heads as well as representatives of nondefense business and labor, with a director appointed by the president. The existing Office of Economic Adjustment within the Department of Defense would be transferred to the Executive Office of the President and provide the necessary staff support. The council would be a high-level executive committee, removing the Office of Economic Adjustment from the Department of Defense and the control of its secretary.

The staff organization would have the kinds of expertise necessary for conversion planning and be empowered to request information from various agencies. For example, the Secretary of Defense would be required to give the council one year's notice of any changes in defense spending that would affect industrial employment or at a military base. This information would then be disseminated by the council to federal, state, and local authorities and to alternative use committees in affected firms and communities. In addition, the Council would plan for civilian-oriented projects; coordinate information on relevant government programs and funding sources; and study the problems of economic adjustment and conversion.

Alternative use committees would be established in every firm that employs at least 100 people under defense contracts. Such committees, which would include both management and labor representatives, would "undertake economic conversion planning and preparation for the employment of personnel" if defense business were reduced or eliminated. Alternative use committees at military facilities would represent both civilian employees and local community interests. The alternative use plans developed would be reviewed and approved by the council. Any defense contractor who failed to submit such a plan or refused to carry out the provisions of any plan approved by the council would be penalized by, among other things, exclusion from future contracts for a period of three years.

The alternative use committees would be charged with evaluating the economic assets of the defense facilities as well as the resources and requirements of the local community and developing and reviewing at least once every two years "detailed plans for the conversion of the facility to efficient, civilian-oriented productive activity" that could be implemented in the event of a cutback at the plant or base. The committee would provide occupational retraining and reemployment counseling services for displaced employees. The conversion plans would be designed to maximize employment of the existing personnel at the facility to be converted—that is, by developing alternatives requiring similar types and levels of skills. The bill also calls for the establishment of the Workers Economic Adjustment Reserve Trust Fund, consisting of payments by defense contractors of 1¼ percent of their gross revenue from military contracts. In addition, 10 percent of the projected savings in defense spending as a result of cutbacks would be deposited in this fund, which in turn would provide special supplementary unemployment benefits to displaced defense workers as well as maintain their pension and health benefits. Supplementary benefits would guarantee maintenance of income up to 90 percent of the first $20,000 of income, declining thereafter. The fund would also pay for retraining programs for comparable civilian employment, job search allowances, and reimbursement of reasonable relocation expenses.

Managerial and technical employees who have spent more than half of the last ten years working in the defense industry would be required to participate in a program of professional retraining. Workers receiving supplementary benefits from the fund would be required to accept comparable employment on the same basis as other workers receiving unemployment compensation. Benefits would cease either when a worker starts a new job with pay levels above the minimum guaranteed percentage of his former salary or two years after loss of his defense job.

The bill also provided for assistance to communities affected by cutbacks in military contracts or at military bases.

The provisions in the McGovern proposal are hardly new ideas. Many European countries—particularly Sweden and West Germany—already have similar programs to deal with mass layoffs and sectoral shifts. The United States, however, has never developed highly sophisticated active labor market policies and sectoral planning, which are necessary to cope with current fluctuations in military demand and critical for the successful implementation of arms limitation and disarmament measures.

Diversification of Defense Industry

Finally, the problems of conversion may also be anticipated and mitigated by altering the structure of specialized military-industrial production. The primary conversion problem at the microlevel is the concentration of specialized military-related production in individual firms and localities; generalized compensatory policies to maintain aggregate demand by expansion of civilian spending or tax reductions are inadequate in these cases. One possible solution is that military and civilian production should be integrated as much as possible both at the firm level and, insofar as practicable at the plant level. Fluctuations in military demand would be offset in part by the civilian activities of the enterprise, and would in any case affect only a smaller percentage of the plant's employment and output.

Many characteristics of the defense-oriented firm that are a barrier to entry into civilian markets might be overcome through experience with civilian products. The efficiency of the military-industrial sector would be enhanced (for example, through better utilization of plant capacity and increased competition).[48] There would also be increased incentives for conversion planning as a normal part of corporate planning for possible shifts in demand.

Such proposals for conversion planning or diversification are reasonable in light of the sharp fluctuations in specialized military production during the postwar period. Yet, they have—at present—no realistic chance of being adopted. Such changes would not only ease adjustment to shifts or declines in military demand; they would also have important political implications. The vested interests of a large number of firms, workers and localities in the arms economy would be weakened and their ties to the Defense Department and current national security policies loosened. The impetus for such reforms can only come as part of a broader challenge to current national security policies and the beliefs and interests that sustain them.

Notes

1. See the discussion of resources released by arms limitations agreements in *Study on the Relationship between Disarmament and Development:* Report of the Secretary General (New York: United Nations, 1981), chapter 6.

2. See this distinction in Roger George, "The Economics of Arms Control," *International Security,* 5:4 (1980), pp. 94–126.

3. See, for example, *Reduction of Military Budgets,* International Reporting of Military Expenditures, report of the ad hoc panel on military budgeting (New York: United Nations, 1981).

4. For an interesting discussion of differential impacts see Leslie Fishman, "The Expansionary Effects of Shifts from Defense to Nondefense Expenditures," in *Disarmament and the Economy,* ed. Emile Benoit and Kenneth Boulding (New York: Harper & Row, 1963), pp. 173–181.

5. An additional upward adjustment would have to be made to take into account production for export.

6. On the following discussion of conversion problems, see the recent surveys by Lloyd Dumas, "Economic Conversion, Productive Efficiency, and Social Welfare," *Journal of Sociology and Social Welfare,* vol. 4:3-4 (January-March 1977), pp. 567-596; and "Conversion and Redeployment of Resources Released from Military Purposes Through Disarmament Measures to Economic and Social Development," chapter 5 of *Study on the Relationship between Disarmament and Development,* pp. 242-328.

7. Dumas, "Economic Conversion," p. 578.

8. Ibid., p. 582.

9. Murray Weidenbaum, *The Modern Public Sector* (New York: Basic Books, 1969), pp. 73-74.

10. U.S. Congress, House Committee on the Armed Services, *The Ailing Defense Industrial Base,* Report of the Defense Industrial Base Panel, 96th Cong., 2d sess., 1980, pp. 14-15. According to testimony reported here it takes three years to train a machinist to work on aircraft engine parts and one year to retrain an auto machinist to work on aircraft.

11. Dumas, "Economic Conversion," p. 583.

12. State of California, Department of Employment, "The Potential Transfer of Industrial Skills from Defense to Nondefense Industries," Sacramento, Calif., April 1968 (Report prepared for the U.S. Arms Control and Disarmament Agency, ACDA/E-102, Vol. 1, 1968).

13. U.S. Arms Control and Disarmament Agency, *The Timing of the Impact of Government Expenditures* (Pittsburgh: University of Pittsburgh, November 1970), ACDA/E-157.

14. Office of the Assistant Secretary of Defense (Comptroller), *National Defense Budget Estimates for FY 1983,* table 7-7, 7-8.

15. Ibid.

16. Jack Stokes Ballard, *The Shock of Peace: Military and Economic Demobilization after World War II* (Ph.D. disseration, UCLA, 1974), p. 183. My account of WW II demobilization is largely drawn from Ballard.

17. Alan S. Milward, *War, Economy and Society, 1939-45* (Berkeley: University of California Press, 1977), pp. 64-72, table 5.

18. U.S. National Resources Planning Board, *After Defense What?* (Washington, D.C.: Government Printing Office, 1941), p. 9. Quoted in Ballard, "Shock of Peace," p. 52.

19. Ibid., chapter 3.

20. Ibid. See chapter 2 for a detailed discussion.

21. *Economic Report of the President, February 1982* (Washington, D.C.: Government Printing Office, 1982), tables B-42, B-8, B-29.

22. Ibid., table B-52.

23. Ballard, "Shock of Peace," p. 112.

24. Ibid., p. 180.

25. Ibid., p. 181.

26. Ibid., pp. 185-186.

27. Ibid., p. 189.

28. Bernard Baruch and John Hancock, *Report on War and Post-War Adjustment Policies* (Washington, D.C.: Government Printing Office, 1944), p. 1. Quoted in Ballard, "Shock of Peace," p. 195.

29. Ibid., pp. 195ff.

30. Ibid., p. 202.

31. Ibid., p. 241.

32. Ibid., pp. 231ff.

33. *Economic Report of the President, February 1982,* table B-73.

34. *National Defense Budget Estimates FY 1983,* tables 7-5, 7-8.

35. Ibid., table 7-5.,

36. Ibid., table 7-7.

37. *Economic Report of the President, February 1982,* table B-1.

38. Ibid., table B-29.

39. Murray Weidenbaum, "Problems of Adjustment for Defense Industries," in *Disarmament and the Economy,* pp. 66-85, 76.

40. Emile Benoit, "Economic Adjustments to Disarmament," in *Disarmarment and the Economy,* pp. 74-75.

41. *National Defense Budget Estimates for Fy 1983,* table 7-7.

42. *Economic Report of the President, February 1982,* table B-31.

43. In *Economic Report of the President, January 1969* (Washington, D.C.: Government Printing Office, 1969).

44. Arthur Okun, in testimony before the Joint Economic Committee, quoted in U.S. Congress, Joint Economic Committee, *1972 Joint Economic Economic Report,* (Washington, D.C.: Government Printing Office, 1972).

45. Economic Adjustment Assistance *Fact Sheet,* Economic Adjustment Office of the Assistant Secretary of Defense (Manpower, Reserve Affairs, and Logistics), January 1981.

46. Economic Adjustment Committee, Office of Economic Adjustment, *Summary of Completed Military Base Economic Adjustment Projects, 1961-79* (September 1979). See also "Cities Find Conversion of Old Military Bases a Boon to Economies," *The New York Times* (April 26, 1979).

47. Weidenbaum, "Problems of Adjustment for Defense Industries," in *Disarmament and the Economy.*

48. Jacques Gansler, *The Defense Industry* (Cambridge: MIT Press, 1980), p. 278, suggests these and other benefits from such changes in defense industry.

Appendix A
Components of the
U.S. Military Burden

The estimates of the components of the military burden in table 3–2 are based on the following assumptions. The use of resources for military purposes is best defined in terms of the National Income and Product Accounts (NIPA), published by the Department of Commerce. They offer a widely used measure of the annual national economic product. It is possible with certain adjustments and estimates to distinguish between the civilian and military product of the United States in a given year. Based on NIPA concepts, the resource burden can then be distinguished from the financial burden as reflected in the federal budget. The civilian and military components of GNP in NIPA terms can be schematically illustrated as follows:

GNP: Civilian and Military Components

1. Government purchases of goods and services (G)
   Federal government (civ and mil)
   State and local government (civ)
2. Gross private domestic investment (I)
   Non-residential structures (civ and mil)
   Producers' durable equipment (civ and mil)
   Residential structures (civ)
3. Personal consumption (C)
   Durable goods (civ)
   Nondurable goods (civ)
   Services (civ)
4. Net exports of goods and services (civ and mil) (E)

Grouping the civilian and military components of GNP separately yields the following summary equation:

$$GNP = GNP_{civ}(G_{civ} + I_{civ} + C + E_{civ}) + GNP_{mil}(G_{mil} + I_{mil} + E_{mil})$$

The military component of government purchases of goods and services (G), defense purchases, is by far the largest component of the allocation of societal resources to military purposes. It is also one of the standard definitions of military expenditure on which NIPA data is readily available. This category differs from the national defense function budget definition primarily in that military retirement pay is excluded and the timing with which such expenditures are recorded is different.

Military retirement pay is excluded on the grounds that it does not represent compensation for current services but a transfer payment based on entitlements acquired through past services. It is a current cost of past military efforts and not a current allocation of real resources to the military effort. The same considerations apply to pensions for retired civilian personnel of the Department of Defense and other agencies with military-related functions.

The exclusion of military and civilian retirment pay from the total of defense purchases as transfer payments is consistent with the effort to specify the current use of real resources for the military effort. Nevertheless, some adjustment has to be made because these exclusions mean that such nonwage compensation is never counted as a personnel cost of military-related employment—that is, the future costs of entitlements to pensions being currently acquired through present service. Because it is difficult or impossible to estimate what these costs are, it seems reasonable to use the current costs of retirement pay for former DOD military and civilian personnel as an estimate of these costs of present employment. The financial burden on the current federal budget reflects only the costs of past military efforts. Beginning in FY 1985, the budget will record military retirement costs on an accrual accounting basis (see chapter 2).

Military assistance in the form of arms transfers to foreign governments is included in the NIPA defense purchases data, clearly a military product in the societal sense used in this book. Similarly, the prorated share of NASA purchases in the NIPA are included because of the military-related nature of these expenditures. They are also a current financial burden on the federal budget.

Veterans Administration expenditures represent in good part transfer payments rather than purchases in NIPA terms and even the purchase element for hospitals and medical services benefits former servicemen. On the other hand, as in the case of retirement pay, the costs of future VA benefits being acquired by current servicemen is nowhere reflected in NIPA or in the federal budget. It seems legitimate to use current VA payments for past services as a crude estimate of this unknown nonwage military personnel cost. Again, the current financial burden on the budget reflects the cost of past military efforts.

Foreign economic assistance represents a transfer payment to foreign countries rather than a direct purchase by the U.S. government. As such, it would appear only indirectly in NIPA as exports of goods and services, although it represents a financial cost in the federal budget. It is thus properly included as part of the military-related burden of the domestic economy and product but would appear in GNP under exports.

Interest payments on the federal debt are also transfer payments that do not represent government consumption for the military effort. Only government purchases of goods and services claim real resources. Government borrowing is a financial mechanism through which societal resources are reallocated from private to government consumption and interest payments merely redistribute claims on the national product via government taxing and spending as do other transfer payments.

Interest payments are a very important financial burden on federal budgets, but even in this case it is necessary to distinguish between military-related debt that is the consequence of past military efforts, such as World War Two, and the debt burden and resulting interest payments attributable to current military efforts. Perhaps the best estimating method is to allocate to current military efforts a share of the interest costs of the current deficit equal to the military share of federal funds expenditures (that is, excluding the largely self-financing trust funds). Although the bulk (75 percent according to Cypher) of the federal debt can be attributed to military expenditures, only a fraction of this debt is attributable to current military efforts.

Gross private domestic investment (I) is another category in the GNP accounts where military-related product appears in nonresidential construction, producers' durable equipment, and inventories. It represents both investment within a given year related to military final demand as well as inventories required to supply military demand. The NIPA defense purchases data only register military product at the stage of final delivery. In fact, military-industrial production, particularly for such hardware as ships, aircraft, missiles, and vehicles, takes place over a number of years before it is delivered and registered in NIPA. Military GNP within the private sector can be estimated roughly for a given year as the difference between obligations incurred for the military and military-related activities and GNP purchases. An additional upward adjustment is required to take into account private sector investment in response to foreign military orders, which now constitute a major proportion of total U.S. production of specialized military equipment.

Military product also appears as exports (E) in (NIPA). The United States sells abroad increasingly large amounts of military product; these sales are estimated as $10 billion in 1980. Under the foreign military sales program, the U.S. government is only an intermediate purchaser through a trust fund account for the ultimate foreign buyer. In addition U.S. firms also make direct commercial sales to foreign governments under the Arms Export Control Act. Foreign military sales thus do not entail any significant budgetary costs for the U.S. government. On the other hand there is a close relationship between foreign military sales and the U.S. military effort, and they do represent the allocation of societal resources and thus military product in a GNP sense. To exclude them would seriously underestimate the impact of military production on the U.S. economy and on U.S. manufacturing in particular. On the other hand the ultimate monetary costs are borne by the foreign purchaser.

Finally, the prorated share of foreign economic assistance attributable to military purposes appears in NIPA as export of goods and services. This category is also a financial burden on the federal budget.

Selected References

Adams, Gordon. *The Iron Triangle*. New York: Council on Economic Priorities, 1982.

――――. *The B-1 Bomber: An Analysis of Its Strategic Utility, Cost, Constituency, and Economic Impact*. New York: Council on Economic Priorities, 1976.

Anderson, Marion. *The Empty Pork Barrel: Unemployment and the Pentagon Budget*. Lansing, Mich.: Public Interest Research Group in Michigan, 1982.

――――. *Bombs or Bread, Black Employment and the Pentagon Budget*. Lansing, Mich.: Employment Research Associates, 1982.

Augustine, Norman. "One Plane, One Tank, One Ship: Trend for the Future?" *Defense Management Journal* (April 1975), pp. 43–47.

Ballard, Jack Stokes. "The Shock of Peace: Military and Economic Demobilization After World War II." UCLA: Ph.D. Dissertation, 1974.

Baran, Paul, and Paul Sweezy. *Monopoly Capital*. New York: Monthly Review, 1966.

Benoit, Emile. "The Monetary and the Real Costs of National Defense." *American Economic Review* 58 (1968), no. 2, pp. 398–416.

―――― and Kenneth Boulding, eds. *Disarmament and the Economy*. New York: Harper & Row, 1963.

Bezdek, Roger. "The 1980 Economic Impact—Regional and Occupational—of Compensated Shifts in Defense Spending." *Journal of Regional Science,* 15:2 (1975), pp. 183–197.

――――. *Long-Range Forecasting of Manpower Requirements*. New York: IEE Press, 1974.

Block, Fred. "Economic Instability and Military Strength: The Paradoxes of the 1950 Rearmament Decision." *Politics and Society,* 10:1 (1980), pp. 35–58.

Bohi, Douglas R. "War in Vietnam and the United States Balance of Payments." *Review of Economics and Statistics,* vol. 51 (1969).

Boretsky, Michael. "Trends in U.S. Technology: A Political Economist's View." *American Scientist* (January/February 1975).

Brzoska, Michael, Peter Lock, and Herbert Wulf. "An Assessment of Sources and Statistics of Military Expenditure and Arms Transfer Data." New York: United Nations report prepared for the Group of Governmental Experts on the Relationship between Disarmament and Development, 1980.

Caputo, David. "New Perspectives on the Public Policy Implications of

Defense and Welfare Expenditures in Four Modern Democracies."
Policy Science, vol. 6 (1975), pp. 423–446.

Chase Econometrics Associates. *Economic Impact of the B-1 Program on
the U.S. Economy.* Bala Cynwyd, Pa., 1975).

Crecine, John, and Gregory Fischer. "On Resource Allocation Processes in
the U.S. Department of Defense." *Political Science Annual,* vol. 4
(1973), p. 189.

———. "Defense Budgeting: Organizational Adaption to Environmental
Constraints." Santa Monica: Rand Corporation RM 6121 (1970).

Cusack, Thomas, and Miroslav Nincic. "The Political Economy of U.S.
Military Spending." *Journal of Peace Research,* 16:2 (1979).

Cypher, James. "The Basic Economics of Rearming America." *Monthly
Review* (November 1981), pp. 11–27.

———. "Capitalist Planning and Military Expenditure." *Review of Radical Political Economics,* vol. 6 (1976), pp. 1–19.

de Grasse, Robert, and Paul Murphy. "The Impact of Reagan's Rearmament." *Council on Economic Priorities Newsletter* (May 1981).

Dempsey, Richard, and Douglas Schmude. "Occupational Impact of
Defense Expenditures." *Monthly Labor Review* (December 1971),
pp. 12–15.

Denison, Edward. *Accounting for Slower Economic Growth.* Washington,
D.C.: Brookings, 1979.

———. *Why Growth Rates Differ.* Washington, D.C.: Brookings, 1967.

Dresch, Stephen, and Robert Goldberg. "IDIOM: An Inter-Industry,
National-Regional Policy-Evaluating Model." *Annals of Economic
and Social Measurement,* 2/3 (1973), pp. 323–241.

Dudley, Leonard, and Peter Passell. "The War in Vietnam and the
United States Balance of Payments." *Review of Economics and Statistics,* vol. 50 (1968), pp. 438–439.

Dumas, Lloyd J. "The Impact of the Military Burden on the Domestic
Economy." *Current Research on Peace and Violence,* no. 2 (1980),
pp. 73–82.

———. "Economic Conversion, Productive Efficiency, and Social Welfare." *Journal of Sociology and Social Welfare,* 4:3–4 (January/March
1977), pp. 567–596.

Eichenberg, Richard, William Domke, and Catherine Kelleher. "Patterns
of Western Resource Allocation: Security and Welfare." *Publication
Series of the International Institute for Comparative Social Research*
(Science Center Berlin), 1980.

Eisenhower, Dwight David. "Spending into Trouble," *Saturday Evening
Post* (May 18, 1963) p. 17.

Fallows, James. *The National Defense.* New York: Random House, 1981.

Feldstein, Martin. "Fiscal Policies, Inflation, and Capital Formation." *American Economic Review,* vol. 70 (September 1980).

Flash, Edward S. *Economic Advice and Presidential Leadership* New York: Columbia University Press, 1965.

Galbraith, John Kenneth. *The New Industrial State.* Boston: Houghton Mifflin, 1967.

Gansler, Jacques. "Can the Defense Industry Respond to the Reagan Initiative?" *International Security,* 6:4 (Spring 1982).

————. *The Defense Industry.* Cambridge: MIT Press, 1980.

George, Roger. "The Economics of Arms Control." *International Security,* 5:4 (1980) pp. 94–126.

Gold, David, and others. *Misguided Expenditure, An Analysis of the Proposed MX Missile System.* New York: CEP, 1981.

————. "The Rise and Decline of the Keynesian Coalition." *Kapitalistate,* no. 6 (Fall 1977), pp. 129–161.

Gordon, Michael. "Pentagon Contractors Divided Over Foreign Arms Co-Production Deals." *National Journal,* 14:8 (February 20, 1982), pp. 332–333.

Greenwood, David. *Budgeting for Defense.* London: Royal United Service Institute, 1972.

Hitch, Charles, and Roland McKean. *Economics of Defense in the Nuclear Age.* Cambridge, Mass.: Harvard University Press, 1960.

Huisken, Ron. "Armaments and Development." Report prepared for the Independent Commission on Disarmament and Security, New York, 1981.

————. *The Meaning and Measurement of Military Expenditure.* Stockholm: SIPRI Research Report 10, 1973.

Huntington, Samuel. *The Common Defense.* New York: Columbia University Press, 1961.

Hirst, F.W. *The Political Economy of War.* London: J.M. Dent & Sons, 1916.

Kaldor, Mary. *The Baroque Arsenal.* New York: Hill and Wang, 1981.

———— and others. *Democratic Socialism and the Cost of Defense.* London: Croom and Helm, 1979.

Kennedy, Gavin. *The Economics of Defense.* London: Farber & Farber, 1974.

Klare, Michael. "The Political Economy of Arms Sales." *Bulletin of Atomic Scientists* (November 1976), pp. 11–18.

Koistinen, Paul A. *The Military-Industrial Complex. A Historical Perspective.* New York: Praeger, 1980.

Korb, Lawrence J. "The FY 1980–84 Defense Program: Issues and Trends." *AEI Foreign Policy and Defense Review,* 5:4.

———. "The Budget Process in the Department of Defense, 1947–77; The Strengths and Weaknesses of Three Systems." *Public Administration Review* (July/August 1977), pp. 334–346.

Kurth, James. "Why We Buy the Weapons We Do." *Foreign Policy,* vol. 2 (1973), pp. 33–56.

Kuznets, Samuel. *Economic Growth of Nations.* Cambridge, Mass.: Harvard University Press, 1971.

Leontief, Wassily, and others. "The Economic Impact—Industrial and Regional—of An Arms Cut." *Review of Economics and Statistics,* 47:3 (1965), pp. 217–241.

Lewis, Arthur. "The Slowing Down of the Engine of Growth." *American Economic Review,* vol. 7 (1980), pp. 555–564.

Lo, Clarence Y.H. "The Conflicting Functions of U.S. Military Spending after World War II." *Kapitalistate,* no. 3 (Spring 1975), pp. 26–44.

Magdoff, Harry. "Militarism and Imperialism." *American Economic Review* (May 1970), pp. 237–242.

Mandel, Ernst. *Marxist Economic Theory.* New York: Monthly Review Press, 1968.

Melman, Seymour. *Our Depleted Society.* New York: Dell, 1965.

———. *Pentagon Capitalism.* New York: McGraw-Hill, 1970.

———. *Permanent War Economy.* New York: Simon & Schuster, 1974.

Milward, Alan S. *War, Economy, and Society, 1939–1945.* Berkeley: University of California Press, 1977.

Moll, Kendall, and Gregory Luebbert. "Arms Race and Military Expenditure Models." *Journal of Conflict Resolution,* 24:1 (March 1980), pp. 153–185.

Morgan, William F. "Unemployment and the Pentagon Budget: Is There Anything in the Empty Pork Barrel?" Center for Naval Analyses, 1976.

Moss, Milton, ed. *The Measurement of Economic and Social Performance.* New York: National Bureau of Economic Research, 1973.

Nardinelle, Clark, and Gary Ackerman. "Defense Expenditures and the Survival of American Capitalism." *Armed Forces and Society,* 3:1 (1976), pp. 13–16.

Nourse, Edwin G. *Economics in the Public Service.* New York: Harcourt, Brace, 1953.

O'Connor, James. *The Fiscal Crisis of the State.* New York: St. Martin's, 1973.

Okun, Arthur. *The Political Economy of Prosperity.* Washington: Brookings, 1970.

Olson, Mancur. *The Logic of Collective Action.* Cambridge, Mass.: Harvard University Press, 1965.

Piekarz, Rolf, and Lois Stekler. "Induced Changes in Trade and Payments." *Review of Economics and Statistics* (November 1967).

Pigou, A.C. *The Political Economy of War*. London: Macmillan, 1921.

Pite, Chris. "Employment and Defense." *Statistical News,* no. 51 (November 1980).

Pryor, Frederick L. *Public Expenditures in Communist and Capitalist Nations*. London: Allen & Unwin, 1968.

Reich, Michael. "Does the U.S. Economy Require Military Spending?" *American Economic Review,* vol. 62, pp. 296–303.

Rothschild, Kurt, W. "Military Expenditure, Exports and Growth." *Kyklos* (1973), pp. 804–814.

Rosen, Steven, ed. *Testing the Theory of the Military Industrial Complex*. Lexington, Mass.: Lexington Books, 1973.

Russett, Bruce. *What Price Vigilance? The Burdens of National Defense*. New Haven: Yale University Press, 1970.

Schilling, Warren R., ed. *Strategy, Politics, Defense Budgets*. New York: Columbia University Press, 1962.

Smith, Adam. *An Inquiry into the Nature and Causes of the Wealth of Nations*. Edinburgh, 1776.

Smith, Dan, and Smith, Ron. "Military Expenditures, Resources and Development." Report prepared for the Group of Governmental Experts on the Relationship between Disarmament and Development, New York, 1980.

Smith, R.P. "Military Expenditure and Capitalism." *Cambridge Journal of Economics,* no. 1 (1977), pp. 61–76.

———. "Military Expenditures and Investment in OECD Countries, 1954–1973." *Journal of Comparative Economics,* vol. 4 (1980), 19–32.

Solo, Robert. "Gearing Military R&D to Economic Growth." *Harvard Business Review* (November–December 1962).

Stockholm International Peace Research Institute. *World Armaments and Disarmament: SIPRI Yearbook*. London: Taylor and Francis (annual).

Stein, Herbert. *Fiscal Revolution in America*. Chicago: University of Chicago Press, 1969.

Thurow, Lester. "How to Wreck the Economy." *New York Review of Books* (May 14, 1981).

———. *The Zero Sum Society*. New York: Basic Books, 1980.

Udis, Bernard, ed. *The Economic Consequences of Reduced Military Spending*. Lexington, Mass.: Lexington Books, 1973.

United Nations. *Economic and Social Consequences of the Arms Race and Military Expenditures*. New York: United Nations, 1983.

———. *Study on the Relationship Between Disarmament and Development*. New York: United Nations, 1982.

―――. *Reduction of Military Budgets, International Reporting of Military Expenditures.* New York: United Nations, 1981.

Weidenbaum, Murray. *The Economics of Peacetime Defense.* New York; Praeger, 1974.

―――. *The Modern Public Sector.* New York: Basic Books, 1969.

―――. "The Economic Impact of the Government Spending Process." *University of Houston Business Review,* vol. 8 (Spring 1961), pp. 4–47.

Wells, Samuel, Jr. "Sounding the Tocsin: NSC-68 and the Soviet Threat." *International Security,* 4:2 (Fall 1979).

Wildavsky, Aaron. *Politics of the Budgetary Process,* 3rd ed. New York: Little Brown, 1979.

U.S. Government Publications

Executive Office of the President, Office of Management and Budget. *America's New Beginning: A Program for Economic Recovery.* Washington, D.C.: Government Printing Office, 1981.

Department of Defense, Office of the Assistant Secretary of Defense (Comptroller). *National Defense Budget Estimates for FY 1983.* Washington, D.C.: Department of Defense, March 1982.

―――, Office of the Secretary of Defense (Directorate for Information, Operations, and Reports). *100 Companies Receiving the Largest Dollar Volume of Prime Contract Awards: Fiscal Year 1980.* Washington, D.C.: Department of Defense, 1980.

―――, Office of the Secretary of Defense, Washington Headquarters Services (DIOR). *Real and Personal Property of the DOD (Annual).* Washington, D.C.: Department of Defense.

―――, Office of the Assistant Secretary of Defense for Research and Engineering. *Defense Science Board Summer Study Task Force on Industrial Responsiveness.* Washington, D.C.: Department of Defense, January 1981.

―――, Security Assistance Agency. *Foreign Military Sales and Military Assistance Facts.* Washington, D.C.: Department of Defense, December, 1980.

―――, Office of the Secretary of Defense (Comptroller). *The Economics of Defense Spending.* Washington, D.C.: Department of Defense, 1972.

U.S. Arms Control and Disarmament Agency. *The Economic Impact of Reductions in Defense Spending.* Washington, D.C.: U.S. Arms Control and Disarmament Agency, 1972.

U.S. Department of Labor, Bureau of Labor Statistics. *Factbook for Estimating the Manpower Needs of Federal Programs* (Bulletin 1832). Washington, D.C.: Government Printing Office, 1975.

U.S. Congress. House Committee on the Armed Services. *The Ailing Defense Industrial Base. Report of the Defense Industrial Base Panel.* Washington, D.C.: Government Printing Office, 1980.

Congressional Budget Office. *An Analysis of President Reagan's Budget Revisions for FY 1982.* Staff Working Paper, March 1981.

——. *The Effects of Foreign Military Sales on the Economy.* Washington, D.C.: Government Printing Office, 1976.

Index

ABM program, 162
Aerospace industry, 71, 72–73, 78, 82–83, 128, 150, 175; conversion, 168, 169, 170, 172; employment, 100, 101, 170
Agricultural sector, 75
Alaska, 53
Alternative use committees, 178–179
Aluminum, 168, 172
Anaheim, Calif., 52
Anderson, Marion, 34, 89–92, 105, 107, 108
Arizona, 53
Armed forces personnel, 2, 48, 156, 173, 176
Arms control agreements, 161–162
Arms Control Export Act, 43, 185
Arms race, 158–159
Arms sales, 43, 139–141, 142, 184, 185
Assets, personal, 171
Atomic Energy Commission, 77
Augustine, Norman, 124
Auto industry, 150, 156, 171, 172

B-1 bomber, 2, 98–100, 162
Balance of payments, 135, 139–141, 142, 158
Ballard, Jack Stokes, 169, 171
Baran, Paul, and Paul Sweezy, 2
"Baroque technology" (Kaldor), 81–83
Belgium, 141
Benoit, Emile, 32
Bezdek, Roger, 92–94, 98, 101, 103–105, 107, 108
Boeing, 82
Boretsky, Michael, 76, 78
Borrowing, federal, 156, 172
Boston, 52
Bottlenecks, 66, 71–73, 157
Boulding, Kenneth, 68, 71
Bradley, Omar, 7
Budget-making process, 56–58
Business profits, 171, 173

Cabinet Coordinating Committee on Economic Planning for the End of Vietnam Hostilities, 176
California, 53, 102, 156
Canada, 76, 86 n.19, 141
Capital, 150, 156, 171. See also Fixed capital formation; Investment
Caputo, David, 64–65
Carnegie Foundation Endowment for International Peace, 1
Carter administration: defense budget, 17, 38 n.22, 58, 145, 146, 147, 148; and MX missile, 54, 73
Center for Defense Information, 3 n.1
Central Midwest region, 105
Chase Econometrics, 98
Chemical exports (OECD), 138
Chicago, 52
Chinese intervention in Korea, 11, 151
CIA, 17
Civil service, 48; employment of veterans, 169, 175; pensions, 27, 42–43, 184
Committee for Economic Development, 131 n.2
Competitiveness, international, 2, 137–139, 148, 150, 158
Construction industry, 75, 101, 171
Consumer demand, 171, 172, 173
Consumer Price Index (CPI), 127, 133 n.29, 151, 169, 175, 176
Consumption, personal, 2, 68
Contract settlement, 170, 171
Contractors, defense, 50, 164
Convention on the Prohibition of Bacteriological Weapons, 161
Conversion, 162–180; and diversification, 179–180; Economic Adjustment Office, 177–178; after Korea, 173–175; McGovern bill, 178–179; planning, 123, 173, 177–180; after Vietnam, 175–177; after WW II, 167–173
Coproduction agreements, 141

"Cost maximizing/subsidy
    maximizing" management
    (Melman), 123, 126
Cost-plus contracting, 164
Cost-push inflation, 122–131
Council of Economic Advisers, 10
Council on Economic Priorities, 3 n.1
Crecine, John, 57
"Crowding out" (investment), 66,
    85 n.9
Cusack, Thomas, and Miroslav Nincic,
    65
Cypher, James, 31, 41, 42, 185

Debt burden, 42, 185. See also Deficit
    spending
Defense Appropriations Act, 164
Defense budget: and budget-making
    process, 56–58; percentage
    breakdown of items, 20. See also
    under Carter/Reagan/Truman
    administrations
Defense Economic Adjustment Council
    (proposed), 178
Defense Logistics Agency, 123
Defense Production Act (1950), 12, 152
Deficit spending, 115–118, 122, 146,
    147, 148, 150, 155–156, 158,
    171–172
Deflators, DOD/GNP, 28–29,
    126–129
DeGrasse, Robert, Jr., 110 n.14
Demand-pull inflation, 113–115
Denison, E.F., 75
Denmark, 141
Depreciation taxes, 146, 156, 171
"Direct defense expenditures"
    (international transactions),
    135–136
Disarmament, socioeconomic impact
    of, 161–182
Dollar, overvaluation of, 158
Dresch, Stephen, and Robert
    Goldberg, 94–95, 105, 107, 108
Drugs, cleaning, and toilet
    preparations, 101

Dudley, Leonard, and Peter Passell,
    139, 143 n.4
Dumas, Lloyd, J., 77, 164–165

Eastern Midwest region, 105
Economic Adjustment Committee
    (EAC), 177
Economic growth, 1–2, 63–87; and
    bottlenecks, 66, 71–73, 157;
    components of, 65–66; of OECD
    countries, 70–71
Economic planning, 123, 173, 177–180
Economic Report of the President
    (1951), 151 (quoted), 152 (quoted)
Economic utility, 18–20. See also
    Opportunity costs; Resource
    allocation
Economy, the (recessions and
    recovery), 73, 148, 154, 155,
    156–157, 169, 175, 177
Egypt, 41–42
Eisenhower administration, 6, 7, 14,
    15, 33, 57, 152, 175, 176
Electrical and electronics industry, 71,
    78, 82–83, 101, 128, 150, 156
Employment: of veterans, 169, 170,
    175; of women, 168, 169, 172; of
    the young and old, 168, 170, 172.
    See also Labor force participation
Employment, military-related, 2, 91,
    109 n.4; direct/indirect, 48–49;
    impact on industries, 100–102; labor
    force effects, 108; and labor
    market, 66; multiplier effect, 2,
    49–50; occupational effects,
    105–108; occupational groups,
    52–53; opportunity costs, 89–100,
    157; regional distribution, 52,
    102–105, 157; R&D, 76–78, 83–84,
    100. See also Labor force
    participation
Employment Research Associates, 3 n.1
Empty Pork Barrel, The (Anderson),
    89–92, 107
Engineering and scientific instruments,
    71

Engineers, 72. *See also* Scientists and
  engineers
Export-led growth model, 137–139

F–16, F–18, 141
Faini, Richard, 84 n.3
Federal budget: and budget-making
  process, 56–58; deficit spending,
  13, 115–118, 122, 146, 147, 148,
  150, 153, 155–156, 158, 171–172;
  surpluses, 13, 172, 175
Federal Reserve System, 85 n.9, 117,
  120, 147, 148, 153, 155
Feedback effect (foreign purchases),
  136
Feldstein, Martin, 122
Fixed capital formation, 45–47. *See
  also* Capital; Investment
Flood control projects, 171
Florida, 156
Ford administration, 58
Foreign capital, 156
Foreign exchange loss, 135–137,
  141–142
Foreign military and economic
  assistance, 41–42, 136–137, 184
Foreign military sales, 43, 139–141,
  142, 184, 185
Foreign Military Sales Financing
  Program, 41, 50
Foreign trade deficit, 135, 139–141,
  142, 158
France, 56, 86 n.19
Frost Belt, 157
Fuel, 53, 127–128, 136, 141
Furman, Robert, 157–158

Galbraith, John Kenneth, 14, 123
Gansler, Jacques, 71–73, 114, 123
General Dynamics, 141
GI Bill, 168, 169, 170
GNP accounting, 20–22
GNP deflator, 28–29, 126–127
GNP statistics, 8, 152, 167, 169
Gold, David, 97–98, 115
Great Society Programs, 153
Greider, William, 123

Gross capacity product (GCP), 68
Gross domestic product (GDP), 70
Gross private domestic investment, 68,
  185

Highway construction, 171
Hollenhorst, Jerry, and Gary Ault, 68
Housing industry, 171
Huntington, Samuel, 6

IDIOM (Dresch and Goldberg), 94 95
*Impact of Military Spending on the
  Machinists Union, The,* 107
Imports, 136, 137, 142
Industrial chemicals, 168
Industry: and cost-push inflation,
  122–126, 131 n.10; diversification,
  179–180; impact of military-related
  employment on, 100–102; lag times,
  166; lead times, 157; plant
  utilization, 170; production 8,
  50–53, 168; production costs, 83,
  123, 126, 164; profits, 171, 173;
  WW II and after, 168, 169, 171, 173
Inflation, 113–133, 148; cost-push
  inflation, 122–131; demand-pull
  inflation, 113–115; indexes
  (DOD/GNP deflators), 28–29,
  126–129; Korean war, 151, 158;
  mark-up inflation, 123; monetary
  inflation, 115–118; Nixon
  administration, 154–155; Vietnam
  war, 114, 119–121, 153, 158, 176,
  177; wage inflation, 123; after
  WW II, 171
Information transfer, 84
"Inside lag," 166
Interest on public debt, 42, 185
Interest rates, 148, 150, 155, 156,
  158, 171
International Association of Machinists
  (IAM), 108
International Institute of Strategic
  Studies, 30
"International security assistance,"
  41–42

Investment, 65–73, 74; OECD countries, 70–71; tax incentives, 146, 156, 171. *See also* Capital
Israel, 41–42
Italy, 76

Japan, 17, 138; defense burden, 45, 63, 142; electronics industry, 84, 158; R&D, 76, 78
Johnson, Louis, 6
Johnson administration, 14, 57, 119, 176; economic policy, 152–153, 154

Kaldor, Mary, 81–83
Kennedy administration, 7, 14, 57, 152
Keynesianism, 1–2; and Korean war, 12–15, 152; and NSC-68, 7–12
Keyserling, Leon, 8, 10, 12
Korb, Lawrence J., 58
Korean war, 11–13, 63, 68, 119; military buildup, 151–152; post-war conversion, 173–175

Labor force participation, wartime/post-war: age factor, 168, 170, 172; Korean war, 173–175; sex factor, 168, 169, 172; Vietnam war, 176; WW II, 167–168, 169, 170, 172. *See also* Employment, military-related
Labor intensity, 99, 110 n.15
Labor market, 66
Laffer Curve, 123
Lag times (production), 166
Laird, Melvin, 58
Land use, 53–55
Lead times (production), 157
Leontief, Wassily, 100, 101, 102, 103, 105, 110 n.15
Living standard, 8, 32
Lockheed Corporation, 164
Locomotives, 168
Los Angeles, 52, 72

Machinery and transport equipment exports (OECD), 138
Magnesium, 172

Management, cost inefficient, 83, 123, 126, 164
Mandel, Ernest, 129 (quoted)
Manufacturing sector, 101, 157, 168. *See also* Industry
Marginal tax rates, 146
Mark-up inflation, 123
Marshall, George, 6
Massachusetts, 156
McDonnell Douglas, 141
McGovern, George: and conversion bill, 178–179
McNamara, Robert, 57, 58
Measure of economic welfare (MEW) (Nordhous and Tobin), 22
Medical, educational, and nonprofit organizations, 101
Melman, Seymour, 3 n.1, 45–47, 123, 126, 137, 139
Middle Atlantic region, 105
Midwest, the, 156
Military Balance, The, 30
Military bases: foreign exchange costs, 135–136, 141–142
Military buildup: Korean and Vietnam wars, 151–155, 156; Reagan administration, 148–151, 155–159
Military burden, 45–47, 63–65, 68, 113, 183–186; Korean war, 63, 68, 151, 155, 173; Reagan's military buildup, 150, 155; U.S. and its allies compared, 63, 150; Vietnam war, 68, 155, 176; WW II, 68, 167
Military expenditures: defined, 23–32; statistics, 28, 43, 45, 126, 132 n.26, 136, 148, 152, 153, 172, 173, 176
Military pensions, 26–27, 184
Mineral resources, 53
Mining industry, 75
Missiles industry, 71, 100, 162
Monetary inflation, 115–118
Monetary policy: Reagan administration, 147, 148, 150, 155
Morgan, William F., 92, 109 n.5
Multiplier effect employment, 2, 49–50
Munitions industry, 168, 170, 172
MX missile, 54, 73, 81, 97–98, 115

Nardinelli, Clark, and Gary
    Ackerman, 65, 85 n.13
NASA, 31, 42, 49–50, 77, 80
Nassau-Suffolk, N.Y., 52
"National defense function," 23–24,
    41, 43
"National defense tax," 116
National Income and Product
    Accounts (NIPA), 23, 24–26,
    183–186
National Resources Planning Board
    (NRPB), 168
National Security Council: NSC-68,
    7–12
NATO, 17, 23, 26, 42
Netherlands, 76, 141
Nevada, 53, 54
New Mexico, 53
Nitze, Paul, 7
Nixon administration, 58, 154–155, 177
Nonproliferation Treaty, 161
Nordhaus, William D., and James
    Tobin, 22
Norsworthy, J.R., Michael Harper,
    and Kent Kunze, 75
Norway, 141
Nourse, Edwin G., 6
Nuclear weapons, 14, 24

Occupational effects, 105–108
Occupational groups, 52–53
OECD countries: export-led growth,
    138; military expenditures/economic
    growth, 70–71; productivity,
    73–74; R&D, 76, 78
Offset agreements, 136, 141, 142
Oil, 53, 127–128, 136, 141
Okun, Arthur, 119, 120, 121
Opportunity costs, 32–35, 89–100,
    155–159. See also Economic utility;
    Resource allocation
Ordnance, 101
"Outside lag," 166

Pace, Frank 6
Partial Test Ban Treaty, 161
Patents, 76

Pensions: civilian, 27, 42–43, 184;
    military, 26–27, 184
Personal assets/savings, 171, 172, 173
Personal consumption, 2, 68
Philadelphia, 52
Plant utilization, 170
Price controls, wage and price, 152,
    154, 171
Price indexes: CPI, 127, 133 n.9, 169,
    175, 176; DOD/GNP deflators,
    28–29, 126–129
Procurement, 50, 100, 150, 156, 164
Production costs, 83, 123, 126, 164
Productivity: OECD countries, 73–74;
    U.S. decline, 2, 66, 73–80
Public works projects, 171, 173

Radio and TV communications
    equipment, 71
Raw materials, 53
Reagan administration, 17, 142;
    defense budget, 2–3, 58, 145, 146,
    148–151; economic policy, 2–3, 58,
    145–148; and socioeconomic impact
    of military buildup, 155–159
Recessions, economic, 73, 148, 154,
    155, 156–157, 169, 175, 177
Recovery, economic, 148, 155,
    156–157, 175
Regional impact of military spending,
    52, 102–105, 156–157
Regulatory burden, 146
Research and development, 2, 66, 100,
    150; military vs. civilian, 75–80;
    personnel, 76–78, 83–84, 101;
    sectoral distribution, 78–80;
    spinoffs/spillover benefits, 80–84
Resource allocation, 183–186. See also
    Economic utility; Opportunity costs
Retirement pay: civilian, 27, 42–43,
    184; military, 26–27, 184
Revenue Act (1945), 171
Ricardo, David, 121–122
Rockwell International, 2, 98
Roosevelt, Franklin D., 168
Rothschild, Kurt W., 138–139

Rubber products, 168
Russett, Bruce, 55, 67–68, 90, 92, 107

SALT, 161, 162
San Jose, Calif., 52
Savings, personal, 171, 172, 173
Say, Jean Baptiste, 19
Schultze, Charles, 156
Scientists and engineers, 52–53, 100; in
   R&D, 76–78; transfer from military
   to civilian employment, 84, 164, 165
Semiconductor/computer industry,
   156, 158
Service sector, 74, 75, 101
Servicemen's Readjustment Act (1944)
   (GI Bill), 168, 169, 170
Shipbuilding, 128, 168, 172
Sivard's *World Military and Social
   Expenditures,* 33
Skilled labor, 53, 158
Smith, Adam, 19, 32
Smith, Ron P., 33, 39 n.38, 64, 70
Smith, Ron P., and Dan Smith, 70
Social Security, 47, 116
Social welfare programs, 55, 56,
   115–116, 145–146, 150, 153, 157
Socioeconomic impact: of
   disarmament, 161–162; of military
   spending, 18–20, 155–159
Solo, Robert, 76, 83
South, the, 105
Southeast, the, 102, 103
Southwest, the, 102, 103, 105
Space program, 42, 71, 76, 77, 78, 152
Spinoffs/spillover benefits, 2, 20,
   80–84
St. Louis, 52
Stagflation, 154, 156–157
Starfighter (F-104), 132 n.26
Steel industry, 150, 156, 168, 171
Stockholm International Peace
   Research Institute (SIPRI), 17, 75
Strategic Computing program, 158
Strategic programs R&D, 81
Substitution effect, 55, 56
Sun Belt, 157

"Supply-side" economics, 147–148
Sweden, 179

Tactical programs R&D, 81
Tax policy: after Korea, 175; Reagan
   administration, 146, 148, 150;
   during Vietnam, 120–121; after
   WW II, 171, 172, 173
Technology, process vs. product, 83
Texas, 156
Thurow, Lester, 74–75, 114 (quoted),
   156–157
Titanium, 53
Tornado (MRCA) fighter, 132 n.26
Tradeoffs, civilian, 55–56
Transfer, information/personnel, 84,
   164, 165
Transfer payments, 184–185. *See also*
Social welfare programs; Trust fund
   expenditures
Trident, 162
Truman administration, 7, 9, 10, 13,
   151, 152; defense budget, 5–6, 57
Trust fund expenditures, 27, 47,
   115–116

Unemployment, 8, 148, 150, 167,
   169, 175, 176
Unemployment insurance, 170, 175
United Kingdom, 56, 73, 86 n.19
United Nations, 30, 94, 161, 162
U.S. Air Force, 175
U.S. Arms Control and Disarmament
   Agency, 17, 41, 166
U.S. Army Corps of Engineers, 20, 23,
   48
U.S. Border Patrol, 48
U.S. Bureau of the Budget, 10–11
U.S. Coast Guard, 48
U.S. Congress, 120–121
U.S. Department of Energy, 24
U.S. Employment Service, 169, 170
U.S. Office of Contract Settlement,
   170
U.S. Office of Economic Adjustment,
   177–178

U.S. Office of War Mobilization and
    Reconversion, 168, 170
U.S. Selective Service System, 24, 41
U.S. Social Security, 47, 116
Utah, 53, 54
Utilities industry, 75

Very High Speed Integrated Circuit
    (VHSIC) program, 158
Veterans Administration, 42, 49–50,
    184
Veterans benefits, 31, 42, 45, 175;
    GI Bill, 168, 169, 170, 172
Vietnam war, 68, 139; inflation, 114,
119–121; military buildup, 152–153;
    post-war reconversion, 175–177

Wage and price controls, 152, 154, 171
Wage inflation, 123
Wage rate, military/civilian, 165
War Mobilization and Reconversion
    Act (1944), 168

Weapons, decline in number of,
    124–126
Weapons systems, 95–100, 150
Weidenbaum, Murray, 43, 165
Weinberger, Caspar, 55, 61 n.28
West, the, 103
West Coast region, 102, 105
West Germany, 56, 76, 136, 138,
    179; military expenditures, 38 n.22,
    45, 55, 63, 132 n.26, 142
Wiesner, Frederich von, 32
Wilson, Charles, 171
Women in labor force, 168, 169, 172
Work week, 170
Workers Economic Adjustment
    Reserve Trust Fund (proposed), 179
*World Military and Social
    Expenditures,* 33
*World Military Expenditure and Arms
    Transfers,* 41
World War Two, 2, 10, 68, 108;
    post-war reconversion, 167–173

About the Author

Hugh Mosley received the Ph.D. in political science from Duke University. He teaches government and politics at the University of Maryland European Division program in Berlin.

His special interests are political theory, comparative social policy, and the political economy of the military sector. His work has appeared in *Policy Studies Journal, Politics and Society, Contemporary Crises, New German Critique,* and other journals.

In 1980 1981 he served as a research consultant at the United Nations Centre for Disarmament in New York for a UN study on the economic and social consequences of the arms race.